Christina Stoddard

The Trail of the Serpent

By Inquire Within

OMNIA VERITAS.

Christina Stoddard
(Inquire Within)

For some years a Ruling Chief of the Mother Temple
of the Stella Matutina and R.R. et A.C.

Author of *Light Bearers of Darkness*

Trail of the
Serpent

First published by Boswell Publishing Co. Ltd.
10 Essex Street, London, W.C.2 - 1936

Published by Omnia Veritas Limited

© Omnia Veritas Ltd – 2024

OMNIA VERITAS.

www.omnia-veritas.com

"That which is above is like that which is below, and that which is below is like that which is above for the accomplishment of the wonders of one thing.

"Its father is the Sun: its mother is the Moon; The wind beareth it in the belly thereof; the earth is its nurse;

It is the Universal Principle, the Telesma of the World."

The Emerald Tablet of Hermes.

"The Serpent, inspirer of disobedience, of insubordination, and of revolt, was cursed by ancient Theocrats, although it was honoured among initiates...

To become like unto Divinity, such was the goal of the Ancient Mysteries... To-day the programme of initiation has not changed."

OSWALD WIRTH — Le *Livre du compagnon.*

FOREWORD

FIVE years ago we published *Light Bearers of Darkness*,[1] largely based on articles appearing in the *Patriot* from 1925 to 1930, being the result of our own experiences and investigations into various individual secret societies, their affiliations, their occult practices, their pseudo religious and political activities.

To-day, in *The Trail of the Serpent,* we issue a further instalment of these researches, built up almost wholly from contributions to the *Patriot* from 1930 to 1935. Going back to Patriarchal times, we attempt to trace, step by step, the worship of the ancient Serpent, the Creative Principle, the God of all initiates, from the early Cabiri, through Paganism to the pseudo-Christianity of the Gnostics and Cabalists, these latter largely emanating under the influence of the Hellenised Jews of Alexandria.

We have endeavoured to prove that the aim, in the higher grades of these varied mysteries and cults, is to awaken this serpent, the sex-force or "God within" man, raising it by processes and yogic methods, uniting it with the Universal Creative Principle without developing the latent senses or, so to say, deifying the adept, but only that he may be enslaved by some astute, outside, and stronger mind or group of minds, who, it would seem, seek to rule the nations through hypnotically controlled adepts. For one and all of these modern mysteries are dominated and ruled by some unknown hierarchy, just as in the Ancient Mysteries the Egyptian high-priests were the masters of the old world through

---

[1] *Light Bearers of Darkness,* by Inquire Within, Published by Omnia Veritas Ltd, www.omnia-veritas.com.

their knowledge and power to manipulate these invisible serpent forces, the magnetic forces of all nature, by means of which they bound and dominated the mystes and even the epoptes and through them the masses.

These revolutionary mysteries first appear as pseudo religions, until by means of some kind of seemingly religious uplift the necessary link with the master-mind is formed. Then it becomes openly political and revolutionary, subverting all aspects of the nation's life, seeking by internationalism and universalism to unify all peoples, socially, economically, politically, in arts and religion, preparing for some New Era, some New Heaven and New Earth.

We have finally sought to materialise these invisible masters and, allowing the Cabalists to speak for themselves, we arrive at the revolutionary and cabalistic Jew, the most cosmopolitan of peoples, who look for the Coming of their Messianic Era. To some of these the Messiah is their race and their race is their God, the Tetragrammaton, the Creative Principle, this Serpent Power, binding and unifying, leading to the hope of merging all races, all faiths under the Law of this their Unity of Race, thus creating the "Greater Judaism" spoken of by the *Jewish World,* 9 and 16 February, 1883.

CHAPTER I

SABEISM ELEUSIS AND MITHRAS

IN 1871 General Albert Pike, Grand Master of the Scottish Rite, Southern Jurisdiction, U.S.A., wrote in *Morals and Dogmas:*

"Among the early nations a wild enthusiasm and a sensual idolatry of nature soon superseded the simple worship of the Almighty God... The great powers and elements of nature and the vital principle of production and procreation through all generations; then the celestial spirits or heavenly host, the luminous armies of the stars, and the great Sun and mysterious, everchanging Moon (all of which the whole ancient world regarded, not as mere globes of light or bodies of fire, but as animated living substances, potent over man's fate and destinies); next the genii and tutelar spirits, and even the souls of the dead, received divine worship... the heavens, earth, and the operations of nature were personified; the good and bad principles personified became also objects of worship."

Further, in New York, 15 August, 1876, at the Supreme Council of the 33rd degree, he declared:

"Our adversaries, numerous and formidable, will say, and will have the right to say, that our *Principe Créateur* is identical with the *Principe Générateur* of the Indians and Egyptians, and may fitly be symbolised as it was symbolised anciently, by the lingam... To accept this in lieu of a personal God is to abandon Christianity and the worship of Jehovah and return to wallow in the styes of Paganism."

In his book, *Dieu et les Dieux*, 1854, Le Chevalier Gougenot des Mousseaux gives an exhaustive account of these many pantheistic, pagan, and phallic forms of ancient worship. He tells us that Sabeism thrust its roots deep into the heart of Patriarchal traditions, perverting the early revelations. This Sabeism, which took its name, not from the country of Saba, but from *Tzaba*, an armed troop, made men bow the knee to the starry army of the firmament; it was Stellar before it became Solar and worshipped the Pole Star, known in Chaldea as I.A.O., the creative principle. Somewhat later it mingled with the more corrupt cult of Nature-Sabeism, or the cult of the Stars and Naturalism. To follow the gradual corruption of the early Patriarchal traditions, the Stone is one of the surest guides, for at the time of its splendour it was worshipped from the Empire of China to the extreme confines of the West. It began by being the rude block detached from the rock; it became the column, the flange, the pedestal surmounted by first one and later two human heads (hermaphrodite god), and was finally shaped in the magic lines of Apollo and Venus.

The religion of the Jews is based on revelation: their writings and traditions say that God appeared in diverse places to the Patriarchs and spoke to them; there the Jews raised altars, taking the form of rude stones, generally called Beth-el — the House of God. But soon it was imagined that God resided in these Stones; thus it became the Beth-aven — the House of Falsehood — entirely material. The Beth-el abounded in Chaldea, Asia, Egypt, Africa, Greece, even in the remotest parts of Europe, among Druids, Gauls, and Celto-Scythians, and in the New World, North and South. Man's sensual imagination soon allowed him "to collect his gods in the dust and fashion them as he pleased." The Pagans imitated the Beth-el of Jacob and consecrated them with oil and blood, making them gods, calling them Betyles or Both-al-Jupiter, Cybele, Venus, Mithras. The greater part of the natural Betyles were the black meteorites or fire-balls fallen from the heavens and regarded by the Sabeists as heavenly divinities. These meteorites were the Cabiri, and the Pelasgi — wandering or dispersed men — were their most noted worshippers. Further, in these Cabiri, even as in Sabeism, we recognise the cult of the stars. Sabeism came from the Principle of Unity transferred from the Invisible God to the God of Nature, the Sun-God; then followed duality, male-female, Sun-Moon, God-Goddess of Nature. This passed on to multiplying the gods by the number of the stars, and led back to unity. For, "soon all the stars together were merely the God of Light, the God of Nature, the God of Phenomena... everything was emanation, each thing was *God-*

part-of-God — Pantheism was created!" M. Creuzer held the idea that the Cabiri of Egypt and Phoenicia, as well as the Pelasgic Greek Cabiri (Japhetic), are the great Planetary Divinities: that is, the Gods of Heaven, universal gods, the many gods in One which dominate air, earth, and the waves, and they mingled with those of the Betyles. They were always the seven Planets — Saturn, Jupiter, Mars, Sun, Venus, Mercury, and the Moon — which together with the Earth formed the eight Cabiric Gods.

Having made the Creator the God of Matter the God of Nature, his principal function was to produce; therefore, the organs of generation became the symbol of divinity. The Stone took the form of the Phallus and the Cteis, the Lingam-Yoni of India. Thus Naturalism uniting with the Stone of the Patriarchs became for the learned men of idolatry the *Principe Générateur* of all things. As the learned converted Rabbi Drach wrote:

> "Our fathers, sons of *Sem,* preserved in the sanctuary of the Temple of Jerusalem the Beth-el Stone of Jacob, and in this Stone they worshipped the Messiah. This cult was imitated by our neighbours of Phoenicia, sons of *Cham,* who had a common language with us. From thence spread the cult of the Stones called Betyles or Beth-el, which the race of *Japhet* called also *lapides Divi,* divine or living stones, and these Betyles were similar to the animated stones of the Temple of Diana in Laodicea, mentioned by Lampridius."

Between the stone, tree, spring, or well a singular and close alliance never ceased to exist; therefore, having enclosed their gods in Stone-Betyles, they then enclosed them in Tree-Betyles, such as the ancient Oak, with its spring, worshipped at the Temple of Dodona, representing I.A.O. — the creative principle — and which had its oracles and blood sacrifices. Again we find the Betyle under the oldest form, that of the Egg, the universal germ of all things, and often along with it the Serpent of the dual forces of life. The combined result of all these forms was Pantheism. Man then sought to manipulate this divinity, these dual forces, and by magic, incantations, and evocations the people were seduced and led astray. Further, the Cabiri, Cybele and Atys, Venus and Adonis, Isis and Osiris, Ceres and Iacchus, were represented in all places by the Phallus Betyle, and as the bases of all their myths are so strikingly connected, one cannot fail to see under the diversity of names the same personification of Nature, celestial and terrestrial — the Universe — therefore material god.

The most ancient of these God-Titans or Cabiri was *Axieros-Unity*, the Demiurge, the Creative Principle; from him proceeded *Ariokersos-Axiokersa duality* of the generative principles, Heaven and Earth: from this duality came forth *Cadmillus*, Eros or Hermes, thus completing the Cabiric Trinity in Unity. In the more debased forms it was the cult of the lingam and the deification of sensual and erotic desires. Moreover, in their feasts the passions of the people were often set on fire only to be extinguished in orgies and bacchanalias impossible to describe.

In the ceremonies, des Mousseaux says, the Cabiric priests united themselves so closely with their gods that they took their names, numbers, and attributions, and on solemn occasions even gave up their own personality; also if the cult demanded it, they imitated them in exact mystic mummery. Further, General Albert Pike writes of these Cabiri:

> "The little island of Samothrace was long the depository of certain august Mysteries… It is said to have been settled by the ancient Pelasgi, early Asiatic colonists in Greece, the Gods adored in the Mysteries of this island were termed Cabiri, called by Varro, 'potent gods-Heaven and Earth,' symbols of the Active and Passive Principles of universal generation… In the ceremonies was represented the death of the youngest of the Cabiri, slain by his brothers, who fled into Etruria, carrying with them the ark that contained his genitals; and there the Phallus and the sacred ark were adored."

All these Mysteries, writes Clemens of Alexandria, displaying murders and tombs, had for basis the fictitious death and resurrection of the Sun, the life-principle.

To-day this Sabeism can be traced in all modern Mysteries—occult and illuminé. Take, for example, the Stella Matutina, a Rosicrucian and Martinist Order, and its 3 = 8 grade, attributed to water and in which *Elohim Tzabaoth* is invoked and adored. The three chief officers and the candidate together represent the Samothracian Cabiric Trinity in Unity; in the ritual we read: *Hierophant — Thus* spake Axieros, the first Cabir: "I am the apex of the Triangle of Flame; I am the Solar Fire pouring forth its beams upon the lower world. Life giving, light producing" (Zeus and Osiris). *Hiereus-Axio*kersos, the second Cabir: "I am the left basal angle of the Triangle of Flame; I am Fire, volcanic and terrestrial, flashing, flaming through the abysses of earth; firerending, fire-penetrating, tearing asunder the curtains of matter; fire-constrained, fire-tormenting, raging, and whirling in lurid storm" (Pluto and Typhon). *Hegemon*-Axiokersa, the third Cabir: "I am the right basal angle of the Triangle of Flame; I am Fire, astral and fluid, winding and coruscating through the firmament. I am the life of beings, the vital heat of existence" (Proserpine and Isis). They represent Fire or the generating principle, acting in earth, water, and air. The candidate is Casmillos or Cadmillus (Horus), and receives the mystic name of "Monokeros de Astris" the "Unicorn from the stars." Moreover, Cabiric godforms, built up according to the instructions of their mysterious Master in Mesopotamia, were astrally assumed by these chief officers in the ceremony, and for the time being they, in thought, became these gods or nature's forces, and like these Cabiric priests they practised theurgy and magnetic healing.

It is, therefore, interesting to find Dollinger, in *Paganism and Judaism,* writing of the Chaldean-Sabeist astrologers: that these men found a support in the Stoic philosophy which, identifying God with Nature, had come to regard the stars as eminently divine and placed the government of the world in the immutable course of the heavenly bodies. These men taught that a secret force descended uninterruptedly upon the earth; that a close sympathy existed between the planets, the heavenly bodies, and the earth, and with the beings who lived there. Further, they believed man had the power to augment the good influence or avert the evil by means of invocations and magical ceremonies. In their magical ceremonies and conjurations, all modern secret occult orders are said to awaken and reawaken powers by means of invoking planetary, Zodiacal, and elemental spirits and influences, always using the required so-called potent, divine, or "barbarous" names.

DACTYLES, CORYBANTES, AND TELCHINES

In *Psychologie des sentiments,* M. Ribot writes of these more or less primitive sects:

> "History at all times abounds in physiological processes, employed to produce artificial ecstasy ... so to say, having divinity within oneself. There are inferior forms, mechanical intoxication produced by the dance, rhythmic music of primitives, which excites them and puts them into a condition ripe for inspiration. Intoxication by drugs, soma, wine, the Dionysia, the orgies of Menades; the shedding of blood so widespread in the cults of Asia Minor: Atys, the Corybantes, the Gauls mutilating and cutting themselves with swords; in the Middle Ages the Flagellants, and in our day the fakirs and dervishes."

Also, as found in the frenzied dances of the Khlysty and other primitive Gnostic sects and even in the modern Eurhythmy of Dr. Steiner's followers, all aiming at deification. In *Les Mystères du Paganisme,* revised and edited by Silvestre de Sacy, 1817, Sainte-Croix gives us much valuable information on these early Mysteries. As he says, "There is nothing more intriguing in antiquity than what concerns the Cabiri, Dactyles, Curetes, Corybantes, and the Telchines. Designated under diverse names, were they gods, genii, legislators or priests? ... They have often been mistaken the one for the other." No doubt it was the case of the priests assuming the name as well as the attributions of their gods, for it is said by the Druidic priest: "I am a Druid, I am an architect, I am a prophet, I am a Serpent," the Serpent being a potent power in his cult. According to Strabo:

> "Some suppose that the Curetes are the same as the Corybantes, the Dactyles of Mount Ida, and the Telchines. Others assert that they are of the same family, with some differences. In general they are all alike as to ecstasy, bacchic frenzy, tumult, the noise they make with their arms, drums, flutes, and their extraordinary cries during their sacred feasts... all had to do with religion and was not foreign to philosophy."

According to Sainte-Croix, the Cabiric ceremonies took place at night, often in a cave, and all knowledge concerning them and the gods was as an inviolable secret hidden from the profane. The Dactyles of Asia, at times confounded with the Cabiri, were originally Children of Heaven and Earth, and by spells, illusions, and bewitchments, used also in their mysteries, they won over the people of Phrygia and Samothtace, making themselves indispensable by practising medicine and teaching them to work in metals. However, it is said that the Phrygians owed their first civilisation to the Corybante jugglers and soothsayers, who also ardently cultivated music and the dance, so much so that their name came to mean a kind of violent passion for these exercises which, according to de Sacy, "Really meant the idea of a supernatural agitation, a divine frenzy, real or simulated, which sends a man out of himself and leaves him no longer master of his actions and movements. It expressed a kind of madness or ecstasy, of a divine origin, which appears to produce effects such as those of a really unbalanced mind." Until the end of Paganism something of the mysteries of the Corybantes still existed.

Like the Cabiri, Dactyles, and Corybantes with whom they had so many links of habit and occupation, the Telchines were at first simple diviners, then Pelasgi priests. To increase their numbers and power they used the arts of illusion and sorcery accompanied with threats of future punishments, thus enticing the people from their mountains and forests, getting them to cultivate the land and adopt a new religion, giving up their ancient cult of Saturn. In time the name Telchine became synonymous with charlatan, sorcerer, poisoner, and even evil spirit.

MYSTERIES OF ELEUSIS

In the same book Sainte-Croix gives a long account of the Mysteries of Eleusis which were said to go back to 1423 B.C.; they were of Egyptian origin, though changed and disguised by the Greeks to cover the source of their borrowings. Like those of the Egyptians, these Mysteries of Eleusis were divided into the Lesser and Greater, the Mystes and Epoptes, with about five years' tests in between. Eusebius gives the officers as: *Hierophant,* Father of generation, or Demiourgos; *Dadoukos,* incense-bearer, representing the Sun; *Epibomos,* altarbearer, representing the Moon; *Hieroceryx,* the Sacred Herald carrying the Caduceus — the twin serpents of generation — representing Mercury. All ceremonies were held in a secret subterranean temple, closed to the profane. Many ceremonies were practised, one of the principal being the elevation of the Phallus, a strange rite of Egyptian origin often spoken of by Clemens of Alexandria, Tertullian, and others. According to Diodorus Siculus, it was held in memory of the virile parts of Osiris thrown into the Nile by Typhon, and which Isis had desired should receive divine honours in sacrifices and mysteries. It was represented in the Greater Mysteries by the figure of the ancient fecundating Mercury — said to be the Logos, at once interpreter and fabricator of the things that have been, that are, and will be; the spirit of the seed, according to the Nasseni, is the cause of all existing things, and is the secret and unknown mystery of the universe concealed among the Egyptians in their rites and orgies.

The women had their own Mysteries, known as *Thesmophories*, from which all men, it is said, were excluded. The members had to be virgins or legally married women, all legitimately born. The *Thesmophories* in Athens were celebrated at night during the month of October, lasting about five days. In place of the Phallus the women venerated the Cteis or female sex-organ, and during the ceremonies there was a gay dance, similar to those in Persia, where they all took hands, forming a circle, and dancing in rhythm to the sounds of a flute. Few details about these Mysteries were known, but all were built upon the myth of Ceres and Proserpine.

The adventures of Ceres and Proserpine were identical with those of Osiris and Isis. We have, therefore, Isis — Mouth or Mother of the world; Ceres — Demeter, the Earth-Mother — both signifying the fecundity of the earth. Proserpine was daughter of Ceres and Jupiter, and we know how the myth describes her abduction to the underworld by Pluto, her compulsory sojourn there for six months in the year followed by six months above with her mother. She was symbolically called "the seed hidden in the earth." Moreover, the most learned of the Egyptian priests, according to the philosophers, regarded Osiris as the spermatic substance, and several assert that the burial of the God was emblematic of the seed hidden in the bosom of the earth. He was equally considered as the Solar force, principle of fecundity in relation with the Moon — also Ceres and Isis — which rules generation.

According to the subtle philosophy of the Neo-Platonists on the origin of human souls and their emanation from the soul of the world or universal life-principle, the abduction of Proserpine by Pluto represented the descent of the soul, leaving the higher regions, precipitating itself into matter, uniting with a body. Iacchus and Bacchus cut to pieces by the Titans was the Universal Mind divided and scattered by generation in a multitude of beings (pantheism), and Plato taught that the aim of the Mysteries was to lead back the souls to the region above and to their primitive state of perfection from which they had originally descended. No doubt the secret knowledge of the priests, imparted to the few, was the Hermetic power, personified by Mercury and his caduceus, of acting upon man's sex-force, raising and uniting it to the universal life-force, their Deity, producing a form of so-called illumination.

Christianity having spread in Greece, the priests were obliged to become more careful in the choice of epoptes, in case of admitting men, inclined to leave paganism and become Christians, who might reveal the secrets of Initiation. Therefore at the opening of the ceremony a warning was given: "If any atheist, Christian or Epicurean is present, witness of these Mysteries, let him leave and allow those who believe in God to be initiated under happy auspices."

MYSTERIES OF EGYPT

In *Les Sectes et Sociétés Secrètes* — political and religious — Le Couteulx de Canteleu, 1863, remarks that the aim of secret societies

> "as a whole was, is and will always be the struggle against the·Church and the Christian religion, and the struggle of those who have not against those who have… All secret societies have almost analogous initiations, from the Egyptian to the Illuminati, and most of them form a chain and give rise to others."

Among modern Illuminati, "The Brotherhood of Light," Los Angeles, California, profess to be "a Western Fraternity of Hermetic students who, realising the truth of Universal Brotherhood, are devoting their energies to the physical, mental, and spiritual uplift of Humanity. They investigate all realms of nature that the latent and active forces may be discovered and subjected to the Imperial Will of man."

Their teaching is for

"the definite purpose of reviving the *Religion of the Stars* which is a religion of natural law — as understood and taught by the Hermetic initiates of Ancient Egypt and Chaldea."

The high Mason Albert Pike states: "The seven great primitive nations, from whom all others are descended, the Persians, Chaldeans, Greeks, Egyptians, Turks, Indians, and Chinese, were all originally Sabeists and worshipped the stars." The Chaldeans regarded Nature as the great divinity that exercised its powers through the action of its parts, the sun, moon, planets, and fixed stars, the revolution of the seasons, and the combined action of heaven and earth — that is, the cosmic forces and the magnetic forces of the earth. Herodotus, Plutarch, and all antiquity unanimously consider Egypt as the origin of the Mysteries. In that anonymous book the *Canon* we are told that the Egyptian priests were practically the masters of the old world, everything and everybody was subservient to their jurisdiction, and the old Greek historians emphatically assert that the essential doctrines of the Greek religion came from Egypt. The mystical secrets of the old priests were passed from generation to generation by initiates and mystics, and this mysticism was synonymous with Gnosticism and was common to Egyptian, Greek, and Hebrew.

According to Le Couteulx de Canteleu, these Egyptian priests formed a Confederation of Philosophers united to study the art of governing men and to concentrate on what they conceived as truth. It was composed of three classes: (1) that of the priests who alone could contact the gods, using illusion and oracles to impose them upon the people; (2) that of the Greater initiates, chosen, as were the priests, from among the Egyptians and from whom there was nothing to conceal; (3) that of the Lesser initiates, the greater part strangers, to whom was confided what the Supreme Pontiffs deemed proper to tell them. The Mysteries were directed by a Supreme Council of five ministers, of whom the chief was called

King, Hierophant, or Sacred Orator. They were divided into the Greater Mysteries, the Epoptes, and the Lesser Mysteries, the Mystes; the celebration of the Greater Mysteries was the initiation of those who had been received into the Lesser, after having been subjected to the necessary tests. According to Faber, in his *Pagan Idolatry*, "the epoptes were supposed to have experienced a certain regeneration ... and were deemed to have acquired a great increase of Light and knowledge"—that is, Illumination, or deification. As soon as the priests heard of a man whose genius, talents, and worth had gained consideration among the peoples, the Confederation used every possible means to attract and initiate him, and all were made to act according to its system and views. The knowledge of the Egyptian priests was immense. They were fathers of astronomy and geometry and the study of nature was familiar to them; they had halls for botany, natural history, and chemistry, also immense libraries where were books of science and history and even sacred books communicated only to initiates. Egypt was the *rendezvous* of all celebrated men who sought instruction.

All these Mysteries appear to come from the same source—, having a complete cosmogony and an explanation of the primitive nature and origin of man. Everywhere appeared the impure genii of paganism, for all their myths had their obscene side as well as cosmogonic, and these nocturnal festivals were full of impure songs and ceremonies. The Initiate was first subjected to horrifying trials by darkness, fire and water, long fasts, visions, etc., and if he surmounted these and remained sane, which many did not, he was received among the priests. Hallucination was one of the great methods of Egyptian theurgy; burnt opium, datura, henbane, hasheesh, cinnamon, and laurel formed these vapours, which caused the frenzy of the pythoness or initiate.

> "The ideas of mystery, of magic, the invocation of the dead and of the spirits were so powerful at that time that the minds of the wisest could not resist them, the greatest geniuses and great philosophers came to be initiated. But the epicurean negation and the stoic pantheism mixed with the Mysteries of Ceres ... the poetry of religion which they invoked gradually disappeared, their beautiful dreams became sinister pantheism, the elements were the only true

gods, and the poetic visions of the night of initiation gradually vanished, leading the initiate to scepticism."

As Le Couteulx de Canteleu continues, generation was the basis of all Mysteries. In the whole universe, to be born, to die, and reproduce its kind, such is the law imposed upon all that exists. It is a perpetual rotation of creation, destruction, and regeneration, and that was the basis and origin of all ancient mythologies and religions. The Egyptians, says Diodorus Siculus, acknowledge two great gods, the Sun and Moon, or Osiris and Isis; through them the generation of beings is effected. All nature is maintained by them in combination with their five qualities — ether, fire, air, water, and earth. Or as Le Couteulx de Canteleu explains, five distinct principles unite in the generation of beings:

(1) *The Cause* — the father, active principle, male, creator; represented among the ancients by the Sun, fire, Osiris, father of light; symbolised by Ptah of the Egyptians, the triangle, and the pyramid.

(2) *The Subject* — the mother, matter, female, passive nature, represented by water. It is Nature adored among all peoples under many forms: the Moon, Cybele, Venus, Ceres, and Isis of the Egyptians.

(3) *The Intermediary* — the seed, ether, the vital fluid, the instrument of reproduction; represented by the Phallus or air, the spirit of life, the magnetic fluid of the Sun, Eros, Bacchus, Hercules, Hermes, and Thoth of the Egyptians.

(4) *The Effect* — fertilisation, producing fermentation, putrefaction, disintegration, out of which comes life; it is represented by Earth, the mother of all bodies, and in which vegetables and minerals develop.

(5) *The Result* — the creation of a new life destined to reproduce its kind; it is ether, the fifth element, the Horus of the ancients, the Blazing Star of the Freemasons, the pentagram, the deified adept.

Initiation, illumination, or deification means fixation of the ether or astral light in a material basis, by dissolution, sublimation, and fixation, the work being accomplished in conformity with its principle reproducing the said principle. Therefore, among subversives these principles of generation or regeneration are applied to religious, political, social, moral, and mental life. As the cabalist says: "The formulate must first become unformulate so it can reformulate in new conditions" (death and disintegration); or as the revolutionary puts it: "Everything must be destroyed since everything must be renewed." In Illuminism the adept's personality must be killed out and a new being formed — the controlled tool by fixation of the astral light, the etheric link!

Mr. H. P. Cooke, in his study of *Osiris,* when speaking of Amen or Amoun says: "The word or root *Amen* certainly means 'what is hidden' ... and has reference to something more than the 'sun which has disappeared below the horizon'; one of the attributes applied to him was that of *eternal.* He looks much like the source of all life."

Now Albert Pike tells us that Amùn or Amoun, the God of Lower Egypt, was "the celestial Lord who sheds light on hidden things." "He was the source of that divine life of which the *crux ansata* is the symbol, the source of all power... He was the Light, the Sun-God." The crux ansata was the Egyptian symbol of life, the dual forces of generation in all things.

As a further elucidation of these Egyptian Mysteries, let us turn to the modern Rosicrucian Order of the Stella Matutina and its Inner Order of the R.R. et A.C. In the initiation ceremony of the S.M. the Hierophant on the Dais, in the East, represents Osiris; his power, represented by the colours of his lamen — red and green — is "as the blazing light of the fire of the Sun bringing into being the green vegetation of the otherwise barren earth." Also by its symbol, the calvary cross with the rose in the centre, "it represents the power of self-sacrifice requisite to be attained by him who would be initiated into the sacred Mysteries." He is Osiris of the Nether Land. Again, Hiereus in the West is Horus, the avenger of the Gods; he is Guardian of the Mysteries against those who dwell in darkness. The four elements, the "living creatures" of Ezekiel's vision, the lion, bull, man, and eagle, represent the Sphinx. Their vicegerents are the Children of

Horus-Amset, south; Hapi, north; Taumutef, east; Qebhsennuf, west. Further, the S.M. Mystic Repast represents communion in the body of Osiris, and when inverting the cup at the end, the Kerux — Anubis, the Watcher of the Gods — cries aloud: "It is finished," regeneration through self-sacrifice is accomplished. Finally, in the Inner Initiation after rising from the tomb, the Chief Adept declaims: "I am the Sun in its rising. I have passed through the hour of cloud and of night. I am Amoun, the Concealed One, the Opener of the Day. I am Osiris On-nopheris, the Justified One. I am the Lord of Life triumphant over death. There is no part of me that is not of the gods." The Concealed One, or the "hidden god" within man, is the kundalini, and by its union with the universal lifeforce the adept is said to become one with the gods. As Lepsius said: "When freed from the body thou wilt ascend to the free ether, thou wilt be an immortal God escaped from death."

Now, the R.R. et A.C. ritual tells us that the gods represent a certain symbolical material action of Nature's Forces, and all magical ceremonies are for the purpose of attracting the Solar Forces and the Light of Nature, using them for a given purpose, in the case of initiation, freeing the bewitched or "hidden god" within man. It is entirely pantheistic, and as we know, the ancient Magi considered the Sun to be the great magnetic well of the universe. Through their deep and secret knowledge of these forces the priests of Egypt might become masters of the old world even as to-day some mysterious hierarchy working behind and through all modern mysteries is seeking to unite and dominate mankind by means of the same secret knowledge.

In *Morals and Dogma*, Albert Pike tells us that Apuleius represents Lucius, still in the form of an ass, addressing his invocations to Isis, who is Ceres, Venus, Diana, and Proserpine, substituting, as the Moon, her quivering light for the bright rays of the Sun. Addressing Lucius, Isis says:

> "The parent of Universal nature attends thy call. The mistress of the elements, initiative germ of generations... She governs with her nod the luminous heights of the firmament, the salubrious breezes of the ocean; the silent deplorable depths of the shades below; one Sole

Divinity under many forms, worshipped by the different nations of the Earth under many titles, and with various religious rites."

Describing the Initiation into the Mysteries of Isis, Apuleius continues:

"I approached the abode of death; with my foot I pressed the Threshold of Proserpine's Palace. I was transported through the elements and conducted back again. At midnight I saw the bright light of the Sun shining. I stood in the presence of the Gods, the Gods of Heaven and of the Shades below; I stood near and worshipped."

Osiris he calls

"the Great God, Supreme Parent of all the other Gods, the invincible Osiris…"

In the 6 = 5 grade of the R.R. et A.C., the adept is ceremonially buried in the tomb, passes into a trance with its inevitable visions, is awakened by the Shekinah, veiled, with the crescent moon upon her forehead, who, holding aloft a lighted lamp, says: "Arise, shine, for thy light has come and the Glory of thy Lord is upon thee." It is Illumination or Initiation, a power to be used, not for the adept's self, but to be placed at the service of his unknown Lord and Master.

MITHRAISM

After the rise of Zoroastrianism-sometimes called the faith of Ormuzd or Mazdaism — Mithras, a Persian God of Light, took his place between Ormuzd and Ahriman or Pluto of the Persians — the eternal Light and the eternal Darkness — to aid, it is said, in the destruction of evil and administration of the world. He was the god of vegetation, the god of generation and increase, and was accepted in the official religion of Persia. He was also regarded as mediator between humanity and the unknowable God, who reigned in the ether. His cult spread, with the Empire of Persia, throughout Asia Minor, and Babylon was an important centre; it grew in strength following the conquests of Alexander. The beginning of its downfall was about A.D. 275, but it still survived in the fifth century. It was modified in Asia by contact with the Chaldean star-worshippers, who identified Mithras with

Shamash God of the Sun, and by the Greeks of Asia, who looked upon him as Helios. It was not until the end of the first century that it gained ground in Rome, where both its politics and philosophy helped its success. Hadrian, however, prohibited these Mysteries in Rome because of the cruel human sacrifices accompanying some of their rites, when future events were divined in the entrails. Nevertheless, they reappeared under Commodus, and spread even to Britain.

Mithraic legend, theology, and symbology have been reconstructed by Franz Cumont in his *Textes et monuments figures relatifs aux mystères de Mithra*, 1896. The legend, as shown on these famous Mithraic reliefs, also described by Sainte-Croix, is briefly: Born of a rock, Mithras ate of the fruit of a fig tree and clothed himself with its leaves. The relief shows Mithras's adventures with the sacred bull, created by Ormuzd; he seized the animal by the horns, was carried along until, subduing it, he finally dragged it into a cavern, and by order of the Sun-God sacrificed it. The central relief represents Mithras with flowing garments and Phrygian cap, slaying the sacred bull; the bull sacrificed to bring forth terrestrial life. The scorpion attacking its genitals was sent by Ahriman from the lower world to destroy the generative power, and so prevent fertility; the dog springing towards the wound in the bull's side was venerated by the Persians as Mithras's companion; the serpent is the symbol of the earth made fertile by drinking the blood of the sacrificial bull. The raven who directs Mithras is the Herald of the Sun-God who ordered the sacrifice; various plants near the bull and heads of wheat symbolise the fruitful result. The torchbearers represent one in three aspects: the sun at the vernal and autumn equinoxes and the summer solstice, the renewal of nature and its fecundity. The Mithraic Mysteries were celebrated at the winter solstice — "the day of the Nativity of the Invincible."

The cave or artificial grotto used in their initiations represented the Universe, that is, the seven planets, twelve signs of the Zodiac, four elements, etc., for the science of the Mysteries had intimate connection with astrology and physics; further, the mystic symbolic Egg represented their dualism of Light and Darkness, Good and Evil, Night and Day, negative and positive.

A text of St. Jerome and inscriptions preserve the knowledge of the seven degrees of initiation. The ladder of seven planets represents, they say, the seven stages by which man descended into matter and through which he must return to the ether and illumination. According to Celsus the order of return is: Saturn, Venus, Jupiter, Mercury, Mars, Moon, Sun, thus differing from the cabalistic system, which is from Earth to Moon, Mercury, Venus, Sun, Mars, Jupiter, and Saturn. The Mithraic degrees were:

(1) *Raven,* the servant of the Sun;

(2) *Occult* or veiled;

(3) *Soldier,* the warfare against evil in service of Mithras;

(4) *Lion,* the element of fire;

(5) *Persian,* clothed in Asiatic dress;

(6) *Heliodromus,* courier of the Sun. *Pater* or *father* — *Patres Sacrorum,* directors of the cult.

In the first three degrees they were servants only.

In the first an oath of secrecy was taken, preceded by purification and fasts. In the Soldier degree, according to Tertullian, the myste was marked or branded on the forehead with a Tau. In the Lion and Persian honey was applied to hands and tongue. There was also a mystic communion of consecrated bread and water; later wine possibly replaced the soma used in similar rites of Mazdaism. In the higher degrees, among participants, the effects of drinking the sacred wine, the manipulation of the light in the crypt, the administration of the oath, and the repetition of sacred formulae all contributed to induce a state of ecstatic exaltation. Springett, in his *Secret Sects of Syria,* speaks of lustrations with fire, water, and honey, and after many tests ending with a fast of fifty days' continuance, spent in perpetual silence and solitude. "If the candidate escaped partial or complete insanity, an occurrence of great frequency, and surmounted the trials of his fortitude, he was eligible for the superior degrees." Yarker, in his *Arcane Schools,* tells us that in some of the Mithraic monuments Mithras appears with a torch in each hand, whilst a flaming sword issues out of his mouth; in others he has a man on each side, one holding a flaming torch upwards, the other holding it reversed. The latter might represent their principles of Light and Darkness; the flaming sword is also a symbol among modern Rosicrucian and Cabalistic sects, where, on the Cabalistic Tree of Life, Adam Kadmon, the Logos, is depicted with the flaming sword issuing out of his mouth; it is the astral light, which can slay or make alive, set in motion by a powerful will and a trained adept controlling it.

In these Mysteries, therefore, we again see the cult of nature and generation applied to the so-called regeneration of man, mental illumination through the action of the astral light, which in many cases leads to illusion, fanaticism, and at times even madness.

CHAPTER II

CABALISTS, GNOSTICS, AND SECRET SYRIAN SECTS

A VALUABLE series of articles on subversive movements throughout the centuries, *The Anatomy of Revolution,* by G. G., better known as "Dargon," author of *The Nameless Order,* was published by the *Patriot,* October 1922. In one of these he writes:

> "For centuries there have existed certain esoteric schools of mystical philosophy originating apparently in several Oriental currents of thought meeting in the Levant, Egypt, and the nearer East. We find in these schools elements of Buddhism, Zoroastrianism and Egyptian occultism mingled with Grecian mysteries, Jewish Kabalism, and fragments of ancient Syrian cults. Out of the hotch-potch of Oriental philosophy, magic, and mythology arose in the earlier centuries of the Christian era numerous Gnostic sects, and after the rise of Mohammedanism, several heretical sects among the followers of Islam — such as the Ismaelites, Druses, and Assassins — which found their inspiration tin the House of Wisdom in Cairo. To the same sources may be traced the ideas that inspired such political-religious movements of the Middle Ages as those of the Illuminati, Albigenses, Cathari, Waldenses, Troubadours, Anabaptists, and Lollards. To the same inspirations must be assigned the rise of early secret societies. The Templars are said to have been initiated by the Assassins into anti-Christian and subversive mysteries, and we find similar traces of an old and occult origin in the Alchemists, the Rosicrucians, and the later mystical cults of which the Swedenborgian is a familiar example."

Further, Albert G. Mackay, Secretary-General of the Supreme Council 33° for the Southern Jurisdiction, U.S.A., writes in his *Lexicon of Freemasonry:*

"The Kassideans or Assideans... arose either during the Captivity or soon after the restoration... The Essenians were, however, undoubtedly connected with the Temple (of Solomon), as their origin is derived by the learned Scaliger, with every appearance of truth, from the Kassideans, a fraternity of Jewish devotees, who, in the language of Laurie, had associated together as 'Knights of the Temple of Jerusalem.'... From the Essenians Pythagoras derived much, if not all, of the knowledge and the ceremonies with which he clothed the esoteric school of his philosophy."

He also says that Pythagoras met the Jews at Babylon, where he visited during the Captivity, and, Oliver says, "was initiated into the Jewish system of Freemasonry." Of the Cabala Mackay writes:

"The Cabal is of two *kinds* — *theoretical* and *practical* — with the practical Cabala, which is engaged in the construction of talismans and amulets, we have nothing to do. The theoretical is divided into the literal and dogmatic. The dogmatic is nothing more than the summary of the metaphysical doctrine taught by the Cabalist doctors. It is, in other words, the system of the Jewish philosophy."

Writing of the S*epher Yetzirah*, which is older than the *Zohar*, Adolphe Franck in his book *La Kabbale*, 1843, says:

"The clouds with which the imagination of commentators have surrounded it will dissipate of themselves if, instead of seeking in it, as they did, mysteries of ineffable wisdom, we merely see an effort of reason, at the moment of awakening, to perceive the plan of the universe and the link which attaches all elements to a common principle, the assemblage of which it offers to us."

It represents and expounds the thirty-two paths on the Cabalistic Tree of Life — the ten Sephiroth or centres of light, united together by the twenty-two paths to which the Hebrew letters are attributed, these being looked upon as potent forces. These letters are divided into three *Mother letters* — *shin*, fire; *mem*, water; *aleph*, air; seven *double* letters, attributed to the planets; twelve *single* letters, attributed to the signs of the Zodiac. And above, uniting all, is the spirit or ether. By some it is said to depict the descent of the soul into matter and its return and union with the universal life-force, producing illumination, ecstasy, deification, and similar conditions. As to the Cabalistic God, he is first *Ain*-negative; then *Ain Soph* — limitless space; finally, *Ain Soph Aur*

— boundless light. The negative God was awakened, he became active. Again, Jehovah, the Jewish Tetragrammaton, so greatly used in cabalistic and magical operations, is Yod, He, Vau, He, the Creative Principle in unity — the father, mother, son, and daughter or material basis, sometimes called the bride. As it is said: the Absolute Being and Nature have one name only, which signifies God; it represents all forces of nature. In creation first, they say, there was merely emanation, like the sparks flying from an anvil, but being unbalanced they all vanished, as did the Edomite kings; then the dual sexes appeared as separate forces, and with them came balanced creation.

Franck holds that the Zohar or Book of Light, the genesis of the light of nature, begins where the Sepher Yetzirah left off. From the cabalistic point of view the Absolute is called the *White Head*, for all colours are mingled in its light. He is the Ancient of Days or first Sephira on the Cabalistic Tree of Life, he is the Supreme head, the source of all light, the principle of all wisdom-unity. From this unity issues two parallel but apparently opposed principles, though in reality inseparable; the male, active, called Wisdom, the other, passive, female, the Understanding, for "all that exists, all that has been formed by the Ancient of Days can only exist through a male and a female." The Ancient of Days, compared by Franck to Ormuzd of the Persians, is the father engendering all things by means of the marvellous paths, by which the force spreads throughout the universe, imposing a form and limits on all that exists. Understanding is the mother, receiving and reproducing. From their mysterious and eternal union issues a son, having the traits of father and mother, thus bearing witness to both. This son is knowledge and science. These three persons enclose and unite all that is and in turn are united in the White Head. They are sometimes shown as three heads forming one, sometimes they are compared to the brain which, without losing its unity, is divided into three parts, and by means of thirty-two pairs of nerves acts throughout the body, the *microcosm*, just as aided by the thirty-two paths of wisdom, divinity is diffused throughout the universe, the *macrocosm*. It also represents three successive and absolutely necessary phases in universal generation.

Quoting Corduero, Franck continues: The first three Sephiroth-Crown, Kether; Wisdom, Chokmah; Understanding, Binah-should be considered as the Three in One, for they are the Father, Son, and Holy Ghost or mother. The other seven Sephiroth of construction develop also in trinities, in each of which two extremes are united by a third. The second trinity is: Mercy, Chesed, male; Severity, Geburah, female, that is, expansion and concentration of will. These are united by Beauty, Tiphareth, or the Sun, the trinity representing moral force. The third trinity is purely dynamic, showing divinity as the universal force, the *Principe Générateur* of all beings; it is Victory, Netzach, female; Splendour, Hod, male; meaning the extension and multiplication of all forces in the universe. These again are united by Foundation, Yesod, the Moon, and are represented by the organs of generation, root of all that is. The tenth Sephira is Malkuth, the Kingdom or material basis, in which is found the permanent and immanent action of the united Sephiroth, the real presence of God in the midst of creation as expressed by the Shekinah. The work of the Sun and Moon is to spread and perpetuate by their union the work of creation. The third trinity is the kundalini or caduceus, and by mysticism and yoga it is awakened, and rises through the Sephiroth to the Crown, the source of all light, uniting with the universal Creative Principal. Thus, according to the Cabala, every form of existence from matter to eternal wisdom is a manifestation of this infinite power. It is not sufficient that all things should come from God in order to have reality and continuance; it is also necessary that God should be always present in the midst of them, that he should live, develop, and eternally reproduce to infinity under these forms. The Cabala is, therefore, entirely pantheistic.

Of its origin Franck writes: "When examining the *Zohar,* seeking some light on its origin, one is not slow to perceive in its inequality of style, want of unity in its exposition, method, and application of general principles, and finally in its detailed thought, that it is quite impossible to attribute it to one person." It rises to great heights, but again sinks to great puerilities, ignorance, and superstition. "We are therefore forced to conclude that it was formed successively during several centuries and by the work of several generations of cabalists." He points to three fragments forming in themselves, unlike the rest, a co-ordinate whole: (I) the *Book of Mystery,* considered the most ancient; (2) the *Greater Assembly,* the discourses of Rabbi Simon ben Jochai, about A.D. 160, in the midst of his ten disciples; (3) the *Lesser Assembly,* where Simon, on his death-bed, gave instruction to his disciples, now reduced by death to seven. In these is found, sometimes in allegorical, sometimes in metaphysical, language a description of the divine attributes and their various manifestations, the origin of the world and God's relations with man.

Some declare that the Cabala was only developed towards the end of the thirteenth century, but Adolphe Franck holds that, according to proofs which he gives, it must have originated during the seventy years of Jewish Captivity in Babylon, and therefore owes much to the ancient religions of Chaldea and Persia. There, under civil and religious authority, the chiefs of the Captivity built the Synagogue of Babylon, which united with that of Palestine, and many religious schools were founded, in which finally the Talmud of Babylon was produced, the last and complete expression of Judaism. All chronologists, Jewish and Christian, agree that the first deliverance of Israel, captives in Chaldea from the time of Nebuchadnezzar, took place, led by Zorobabel, during the early years of Cyrus's reign over Babylon, about 536-530 B.C. Zoroaster had already commenced his religious mission, teaching the doctrine of dualism Light and Darkness, Good and Evil, in 549 B.C., fourteen years before the first return of the captive Israelites to their own country, and no doubt they carried with them the imprint of this teaching. Apparently no other nation exercised such close influence over the Jews as Persia and the religious system of Zoroaster with its long traditions.

The Practical or Magical Cabala with its combinations and correspondences was the astrological, magical, and magnetic basis used by the Alchemists and Magicians of the Middle Ages in working their transmutations and conjurations. It was impregnated with the "fluidic magic" derived from very ancient cults, and still practised at the time of the Captivity among the Persians and Chaldeans. To-day, all Rosicrucians and cabalistic sects use this Magical Cabala for their works of divining, clairvoyance, hypnotic and magnetic healing, making of talismans, and contacting their mysterious masters. As the Jewish writer Bernard Lazare said:

> "Secret societies represented the two sides of the Jewish mind, practical rationalism and pantheism, that pantheism which, metaphysical reflection of the belief in One God, ended at times in cabalistic theurgy."

CABALISTS AND GNOSTICS

Albert Pike, in *Morals and Dogmas*, tells us that, after the intermingling of different nations, which resulted from the wars of Alexander, the doctrines of Greece, Egypt, Persia, and India met and intermingled everywhere. Gnosis, he says, is the science of the mysteries handed down from generation to generation in esoteric traditions.

> "The Gnostics derived their leading doctrines and ideas from Plato and Philo, the Zend-avesta, the Kabalah, and the Sacred books of India and Egypt; and thus introduced into the bosom of Christianity the cosmological and theosophical speculations, which had formed the larger portion of the ancient religions of the Orient, joined to those of the Egyptian, Greek, and Jewish doctrines, which the Neo-Platonists had equally adopted in the Occident... It is admitted that the cradle of Gnosticism is probably to be looked for in Syria and even in Palestine. Most of its expounders wrote in that corrupted form of the Greek used by the Hellenistic Jews... and there was a striking analogy between their doctrines and those of the Judaeo-Egyptian Philo of Alexandria; itself the seat of three schools, at once philosophic and religious — the Greek, the Egyptian, and the Jewish. Pythagoras and Plato, the most mystical of the Grecian philosophers (the fatter heir to the doctrines of the former), and who had travelled, the latter in Egypt, and the former in Phoenicia, India, and Persia, also taught the esoteric doctrine... The dominant doctrines of Platonism were found in Gnosticism...

> "The Jewish-Greek School of Alexandria is known only by two of its chiefs, Aristobulus and Philo, both Jews of Alexandria in Egypt. Belonging to Asia by its origin, to Egypt by its residence, to Greece by its language and studies, it strove to show that all truths embedded in the philosophies of other countries were transplanted

thither from Palestine. Aristobulus declared that all the facts and details of the Jewish Scriptures were so many allegories concealing the most profound meanings, and that Plato had borrowed from them all his finest ideas. Philo, who lived a century after him, following the same theory, endeavoured to show that the Hebrew writings, by their system of allegories, were the true source of all religions and philosophical doctrines. According to him, the literal meaning was for the vulgar alone.

... The Jews of Syria and Judea were the direct precursors of Gnosticism; and in their doctrines were ample Oriental elements. These Jews had had with the Orient, at two different periods, intimate relations, familiarising them with the doctrines of Asia and especially of Chaldea and Persia... Living nearly two-thirds of a century, and many of them long afterward, in Mesopotamia, the cradle of their race; speaking the same language, and their children reared with those of the Chaldeans, Assyrians, Medes, and Persians, they necessarily adopted many of the doctrines of their conquerors... and these additions to the old doctrine were soon spread by the constant intercourse of commerce into Syria and Palestine...

"From Egypt or Persia the new Platonists borrowed the idea, and the Gnostics received it from them, that man, in his terrestrial career, is successively under the influence of the Moon, Mercury, Venus, Sun, Mars, Jupiter, and Saturn, until he finally reaches the Elysian Fields."

This latter teaching in one form or another is to be found in all modern Gnostic and Cabalistic sects. Thus, in the Stella Matutina Outer and Inner Orders, the grades are placed on the Cabalistic Tree of Life, and the candidate is said to pass successively under the influence of these planets in the above sequence, until at $10 = 1$, the highest grade, he becomes illuminised, and is no longer his own master. These influences represent in their colours the spectrum of the so-called "Divine White Brilliance" — electromagnetic fluid — of the Rosicrucians, which adepts are taught to draw down upon themselves and project for magical purposes. As Albert Pike says:

"The sources of our knowledge of the kabalistic doctrines are the books of Yetzirah and Zohar, the former drawn up in the second century, and the latter a little later; but they contain materials much older than themselves... In them, as in the teachings of Zoroaster, everything that exists emanates from a source of infinite Light."

JEWISH SCHOOL OF ALEXANDRIA

'The Brotherhood of Light,' California, of whom we have already written, claim that 'this venerable Order gave the *impetus to learning in Alexandria* which made that city so justly famous.' And again, 'It was the Brotherhood of Light who preserved the taper of learning from complete extinction during the Dark Ages.' It is therefore interesting to find Dion Fortune, head of the 'Fraternity of Inner Light,' when writing of Hermeticism saying:

> "The highest development was in the Egyptian and Cabalistic systems, and it was blended with Christian thought in the schools of the Neo-Platonists and the Gnostics... Its studies were only kept alive during the Dark Ages among the Jews who were the chief exponents of its Cabalistic aspect ... and it is still alive to-day."

Now the Mason Springett tells us in his book, *Secret Sects of Syria,* that

> "in later times Gnosis was the name given to what Porphery calls Antique and Oriental Philosophy to distinguish it from the Grecian systems. But the term was first used (according to Matter) in its ultimate sense of *supernal* and *celestial* (cosmic) knowledge, by the Jewish philosophers of the celebrated Alexandrian School. A very characteristic production of this Jewish Gnosis has come down to our time in the *Book of Enoch,* of which the main subject is to make known the description of the heavenly bodies and their correct names are revealed to the Patriarch by the angel Uriel. This profession betrays of itself the Magian source from which the inspiration was derived."

In *Le Problème Juif,* Georges Batault writes of these Alexandrian Jewish Philosophers, that they were ardent propagandists, eager to make proselytes, and for this purpose endeavoured to adapt Judaism to Hellenism, persuaded that without the Law and without Israel to practise it, the world would cease to be, the world would be happy only when subject to this universal Law, that is, to the empire of the Jew. As the Jewish writer Bernard Lazare admitted in *L'Antisémitisme:*

"From Ptolemy Philadelphus until the middle of the third century the Alexandrian Jews, with the object of maintaining and strengthening their propaganda, devoted themselves to an extraordinary work of falsification of real texts as a support for their cause. The verses of Aeschylus, Sophocles, Euripides, of the pretended Oracles of Orpheus, preserved in Aristobulus and the Stromata of Clemens of Alexandria, thus celebrated the One God and the Sabbath. Historians were falsified, still more they attributed entire works to them, and it is thus that they placed a History of the Jews under the name of Hécatee d'Abdère. The most important of these inventions was that of the Sibylline Oracles, fabricated entirely by the Alexandrian Jews, which announced the future era, when the reign of One God would eventuate. The Jews even attempted to ascribe to themselves Greek literature and philosophy. In a commentary on the Pentateuch which Eusebius has preserved to us, Aristobulus endeavoured to show how Plato and Aristotle had found their metaphysical and ethical ideas in an old Greek translation of the Pentateuch."

Georges Batault continues:

"The exegesis which consists in distorting texts in order to bring out of them what they desired is the only "science" which can be traced to the Jews. It became in the hands of the Judaeo-Alexandrians, a formidable arm which, by the perfidious force of their veiled lies, enrolled Hellenism, in spite of itself, *into* the service of the exclusivism and the religious proselytism of the Israelites. The attempt to 'Judaise' Hellenism, which to-day appears to us so perfectly absurd and disastrous, has had, nevertheless, the result of obscuring the intelligence of humanity for hundreds of years."

The Italian Mason Reghellini de Schio, writing in 1833, says:

"Alexandria, newly built, was colonised by the Jews, who came in crowds to people the new town. The result was a mixture of men of different nations and religions, who gave rise to several philosophical and religious associations. Platonism was publicly taught by the Greeks in Alexandria, it was eagerly received by the Alexandrian Jews, who communicated it to the Jews of Judea and Palestine... In Egypt and Judea, before the commencement of Christianity the philosophy of Pythagoras and Plato had thrust deep roots among the Jews, which gave rise to the dogmas of the Essenes, Therapeuts, Sadducees, Carpocratians, Cabalistic-Gnostics, Basilideans, and Manicheans; all these dogmatists adapted part of the doctrine of the Egyptian Magi and Priests to the above philosophy. They spread in time into Asia, Africa, and Europe. These different Jewish-Christians preserved the mysteries of the Temple of Solomon with the allegory of the Grand Architect, who was the Jewish Messiah, an idea still preserved by the Jew to-day."

As des Mousseaux notes, the Gnostics and Manicheans preserved the cabala of this primitive Masonry, of which a branch has thrust deep roots among the Druses, and when the Crusaders inundated Asia, they infected the ancestors of our Freemasonry with it — the Templars, the Rose-Croix, and the organs of Western Occultism.

MANICHEANS

The Manicheans taught both Pantheism and Dualism — good and evil, light and darkness; the immanence in all living things of their God, the Creative Principle with its negative and positive aspects. According to Matter, the Carpocratians were the most universal communists; their theory was: "Nature reveals the two Great Principles, community and unity of all things. Human laws contrary to natural laws are guilty violations of the legitimate and divine order; therefore, to re-establish this order, it is necessary to institute community of lands, goods, and women." Further, Manes disavowed war even when waged from just motives, and his followers condemned political and civil magistrates as created and established by the Evil God. Manes likewise condemned all possession of houses, land, or money. Finally, both Gnostics and Manicheans were noted for their disordered morals. Manes proscribed marriage whilst allowing its pleasures, some excused themselves, saying, "to the pure all is pure." According to Baronius, the Manicheans seduced men by sublime words and great promises, and entrapped their unfortunate victims in such powerful nets that once caught it was almost impossible to get free. The disciples bound themselves by the most inviolable oath to keep the secrets of the sect. They were allowed to swear and perjure themselves, but never to reveal the secrets, according to their celebrated maxim: *Jura, perjura secretum prodere noli.*

One of the outcomes of Mithraism was Manicheism, which derived its name from Manes, said by some to be Cubricus, a

Persian slave and scholar, and others maintain that he was educated by his father at Ctesiphon, was brought up in the religion of the "Baptists" of Southern Babylon, who were connected with the Mandeans, and later travelled much and far, including China and India, spreading his beliefs. Opposed by dominant Magian priests, he was eventually crucified. Manicheism was an uncompromising system of dualism in the form of a fantastic philosophy of nature entirely materialistic. It is a conflict between Light and Darkness, Good and Evil, male and female; darkness sought to bind men by sensuality, light tried to save them through the knowledge of Nature and her forces. Manes had no "redeemer," only a physical and gnostic process of redemption, freeing the spark of light from darkness or matter, that is, from within man's body, returning it to the universal light. In this we have the whole basis of modern Cabalistic and Gnostic sects.

M. de Beausobre, in his *Histoire Critique de Manichee et du Manichéisme*, 1734, thus summarised this system: Manes claimed authority as Apostle and Prophet of Jesus Christ directly enlightened by the "Paraclete," in order to reform all religions and reveal those truths to the world which had been withheld from the first disciples. He rejected the Old Testament and reformed the New. Denying the inspiration of the Hebrew Prophets, he opposed to them the books of Seth, Enoch, and other Patriarchs, said to be truths received from good angels. This so-called wisdom still exists in books and schools of Oriental Philosophy. Manes thought of the Divinity as a Living Light, a Father of all Lights, immaterial, eternal, residing in a Supreme luminous Heaven, also eternal, for nothing could be made out of nothing, and always accompanied by Eons, emanations of this divine essence but inferior. God was a Cause in perpetual and eternal action (Creative Principle). From the essence of the Father emanated the Son and the Holy Spirit, co-substantial but subordinate to the Father. Since the creation of the world and until the consummation the Son has resided in the Sun as a power, and in the Moon as the reflected wisdom of the Mother of Life; the Holy Spirit resides in the air, both carrying out the orders of the Father. Here we have apparently a variation of the Emerald Tablet of Hermes.

M. de Beausobre then explains Darkness. In a corner of the vast space is a malignant power, also eternal, called philosophically matter, mystically Darkness, and by the vulgar the Devil. Both Light and Darkness were divided into five elements: water, earth, fire, air, and Light or Darkness, otherwise ether; that is, the four properties of dissolving, coagulating, heating, and cooling. Light knew Darkness, but Darkness only became aware of Light when a revolt arose within that Kingdom (Lucifer) upon which Darkness invaded Light, and although the Primal Man (Christ), assisted by the Living Spirit, of five elements, opposed and overpowered it, part of the Light was stolen and Darkness and Light became mixed together. The Living Spirit then separated the luminous substance which had not been seized by matter, and formed it into the Sun and the Moon, and other planets, also our inferior heaven; the rest went to form our sublunary world, with matter and light mixed together. Wishing to retain the spark of Light, the Prince of Darkness or matter formed two bodies on the model of the Primal Man, but with different sexes, and enclosed these sparks or souls, charming them with the emotions of the senses, and as generation resulted more and more were thus entrapped and drank of the cup of forgetfulness. Then, according to Manes, good angels, Sages, and Prophets appeared to teach the forgotten truths, and finally came the "phantom" Saviour. He held the Docetic belief that matter being evil, Christ's body was a mere phantom, that His acts and sufferings, including the Crucifixion, Resurrection, and Ascension, were only apparent and in reality merely mystical teachings. He also denied the Incarnation. For the elect he disapproved of marriage as being invented by Darkness to retard the return to the Light (unused sex-force is required for this return!); austerities, no meat, no wine, were advocated as weakening the flesh and freeing the spark within. The elect had to embrace poverty, and the only pleasures allowed were music and perfumes, both loosening the spark or soul from the shackles of matter. When sufficiently purified, this soul passed into the moon, receiving surface illumination, and from there was discharged into the sun, where it became luminous, and was finally remitted to the "Pillar of Glory," free from all matter. Transmigration was admitted, as one life was not enough to free the spark from the taint of matter.

The final consummation will be when all this luminous substance has been separated from matter; the evil fire will then be freed from the caverns; the angel upholding the earth will let it fall in flames, and the whole mass will be relegated to Outer Darkness. Those who have failed to free themselves in time will be made guardians of the devils, keeping them from again bringing matter into the kingdom of Light. Such is the marvellous fable under which lies the nature-worship of ancient and modern Magism, known to-day as Illuminism, often called Christian! — as, for example, Anthroposophy or Steinerism, with its two opposing forces Lucifer and Ahriman, light and matter, and its solar and illuminising Christ. And the redemption consists with them of a physical and gnostic process of freeing, by means of unused sex-force, the element of light from matter or the body, and uniting it with the universal magnetic agent without, more of ten linking one mind with another in a magnetic chain, the weaker dominated by the more powerful, producing a world-inundation of communications from so-called "Sages and Prophets" destructive both to Christianity and Western civilisation.

Yarker, in *Arcane Schools,* gives the Manichaean grades as: Disciples, Auditors or mystics, and the Perfect or elect, the priests; from these latter was formed the Magistri or Council of Twelve and a thirteenth as President, as in the Chaldean system. Further, they had secret forms of recognition: word, grip, and breast. Finally, it is said that, as the body was considered evil, it had to be defiled or humiliated, hence the erotic and sexual practices found among Manicheans and other Gnostic sects, more of ten after their frenetic dances; all of which were supposed to free the spark and hasten deification.

As Gibbon stated, the great Manichaean system flourished in the Byzantine age from Persia to Spain, in spite of persecutions by Arian and orthodox emperors alike. And Springett tells us, in the *Secret Sects of Syria:*

> "Manichaean doctrines were thus being diffused during the period when the Templars were at the height of their prosperity and power, and King devotes several pages of his work to a consideration of the close resemblance between these Orders.

Gnosticism, he points out, in one shape or another, was still surviving on the very headquarters of the Order, among their closest allies or enemies, the mountaineers of Syria."

ISMAILIS

According to von Hammer, in his *Histoire de l'Ordre des Assassins,* 1835, the founder of the Ismaili sect, Abdallah, son of Maimoun, deeply learned in all sciences and taught by the bloody revolts of his own time, realised the danger of declaring open war against religion and the ruling Dynasties, more especially when supported by the people and a powerful army. Therefore, he formed a carefully considered scheme to secretly undermine what he could not openly attack. His doctrine, subversive to the Khalifat, had to be veiled in mystery, and only revealed when by secret intrigue the power had been captured. Finally, he dreamt of destroying, not only what he called the errors of dogma and positive religion, but also the basis of all religion and all morals. He divided his doctrine into seven degrees, in this way gradually seizing and subverting the minds of his followers. Out of this doctrine arose the sect of the Karmathites, more open and more violent in their revolt against the Khalifat, both politically and morally. For a century the frightful doctrines of the Karmathites held their sway until at last the sect was extinguished in its own blood. Finally, one of their most zealous Dais, Abdallah, who claimed to be a descendant of Mohammed; son of Ismail, escaped from prison, and seated himself upon the throne, founding the Dynasty of the Fatimites at Kairwan about A.D. 910, under the name of Obeid-allah.

HOUSE OF WISDOM

Our authorities on the nine degrees of Initiation, as were given by the Ismailis in the Grand Lodge or House of Wisdom, Cairo, are, von Hammer and *Expose de la Religion des Druzes,* by Silvestre de Sacy, 1838; both quote Macrisi and Nowairi. As van Hammer writes:

"The details which Macrisi has transmitted to us on the origin of this doctrine and the different degrees of initiation, which were extended from seven to nine, are the most precious and most ancient that we have on the history of the secret societies of the East, in whose steps those of the West afterwards trod. The close agreement between this doctrine and that of the Assassins is worth noting."

This doctrine of Abd'allah, son of Maimoun, from the foundation of the Fatimite Empire dominated both court and government, first at Mahadia and then at Cairo. The chief of the *Darol-Hikmet,* or House of Wisdom, was known as the *Daial-Doat,* or Grand Prior of the Lodge. They upheld Ismail as founder of the "Path," and admitted men and women. There, under El Hakem, the sixth Fatimite Khalifa, a veritable monster of cruelty and crime, who to-day is venerated by the Druzes as a god-made man, the secret doctrine was taught and the nine degrees given.

Briefly, summed up from de Sacy, who quotes both Macrisi and Nowairi, who apparently drew their information from one and the same source, they were:

(1)   The Dai, or missionary, affected devotion in order to seduce his proselyte; with the learned he applauded and agreed with their opinions, careful that his designs and secret were not betrayed. To the simple-minded, easily seduced, he explained that religion was a hidden and abstruse science, the inner meaning of which was known to the Imams alone. By questions on the contradictions of positive religion and reason, the obscurities and absurdities of the Koran, he stirred up doubts and perplexities as well as a violent curiosity, refusing to satisfy this curiosity, and before giving further teaching the Dai demanded an inviolable oath, in which the proselyte swore not to betray the secret, not to lie to or league against the Lodge. If he consented, a money pledge, the amount determined by the Dai, was exacted. Should he refuse either to take the oath or pay the money, he was left to his own perplexities and told nothing more.

(2)   He was then persuaded that only through divinely appointed Imams could the doctrine be received.

(3)   Further, that the number of these "revealed" Imams of the Ismailis was seven, as opposed to the twelve Imams of the Imamias, thus discrediting the Imamat and its head Mousa.

(4)　　The proselyte was told that from the beginning of the world there have been seven divine law-givers or speaking prophets — Adam, Noah, Abraham, Moses, Jesus, Mohammed (Mahomet), and Ismail, son of Djafar-who could by divine command abrogate the preceding religion and substitute a new one. To each of these "speakers" was attached another, who received his doctrine and succeeded him after his death; seven such *mutes*, who carried on the existent religion, succeeded uninterruptedly each law-giver, until finally the seventh of these law-givers abrogated all preceding religions. According to the Ismailis, this last was Mohammed; son of Ismail, who instituted and revealed the new science of the inner and mystic meaning of all outward things. He alone was the teacher, and all the world must follow and obey him. Agreeing to this, the proselyte renounced the Law of the Prophet Mahomet, and therefore became an apostate.

(5)　　He was taught the virtue of numbers and some principles of geometry, and told that each Imam had twelve ministers — the twelve signs of the Zodiac. The Dai then prepared the proselyte to abandon all religions established by the prophets, leading him to the doctrines of the philosophers.

(6)　　Sure of his silence and having reoriented his beliefs, the Dai began to undermine his faith, allegorising the precepts of prayer, tithes, pilgrimages, and other religious observances, making them appear as merely means to dominate the masses. The Dai then praised the principles of such philosophers as Plato, Aristotle, etc., speaking on the other hand lightly of those who had instituted these religious observances, criticising and treating the Imams with scorn. Deprived of all his beliefs, the proselyte was an easy prey.

(7)　　He passed from philosophy to mysticism, the Oriental pantheistic mysticism of the Sufees. He was turned from the Unity of God to dualism and materialism.

(8)　　The Dai then expounded the true prophet's mission, which, he said, was to establish certain political institutions forming a well-constituted government, a philosophical system, and spiritual doctrines applied allegorically to intellectual things, and finally a religious system on the authority of this prophet. The teachings of the Koran were explained as meaning nothing "but the periodical revolution of the stars and the universe, the production and destruction of all things, according to the disposition and combination of the elements, conformable to the doctrine of the philosophers" (Cosmic forces and universal generation).

(9) Having got so·far, some adopted the teachings of Manes, the Magi, or the philosophers, or they mixed them together, and ended in abandoning all revealed religions. To suit the new doctrine, the Dai, by allegorical interpretations, twisted the words of whatever religion was professed by the proselyte always in favour of the prophet, Mohammed, son of Ismail, as the sole prophet inspired by God. With regard to this prophet, at first they said he would return to the world, then modifying this, said that "he could be contacted spiritually through meditation on the mystical doctrines; as for his manifestation, it consisted in preaching his doctrines, communicated to men by the tongues of his faithful servants."

As van Hammer wrote:

"As soon as the proselyte arrived at the ninth degree he was ripe to serve as blind instrument to all passions, and above all to a limitless ambition for domination. The whole of this philosophy could be resumed in two words: *believe nothing and dare all*. These principles destroyed from top to bottom all religion, all morals, and had no other aim than to realise sinister projects carried out by clever ministers, to whom nothing was sacred. We thus see those who should have been the protectors of humanity abandoned to an insatiable ambition, buried under the ruins of thrones and altars in the midst of the horrors of anarchy, after having brought misfortune upon nations, and deserving the curse of mankind."

Finally, this curious order was given to the Dai by those above him: "You must practise and gain great sleight of hand so as to fascinate the eyes (hypnotic illusion) in order to work the miracles which are expected of you." As we have already shown, among the Dactyles, Corybantes, and in the Greater Mysteries, illusions, jugglery, and evocations were the means. used to deceive, not only the epoptes and mystes, but the ignorant people.

To-day, in these numerous sects, cabalistic and illuminati, much the same methods as with the Ismailis are used, and the same doctrine taught. It is always a gradual re-orientation, first an attempt to adapt these doctrines of the Magi,. Manes, and the philosophers to Christianity, destroying the very essence of Christian beliefs, leading to pantheism, dualism, and materialism, often ending in pantheistic mysticism. Through mystical meditation and yoga they achieve magnetic but controlled union with their sinister masters, from whom they receive the universal teachings necessary for their master's "Great Work," unification and world control — religious, political, and intellectual.

Speaking of the House of Wisdom, Springett quotes Ameer Ali's book, *A Short History of the Saracens,* in which he says:

> "Makrisi's account of the different degrees of initiation adopted in the Lodge forms an invaluable record of Freemasonry. In fact, the Lodge at Cairo became the model of all the Lodges created afterwards in Christendom."

ASSASSINS AND TEMPLARS

As we would show, modern subversive ideas have their origin in the nearer East, and have been spread largely through the primitive cabalistic sects and their more ancient borrowings. In his book, *Le Juif, le Judaisme et la Judaïsation des Peuples Chrétiens,* 1869, Gougenot des Mousseaux, speaking of the Manichaeans, Gnostics, Yezidis, Druses, etc., writes:

> "Primitive cabalism was what these sectaries are, for they remain Sabeists; they adore the sun, the stars, the spirit of the stars, and the evil principle, called by the Persians Ahriman... Among these sectaries, all passions, even the most shameful, are regarded as sacred... This absolute despotism of the Grand Masters of Chaldean cabalism was that of the Prince of the Assassins, and the Druses preserve the doctrine and the morals of this cabala. It is that of the secret Grand Master of High Masonry which is governed by the Jews."

The Eastern Ismailis or Assassins were founded about 1090 by Hassan Sabah, who, after being admitted into the House of

Wisdom, Cairo, had to fly because of his intrigues. Realising that as a political society it must have a fortress, by further intrigues he purchased the Castle of Alamoot, on the Caspian Sea, where he eventually founded his Order. He gained many castles in Persia, obtaining great power, inspiring terror in the hearts of all by sudden assassinations of caliphs and viziers. Their head or Sheikh was known as "The Old Man of the Mountain," and it was said "the initiates worked with their heads and led the arms of the Fedavis in execution of the orders of the Sheikh who with his pen guided the daggers." Later it was dispersed, but still exists in India and other countries.

In his *Secret Sects of Syria,* Springett traces the influence of the Jewish philosophers of the celebrated Alexandrian School upon Gnostics and Manicheans and through them upon the Templars. He quotes King and von Hammer to prove that the constitution of the Templar Order

> "is a servile copy of that of the Assassins. The statutes of the latter prove the fact beyond gainsaying; they were found upon the captives of their capital Alamoot by the Mogul Halakoo, in the year 1335, when by a singular coincidence, Caliph and Pope were busied in exterminating the model and the copy in the East and West, at one and the same time."

From these documents were verified the "Eight Degrees of Initiation" as established by Hassan, the first Grand Master or "Prince or Old Man of the Mountain." We find in number 3, denial of the truth of the Koran, and of all other sacred scriptures; 4, the trial of silent and perfect obedience; 5, the disclosure of the names of the great Brothers of the Order, royal, sacerdotal, and patrician, in all parts of the world; 7, the allegorical interpretation of the Koran, and of all other scriptures. In this Order the divinity of all founders of religious systems was alike denied. Religion was shown to be a mere step to knowledge, its narratives to be merely allegorical, and exhibiting the progress of civil society; thus, Man's Fall signified political slavery; Redemption his restoration to liberty and equality. 8, that all actions were indifferent, provided only they were done for the good of the Order, there being no such thing absolutely as vice or virtue. These are almost identical with the tenets of the Illuminati.

Von Hammer, in his *History of the Assassins,* further elucidates this "Catechism of the Order," as he calls it. Of the fourth he says that, after taking an oath, the candidate promised a blind obedience, and at the same time swore "to communicate to none but his superiors any doubts he might have about the mysteries and doctrines of the Ismaelites." Curiously enough, the late Dr. Felkin, Chief of the Stella Matutina, desiring, in 1909, further teaching from the "Hidden Chiefs" or Sun Masters, was told he must first take a pledge "by all that he held most awful and sacred, never to betray the method to mortal man." Part of the pledge was: "If hereafter I am assailed by doubts I will reveal such doubts only to the Masters... Should I at any time find myself unable any longer to keep this pledge, I will say nothing to my brothers or sisters of the Order to weaken their faith, but I will quietly pass into abeyance." The pledge was taken.

With regard to the seventh degree, we find the same idea in the Jewish School of Alexandria, for, as we have already said, Aristobulus declared that all the facts and details of the Jewish Scriptures were so many allegories, concealing the most profound meanings. Philo too followed the same theory, and endeavoured to show that the Hebrew writings, by their system of allegories, were the true source of all religions and philosophical doctrines. The literal meaning was for the vulgar alone. Like Philo, Steiner, of Anthroposophy, taught the same interpretation, that the Bible was merely an allegory of the gradual and mystical deification of man as symbolically portrayed in all ancient and modern mysteries. This deification is symbolised by the "hidden God" Amoun of the Egyptians and the *crux ansata,* the latter being the centre of the Theosophical symbol and means the dual forces of generation — the kundalini; again, the Caduceus of Hermes, placed on the lower part of the pantheistic figure Baphomet of the Templar cult, represents the generative forces within man, the means of deification.

Further, among the Khlysty and other primitive gnostics is found this same allegorical interpretation of the Gospels and Old Testament, with the same deification or creation of "Christs" in view. As M. Ribot says, there are many ways of producing artificial ecstasy or having divinity within oneself — rhythmic dances, soma, wine, blood, orgies, and drug intoxication, including no doubt hasheesh, such as was used by "The Old Man of the Mountain" which prepared his fanaticised Fedavis, intoxicated by every lure of the senses, a so called foretaste of paradise, or perhaps hypnotised, thus made ready and willing to carry out by dagger or poison the plotted murders of the Grand Master's victims.

According to von Hammer there were seven grades of Assassins closely akin to those of the Templars:

1. Grand Master, or "Old Man of the Mountain."

2. Dailkebir, or Grand Prior.

3. Dais, or initiated Masters, recruiters.

4. Refik, or companions.

5. Fedavis, blind instruments, the guards of the Order.

6. Lassiks, aspirants.

7. Batini, or secret brethren, affiliates.

Among the seven silent Imams was the "Invisible Imam," in whose name the Grand Master exacted obedience from the people. Like the secret instigators of the French Revolution, according to Louis Blanc, Grand Masters of the Templars linked to Weishaupt's Illuminati, Hassan desired to overthrow thrones and altars, but recognised that anarchy, although often useful to the governed, should never be the aim of the governing. His ambition was to found an empire on the ruins of the Khalifat and the family of Abbas.

The Assassins were not a principality, but merely a confraternity or Order similar to that of the Knights of Saint John, the Teutonic Knights, or the Templars. As von Hammer says:

> "The nature of the functions that in the last-named Order were filled by its·Grand Master and Grand Priors, its religious institutions, the political tendency of its spirit and its doctrines, all even to its clothing gave it some resemblance to that of the Assassins... The fundamental rule of the two Orders was to seize fortresses and castles in the neighbouring countries in order more easily to control

the people; both were dangerous rivals for the princes and formed a state within a state."

To-day it is not merely a state within a state ruled by secret sects, but a Universal World State ruled by unknown "Supermen."

DRUSES

According to Springett, the Druses were said to take their name from Mohammed Ibn, Ismail el-Dorazi, a Persian who came to Egypt about 1017. Causing fanatical riots at Cairo by proclaiming the divinity of the Khalifa El-Hakem, he was forced by the people to fly, and was sent to Lebanon by El-Hakem, where, under his instructions, the Druses acknowledged El-Hakem's divinity. Some years later the real founder of their religion, Hamzeh, a Dai or missionary of the House of Wisdom, further sent Moktana Baha-edeen to replace Dorazi, and prevailed on the Druses to accept the initiation system of the Grand Lodge at Cairo, thus forming. the religion as it is to-day. Dorazi's teaching was a form of mysteries which "threw a cloak over the indulgence of the worst passions of human nature," and these to a certain extent still prevail, dividing the Druses into two sects — the more orthodox moral and religious teaching of Hamzeh and the licentiousness of Dorazi. Mackenzie describes their religion as a compound of Judaism, Christianity, and Mohammedanism; they have a priesthood, a kind of hierarchy, passwords and signs, and both sexes are admitted.

As stated by Mme Blavatsky, who was a member of the Druse Order, it is Gnostic and Magian; they believe in the Unity of God, who is the essence of life, invisible but known through occasional manifestations in human form. She calls it a last survival of the archaic Wisdom religion known to-day as "Kabalism, Theosophy, and Occultism." It is pantheistic. Outwardly, as inculcated in their sacred books, they profess to read the Koran and the Gospels, while secretly following their mystery doctrines. She also claims that there is a close affinity between the Turanian Lamaists and the Semitic El-Hammists or Druses. The Turanians of India are, writes Yarker, a race of builders, tree, and serpent worshippers. In an early issue of the *Theosophist* Mme Blavatsky quotes Laurence Oliphant as writing:

> "The Druse has a firm conviction that the end of the world is at hand... [which] will be signalised by the approach of a mighty army from the East against the contending powers of Islam and Christianity ... under the command of the Universal Mind [Illuminism!] and will consist of millions of Chinese Unitarians. Christians and Mohammedans will surrender and march before it to Mecca, El-Hakem will then appear (as the last divine incarnation)... The Druses are eagerly waiting for an Armageddon in which they believe themselves destined to play a prominent part."

Yarker says of Mme Blavatsky:

> "Blavatsky, who was an initiate of the (Druse) Sect, informs us ... that its basis is the old Ophite (or Nasseni) Gnosticism."

She also, we know, belonged to the revolutionary, Jew-dominated Carbonari, and later claimed to be in touch with Masters in Tibet. A few points about her are worth noting as given by the French orientalist, Rene Guenon, in *Le Théosophisme*. Before she founded the Theosophical Society she was greatly influenced by Palos Metamon, a Copt, or, as some say, a Chaldean, a worker in magic and spiritism; further, Sinnet declared that "Mme Blavatsky crowned a career of thirty-five to forty years of mystic studies by a retreat of seven years in the solitudes of the Himalayas"; this was before she went to America in 1873, at which time she was only forty-two! As Rene Guenon remarks, "We should have to conclude that she must have begun her studies at her birth, if not indeed a little before!" Going back through her life and giving data, he concludes that her visit to Tibet was pure invention. As for her controls, she was for a time member of the Hermetic Brotherhood of Luxor, who taught that *"these phenomena were due, not to spirits of the dead, but to certain forces directed by living men."* He further explains that her "spirit guides" — John King, Serapis, and the Kashmiri brother — merely represent the successive influences using her, and that "it is legitimate to conclude that Mme Blavatsky was, above all, in many circumstances, a "subject" or instrument in the hands of individuals or occult groups, sheltering behind her personality, in the same way as others were in their turn instruments in her hands." And this is what one finds throughout the whole history, ancient and modern, of these sects — illusion, jugglery, magic — the use of this "fluidic magic," going back to the remotest past, it is the fire stolen by Prometheus from the Gods.

SUFEES AND DERVISHES

Again we learn from Springett, in his *Secret Sects of Syria,* that 'the Sufees are a secret society of Persian mystic philosophers and ascetics, whose original religion may have been that of the Chaldeans or Sabeans, who believed in the unity of God, but adored the hosts of heaven (Tsaba), especially the seven planets, as representing Him.' The Sufi Masters mean by God the power underlying all phenomena which is everywhere and in everything. It is pantheistic mysticism. These Sufee principles are held among the higher grades of the Dervishes. The Sufee doctrine, King says, involves the idea of one universal creed which could be secretly held under any profession of an outward faith. The Dervish guide instructs the candidate in the mystic philosophy, and if it in any way shocks the pupil, is supplied with a double sense so that he can turn aside any fears or objections. In the same way the pantheistic teachings of the Stella Matutina of today could be twisted so that even a Christian priest might be persuaded to see Christianity in them.

Speaking of the Initiation of a Dervish, Springett says of the *Kadiri* Order that, after many months of probation in the monastery, the Sheikh, at the assembly of the brethren, places on the candidate's head a white felt cap, having attached to it a cloth rose of eighteen petals with the interlaced triangles of Solomon's Seal in the centre — the Jewish symbol of the dual forces of nature, as above so below. Before being fully accepted as a Dervish, he passes through intermediate stages under the guidance of a Superior or initiate of the highest degree.

> "He is taught to concentrate his thoughts so completely on his 'Guide' as to become mentally absorbed in him as a spiritual link with the supreme object of all devotion. The Guide must be the neophyte's shield against all worldly thoughts and desires (let go the material!); his spirit must aid him in all his efforts, accompanying

him wherever he may be, and be ever present in his mental vision. Such a frame of mind is termed "annihilation into the Murshid," and the Guide discovers, by means of his own visions, the degree of spirituality to which his disciple has attained, and to what extent his soul has become absorbed into his own."

He then enters the "Path," and according to his aptitude and willingness to accept the Guide's mystic philosophy, although against his religious feelings, his advance will be correspondingly rapid.

"He is now supposed to come under the spiritual influence of the *Pir* or founder of the Order, in whom he in turn becomes mentally absorbed to such a degree as to be virtually one with him, acquiring his attributes and power of performing supernatural acts. The·next stage of the mystic life is that termed by the Dervishes "Spiritual Knowledge," and the disciple... is believed by the Sheikh ... to have become inspired... He now enters into spiritual communion with the Prophet himself, into whose soul his own has become absorbed."

Finally, in the fourth degree "during forty days' fasting and seclusion ... in an ecstatic state he believed himself to have become part of the Divinity, and sees Him in all things." The Sheikh then "gently awakens the disciple from his ecstasy, and having restored him to his normal condition, bestows upon him the rank of *Khalifeh* (successor). The mystic now resumes his outward observance of the rites of Islam, and prepares for his pilgrimage to the Holy Cities."

To-day the whole world has become a veritable hive of cabalistic and gnostic sects, and in each and all is found this same system of gradual mental absorption, as with the Dervishes, of the adept's personality as he advances upward, successively by the official teacher of the Order, by a Teacher on the astral plane, in Rosicrucian Orders by its so-called founder Christian Rosenkreutz, and finally complete absorption by some unknown Central Power, still in the material body. Thus oracles are trained, apparently inspired, giving forth teaching, which in turn is passed down through the various grades of the order orienting the members. They finally go out among the people spreading the ideas, often in the name of Liberty, Equality, and Fraternity, leading them astray under the direct or indirect influence of these sects and their outside manifestations, international, universal, socialist, communist, and atheist.

YEZIDIS

As Springett writes:

> "The Yezidis have a tradition that they originally came from Basrah, and from the country watered by the lower part of the Euphrates; that, after their emigration, they settled first in Syria, and subsequently took possession of the Sindjar hill, and the districts they now inhabit in Kurdistan... There is in them a strange mixture of Sabeanism, Christianity, and Mohammedanism, with a tincture of the doctrines of the Gnostics and Manichaeism; Sabeanism, however, appears to be the prevailing feature."

They have a great respect for the Sun and its symbol fire. In *Le Juif,* des Mousseaux, quoting authorities, tells us that Chaldea has always been the cradle of the demonic cabala, descended from the Cainites, and from the Sabeans, who adored the sun, stars, spirit of the stars, and the evil principle. This cabala penetrated among the Yezidis and Druses.

Now W. B. Seabrook, in his *Adventures in Arabia,* says that in the "Black Book" of the Yezidis, Shaitan commands: "Speak not my name nor mention my attributes, lest ye be guilty, for ye have no true knowledge thereof, but honour my symbol and image." Seabrook was told that "Shaitan" was the "Bright Spirit Melek-Taos" (Angel Peacock), the "Spirit of Power and the ruler of the world" — Lucifer! He also speaks of the, seven Towers of Shaitan, or "power-houses," which are said to form a chain across Asia, from northern Manchuria, through Tibet, west through Persia and ending in Kurdistan, and in each tower is a priest who was said to do world-magic. He saw one such at Sheikh-Adi; it was whitewashed, fluted, and cone-shaped, with a polished ball of gold or brass on the pinnacle, which flashed abroad when struck by the sun; often, he was told, a special magic-worker spent many days alone in it. On the entrance to their shrine was a black serpent!

According to des Mousseaux, the Yezidis were governed by a Supreme Emir, who was Patriarch and Pontiff, with absolute power; by means of subordinate emirs he transmitted his orders to all Yezidis (Schamanites) scattered throughout Kurdistan, Media, Mesopotamia, and the Mounts Zindjar. And "it is probable also that by mysterious ramifications his orders reached to the remotest extremities of Asia, and perhaps even Europe." Further,

> "all passions even the most shameful, are regarded as sacred … the devil for them is only a fallen angel… God, they say, is infinitely good, incapable of doing evil to men. The devil, on the contrary, is infinitely wicked, and in his malice his sole pleasure is to torture them. It is, therefore, above all prudent, if one would be happy here below, to abandon the cult of God, who can do no harm… and to place oneself under the protection of the being who alone can exempt men from the evils of this life, since he alone can inflict them…"

It is said that they are given up to the most extraordinary theurgic practices, all that is most diabolical in magic and sorcery. In confirmation of much of this Springett writes further:

> "If, indeed, the Yezidi belief be one deprecatory of the Devil, and if, as Mr. Layard intimates, the peacock be symbolic of Satan, who is in their eyes only the chief of the rebel angels, then the Malek Taoos would represent the bad rather than the good principle, and so far would be akin to the golden calf of the Druses, and imply also Persian origin of the sect, and the ancient ideas of Ahura Mazda (or Ormuzd) and Ahriman."

The Yezidi Chief himself said the "Malek Taoos" was a symbol held in great reverence.

Springett states that the Yezidis are ruled by two Sheikhs, one directing civil affairs, the other presiding over religious rites, especially entrusted with the care of their Sanctuary named after their chief Saint, *Sheikh Adi*. The hierarchy includes four orders of priests — Pirs, Sheikhs, Kawals, and Fakirs, which are hereditary, and women, if in the line of succession, can fill them. As to their beliefs, they believe in a Supreme Being, the essence of goodness,

> "and also revere Satan, though they never pronounce his name or anything approaching it… They appear, therefore, to worship both Good and Evil deities of the ancient Persians, but say, as the latter

can sometimes do good while the former cannot possibly do anything evil, it is the Evil principle they must conciliate."

He also speaks of "the extremely prized sacred book possessed by the Yezidis", and according to Badger and Layard it is written in Arabic, and consists of a poetical rhapsody on the merits and attributes of Sheikh Adi.

As reported by the *Revue Internationale des Sociétés Secrètes,* I May, 1932, Pierre van Passen, of the *Toronto Daily Star,* gave an account of a Black Mass ceremony which he witnessed in the Temple, rue de Montparnasse, Paris. He said there are eleven temples, and, it is estimated, about 10,000 worshippers of the Devil in Paris — men and women who have passed through a long apprenticeship. These worshippers of the Devil are in communion with a sect still existing in the Syrian desert in the neighbourhood of Bagdad, who worship "Shaitan," which name must never be spoken, not even words beginning with the first two letters. There have been, for ten or twenty years, many outside complaints, but, under the "liberty of worship" decree, this cult is allowed by the French Government on conditions that no open propaganda is carried on.

CHAPTER III

ROSICRUCIANS AND ILLUMINES

THE origin of the Rosicrucians is still an unsolved mystery; it is even as Disraeli wrote in 1841:

> "This mystic Order spread among the Germans, a mystic people, where its origin was actually debated in the same·way as those of other secret societies; in fact, its hidden sources defy research." ·

On the other hand, as in all so-called Rose-Croix Orders, the R.R. et A.C. — *Rosae Rubeae et Aureae Crucis* — in its 5 = 6 ritual claims to go back to the remotest, even mythical, ages of antiquity, for it says:

> "Know that the Order of the Rose and Cross has existed from time immemorial, and that its mystic rites were practised and its wisdom taught in Egypt, Eleusis, Samothrace, Persia, Chaldea, India, and in far more ancient lands, and thus handed down to posterity the Secret Wisdom of the Ancient Ages. Many were its Temples, and among many nations where they established, though in process of time some lost the purity of their primal knowledge."

The mysterious Brothers of the Rosy Cross designated themselves as *Invisibles,* and their legendary history was briefly this: the Fraternity was founded by a certain Christian Rosenkreutz, born, it is said, in 1378, of a noble German family. For twelve years, from the age of five, he was educated in a cloister, and thereafter travelled to Damascus, and from thence to a place called Damcar in Arabia, where he was well received by the Magi. These wise men expected him as being the one who, it had been foretold, would regenerate the world, and they initiated him into their Arabian magic. After visiting Fez and Spain, he returned to Germany where, along with three disciples, he founded the Fraternity, and they built their house called "Domus

Sancti Spiritus," in which C. R. lived until his death. There they wrote the book "M" — *Magicon,* according to Dr. Wynn Westcott-compiled, it is said, from the magic taught to C. R. by the Arabs of Damcar. Also the books Axiomata, Rota Mundi, and Protheus.

Christian Rosenkreutz died, we are told, in 1484, at the age of one hundred or more, and for one hundred and twenty years the place of his tomb remained unknown. In 1604, while repairing the building, they came upon the door of the vault, and when opened they there found the body of their founder and much magical property and occult manuscripts. After his death the brothers devoted themselves to the study of the secrets of nature and its hidden forces, besides practising medicine, gratuitously, using some mysterious remedies. Their agreement was: (1) That none of them should profess any other thing than to cure the sick and that *gratis.* (2) None of the Posterity should be constrained to wear one certain kind of habit, but therein to follow the custom of the country. (3) That every year, upon the day C. (Corpus Christi Day, the summer solstice), they should meet together at the house Sancti Spiritus, or write the cause of absence. (4) Every brother should look for a worthy person, who, after his decease, might succeed him. (5) The letters R. C. should be their seal, mark, and character. (6) The Fraternity should remain secret one hundred years.

These Invisibles awaited what they called the purification of the Church, when, before the end of the world, they hoped to re-establish everything in its primitive integrity. After the opening of the tomb, the appointed one hundred and twenty years having more than passed, they issued two manifestos — *Fama Fraternitatis R.C.,* 1614, and *Confessio Fraternitatis Rosae Crucis,* 1615, and sent them to all the learned men and Governments in Europe, inviting them to join with the Order in the universal reform. For a time these made a great stir, but with little outward result. These documents by many were ascribed to Jean Valentin Andrea, although he, himself, always denied the authorship.

In his book, *Les Rose-Croix Lyonnais au XVIIIe Siècle,* 1929, Paul Vulliaud goes into these manifestos, etc., linking them with

Paracelsus and Cornelius Agrippa, Theosophy and Illuminism. Speaking of Ch. Fauvety's *Livre du Monde* (Magic of Nature) Vulliaud writes:

> "In a very interesting study Fauvety maintains it has to do with *Magnetism...* He did well in showing the importance attributed, during the time of Paracelsus, to the *magnetic fluid* in the Theosophico-scientific doctrines... After having observed that the followers of Paracelsus and van Belmont made a mystery of it, Fauvety adds, that the *magnetic power* "might, indeed, according to some writers, have been the secret of the Rose Croix, who in the sixteenth century were said to possess a universal remedy. What supports this supposition is that even the adversaries of magnetism reproached the doctors, followers of Paracelsus, with curing by magnetic processes similar to those of the Rose-Croix."

As Gustave Bord wrote in *La Franc-Maçonnerie en France*, 1908:

> "The doctrine of Paracelsus was drawn from the Cabala, Hermetic philosophy and alchemy. He claimed to know and expound the entire system of the Mysterious forces which act in nature and in man... Man must unite himself to the forces required in order to produce either physical or intellectual phenomena. The Universe was the Macrocosm, man was the Microcosm, and they were similar (as above so below)."

Further, Vulliaud says that J. J. Monnier also knew that in certain lodges the initiates practised magnetism. According to Monnier, 'they magnetised by divine grace *[sic]*, by force of faith and will, through walls to great distances, from Paris even to Dominica.' Finally, Vulliaud concludes:

> "To sum up, Rosicrucianism is composed of mystic illuminism, in combination with alchemy, astrology, magnetism, and communication with spirits [astral!], if not with the Word itself; it is composed of sometimes one, sometimes several of these forms of the marvellous and occult. In certain lodges... they ardently practise theurgy."

In an anonymous book, *Mysteries of the Rosie Cross,* published in 1891, which is full of documented information, we read:

> "Respecting the origin and signification of the term Rosicrucian, different opinions have been held and expressed. Some have thought it was made up of *rosa* and *crux* (a rose and a cross), but it is

maintained by others upon apparently good authority, that it is a compound of *ros* (dew) and *crux* (cross).

... A cross in the language of the fire philosophers is the same as *Lux* (light), because the figure of a cross exhibits all three letters of the word *Lux* at one view... A Rosicrucian, therefore, is a philosopher who, by means of *dew* seeks for *light* that is, for the substance of the philosopher's stone"—

the Quintessence or five elements, earth, air, fire, water, and ether; the illuminised man!

As to the Rosa-Crux interpretation, the R.R. et A.C. ritual informs us the key to the

"Tomb of Osiris On-nopheris, the Justified One (illuminated), the symbolical burying-place of our Mystic Founder Christian Rosenkreutz which he made to represent the Universe ... is the form of the Rose and Cross, the ancient Crux Ansata, the Egyptian symbol of Life, which resume the Life of Nature and the powers hidden in the words I.N.R.I."

As we know, I.N.R.I. is *Igne Natura Renovatur Integra* — the entire nature is renewed by fire. It represents the three phases of universal generation — creation, destruction, and regeneration. The signs given are L.V.X. representing the same idea. Further explaining L.V.X., the same ritual says: Having arrived at the door of the tomb,

"upon more closely examining the door you will perceive ... that beneath the CXX in the inscription were placed the characters L.V.X., the whole being equivalent to 'Post CXX Annos Lux Crucis Patebo' — at the end of 120 years I the light of the Cross will disclose myself. For the letters L.V.X. are made from the dismembered and conjoined angles of a cross +."

Moreover, the Rosicrucians were learned cabalists, and Adolphe Franck, in *La Kabbale,* quotes Simon ben Jochai in the *Zohar,* speaking of the Ancient of Days, the first of the Sephiroth on the Tree of Life:

"He is seated on a throne of sparks which he subjects to his will... From his head he shakes a *dew* which awakens the dead and gives birth within them to a new life. That is why it is written: 'Thy dew is a dew of light. It is the nourishment of the saints of the highest order. It is the manna prepared for the just for the life to come. It descends into the fields of the sacred fruits (adepts of the Cabala). The aspect of this dew is white as a diamond, whose colour includes all colours'."

This dew is the "Divine White Light or Brilliance" of the Rosicrucians, the magnetic fluid of their magic. Furthermore, it is said in the same R.R. et A.C. ritual: "Colours are forces and the signature of forces, and Child of the Children of Forces art thou, and, therefore, about the throne of the Mighty One is a rainbow of Glory and at his feet is the Crystal Sea." It is the force of Illuminism, a light of Nature!

Again, Jane Lead, chief inspiration of the Panacea Society, speaking of the properties of the Cabalistic Tree of Life, describes the fifth as: "The sweetness of the dew, which lies always upon the branches of the Tree... It is all paradisical (or illuminating) power." This same power, magnetic fluid, is the basis of their Rosicrucian universal remedy. Moreover, according to the writer of *The Mysteries of the Rosie Cross:* "A remarkable work was published in Strasbourg in the year 1616, entitled, *The Hermetic Romance, or the Chymical Wedding. Written in High Dutch by Christian Rosencreutz.* This book ... is said to have existed in manuscript ... as far back in fact as 1601, thus making it the oldest Rosicrucian book extant." Some say it was the work of Valentin Andrea; in any case, it appears to depict the adept's union with the Universal agent, and it is possible that the whole legend of Christian Rosenkreutz merely represents the same mystical idea as found among all yogis and mystics, awakening mysterious powers.

As Gustave Bord wrote:

> "In all times there were secret sects who claimed to understand the laws which regulate the Universe; some believed they really possessed the ineffable secret; others, the clever ones, made their mysteries a lure for the crowd, claiming thus to dominate and lead it; at least they found the way to utilise it to their profit."

In the Preface to a curious book, *The Long Livers,* by Robert Samber, writing under the pseudonym "Eugenius Philalèthes Junior," which was dedicated to the Grand Lodge of London in 1722, and has been referred to by the Masonic historians Mackay, Whytehead, and Yarker, it is clearly indicated that above the three traditional grades there is an *illumination* and a hierarchy, whose nature is not revealed, but the language used is entirely that of alchemy and Rose-Croix. Louis Daste, speaking of Freemasonry in the French Revolution, remarks:

> "This mysterious illumination of the low grades of Masonry, this hierarchy of which Philalèthes Junior has so jealously guarded the secret, those 'Unknown Superiors' venerated by the Judaising Martinists and Philalèthes, who claim domination over ordinary lodges — is not all that the unbreakable chain which links the Jewish Cabala to Freemasonry, and have we not henceforth the right to suspect the Occult Power hidden behind the Masonic Lodges to be the brain of Judaism which would conquer and dominate the entire world?"

MARTINES DE PASQUALLY

In his book on the Order of the *Élus Coens* of the eighteenth century, R. le Forestier tells us that this Order was founded— continuing as Martinists to-day — about 1760, by Martines de Pasqually, said to be a Portuguese Jew. It was one of the most interesting occult groups of the time, 'which constituted under cover of Freemasonry one of the last links of the long chain of mysterious and jealously closed associations whose members claimed by magical processes to communicate with the divine in order to participate in a blessed immortality' — Illuminism! The name *Coen* given by Pasqually to his members is an adaptation of the Hebrew term *Cohanim,* which designated the highest sacerdotal caste, constituted at Jerusalem, under Solomon, to assure divine service in the Temple; they were said to be descended in a direct line from Aaron. The Coens thus claimed to be heirs and depositories of the secret Jewish tradition. Pasqually built up a curious metaphysical and mystic system, 'borrowed from secret traditions, it represented a weak but very clear echo of the diverse esoteric doctrines originating in the East during the early centuries of our era after adopting other more ancient traditions, and which later penetrated the West through the intermediary of the Jewish Cabala.' His disciples were the successors of the mystes of Asia, Egypt, Greece, and Italy, of the Valentinians, Orphics, and followers of Mithras; they professed the mystic doctrines of the Neo-Platonists, Gnostics, and

Cabalists, and cultivated at the time of the *Encyclopaedia* the 'Secret Wisdom of the Ancients.'

The Theoretical Cabala, as we know, treats of the nature of the Deity, his relations with man, and the origin of the world. The Practical or Magical Cabala, on the other hand, dealt with 'dynamistic and theurgic magic, taught the art of commanding spirits, divining the future, clairvoyance from a distance, and making amulets.' In its mystic currents were found the influence of Chaldean astrology and demonology, Ionic natural philosophy, Mazdean, Manichaean, Sabean, and Mithraic concepts, also Pythagorean arithmetic and geometry. It was a residue of the primitive cults founded on 'fluidic Magic' — the magical magnetic fluid of the alchemists, Rosicrucians, and Illumines — and which still, during the Captivity, persisted in the Babylonian and Persian religions. In the seventeenth century J. B. van Helmont, in his *Hortus Medicine,* wrote: "A magical force, sent asleep by sin, is latent in man; it can be awakened by the grace of God or by the art of the Cabala." It is the awakening of the kundalini by magical processes or yoga! These theurgic rites of the Practical Cabala had existed until the eighteenth century in the heart of the Jewish sects connected with the Frankists, so widespread in Central Europe.

Finally, le Forestier says that the theurgic process, advocated particularly by the Practical Cabala, was founded on the marvellous power of divine names; it is derived from one of the fundamentals of all kinds of magic, going back to remotest times. Pasqually also emphasised this idea, familiar to cabalists, that the name above all manifests its power when pronounced in a loud voice. Here we have the 'vibratory mode of pronouncing—divine names,' used in the Stella Matutina and the R.R. et A.C., a Martinist Order, which their obligations command should never be revealed! The power is greatly increased, as in magical conjurations, by pronouncing the name together with all its correspondences as shown in Crowley's book *777.* Further, the operations of the Coens, with their diagrams, lustrations, burning of incense, prostrations, invocations, and conjurations, manifestly show the magical ceremonials to which the disciples of Pasqually devoted themselves. We find the same operations in the S.M. and the R.R. et A.C. to-day. To turn to Eliphas Levi, another and later Martinist, who writes in his *History of Magic:*

"Moreover, the law of equilibrium in analogy leads to the discovery of a universal agent which was the Great Secret of the alchemists and magicians of the Middle Ages. It has been said that this agent is a light of life by which animated beings are rendered magnetic, electricity being only a transient perturbation. The practice of that marvellous Kabalah reposes entirely in the knowledge and use of this agent. Practical Magic alone opens the secret Temple of Nature to that power of human will which is ever limited but ever progressive."

The *Zohar,* he says, is a genesis of light (of nature). The *Sepher Yetzirah* is the ladder of accomplishment and application; it has thirty-two steps — ten Sephiroth or centres of light, and twenty-two paths or canals linking the Sephiroth, and through which the light or magical fluid flows. It is the Cabalistic Tree of Life. Applied, as it is in cabalistic and magical Orders, to the Microcosm or man's brain and nervous system, it is full of danger and illusion, mental, moral, and physical. Eliphas Levi further says that the science of fire and its ruling was the secret of the Magi, giving them mastery over the occult powers of nature; 'On every side we meet with the enchanter who slays the lion and controls the serpents. The lion is the celestial (cosmic or starry) fire, while the serpents are the electric and magnetic currents of the earth. To this same secret of the Magi are referable all marvels of Hermetic Magic.'

Finally, these controlling 'Supermen' behind the scenes are, it would seem, past-masters in the knowledge and working of this Practical Cabala built up from cults of the remotest past. Is it not, therefore, justifiable to suppose that these Supermen are magic-working, cabalistic, and revolutionary Jews?

PERNETY

Joanny Bricaud, in *Les Illuminés d'Avignon,* 1927, gives us some curious details on the growth of this movement:

"Strange thing! The era of the *Encyclopaedists* and philosophers was also the era of the prophets and the thaumaturgists. In face with

Voltaire, Diderot, d'Alembert, incredulous and sceptic, arose Swedenborg, Martines de Pasqually, Saint-Martin, Mesmer, and Cagliostro, founders of mystic groups given up to every practice of theurgy, magic, and illuminism."

As said by Bricaud, Dom Pernety, the founder of the Avignon group, was born at Roanne, in Forez, 1716, and became a Benedictine of Saint-Maur. Whilst at the Abbey Saint-Germain-des-Prés, he came across many books on Hermetic lore and Alchemy, and became thoroughly inoculated with this fever of the age. Finding monastic life intolerable, he threw it up and went to Avignon, where he founded his Hermetic Rite, 1766. Later we see him in Berlin, still keeping in touch with his adepts. Gradually his hermeticism became invaded by the mysticism of Swedenborg and Boehme, he became a seer and illumine, having as guide a so-called Angel Assadai, receiving communications from an invisible power known as Sainte-Parole.

M. Bricaud further says that there exists in the Bibliothèque Calvet at Avignon, a strange manuscript of 155 pages in Pernety's own handwriting, which was seized in his house during the Revolution. It dates from Berlin, 1779–1783, and Avignon, 1783–1785, and is an account of the evocations and questions of his initiates to this Sainte-Parole and the replies of that power. The initiates are inscribed by occult numbers, which form the basis of their cabalistic operations, when consulting Sainte-Parole. Nothing was done without the approval of this unknown power. As Weishaupt has said: "We cannot use men as they are; they must be shaped according to the use that is to be made of them." In the same way Pernety and his initiates were tested, admonished, and bemused until the power obtained absolute faith and obedience from them. They were consecrated on a hill above Berlin, regenerated, and illuminised; Pernety was destined to found a society for the "new people of God," and build a new city in preparation for a "new heaven and new earth." He was to be the centre and pontiff, and another adept, Comte Grabianka, was to be king. The six-year-old daughter of the latter was to be isolated from parents and country for seven years to be prepared as oracle through whom he was to rule. Finally, the temple called *Thabor* was established near Avignon, and the group became known as the *Illuminés d'Avignon*. Their cult was absolutely secret, and in a general way their ideas were those of Swedenborg, but they also professed a cult of the Virgin, apparently the Great Mother of the Gnostics. Don Pernety died in 1796, and the last survivors entered Martinism.

SAINT-MARTIN

Martinist Illuminism was founded, as we have seen, by Martines de Pasqually, who taught the doctrine of reintegration; from 1754 to 1768 he propagated his higher grades among the Masonic Lodges of France.

M. de Maistre, in 1810, wrote that the Martinists had a cult and higher initiates or priests called by the Hebrew name of *Cohen*, and he observed that all these great initiates took part in the Revolution, though not to excess. Saint-Martin, the unknown philosopher, was Pasqually's disciple and later considerably developed the movement, establishing his *Loge maçonnique des Chevaliers de la bienfaisance* at Lyons. According to Louis Blanc:

> "Martinism made rapid progress in Paris; it reigned in Avignon; at Lyons it had a centre whence it radiated to Germany and Russia. Grafted on Freemasonry, the new doctrines constituted a rite which was composed of ten grades... through which the adepts had successively to pass; and numerous schools were formed with the sole aim of finding the key to the mystic code and spreading it. Thus, from one book (*Des Erreurs et de la Verité par un philosophe inconnu)* arose a vast crowd of... efforts which contributed to enlarge the mine dug under old institutions." [He adds:] "In the name of pious spiritualism the unknown philosopher rises up against the folly of human cults. By paths of allegory he leads to the heart of the Mysterious Kingdom which man in his primitive state had inhabited."

The Illumines, organised under the law of secrecy, exercised important influences in revolutionary movements, and both Martinists and Swedenborgians allied themselves to the Illuminati of Weishaupt, as seen in the Wilhelmsbad Convent of 1782, the object of which was thus expressed by a horrified delegate, the Comte de Virieu who had been deceived by Saint-Martin's mysticism:

"There is a conspiracy being plotted so well planned and so deep that it will be very difficult for religion and governments not to succumb to it."

In the *Rituel de l'Ordre Martiniste*, edited by Teder, 1913, the adept of the third degree is warned not to reveal the mysteries:

"But if, by the power of thy freewill and the blessing of the Divine One, thou shalt arrive at contemplating the Truth face to face, remember that thou must keep silence on the Mystery that thou hast penetrated, even should thy fidelity cost thy life. Ever remember the fate of the Great Initiators who have, even with the best of intentions, tried to raise, before the multitude, a corner of the sacred Veil of Isis."

"Here follows a few named: Jesus, Jacques Molay, Paracelsus, Cazotte, Cagliostro, Saint-Martin, Wronski, Eliphas Levi, Saint-Yves d'Alveydre, and hundreds of others. And they continue: 'Shouldst thou reveal the least of the Secret Arts or any part of the hidden mysteries that meditation may have led thee to understand, there is no physical torture that is not sweet compared to the punishment that thy folly shall bring upon thee.' No material symbol can express the horror of annihilation both spiritual as well as physical which awaits the miserable revealer of the True Word, for God *[sic]* is without mercy, for whosoever may profane His sanctuary and brutally expose to unworthy eyes the unspeakable Secret.

Finally, the Superior Inconnu in the Second Temple has to swear to 'work with all my strength to establish on earth, the Association of all Interests (Profits), the Federation of all Nations, the Alliance of all cults and Universal Solidarity.' In 1913 'Papus,' Dr. G. Encausse, was Grand Master and President of the Supreme Council of the Martinists.

SWEDENBORG

As for Swedenborgianism, in *Les Sectes et Sociétés Secrètes*, from the pen of Le Couteulx de Canteleu, we find a short but interesting sketch of Swedenborg and his systems: Emanuel Swedenborg was the son of a Lutheran Bishop of Skara in Sweden, and was born in Upsala about 1688. In 1743 he began to spread his beliefs, a mixture of mysticism, magnetism, and magic. As with all such doctrines, he had two systems: one for dupes and fools which was apparently to reform Christianity by a fantastic deism, the reigning faith in his New Jerusalem; his followers believed in his marvellous visions and prophecies, his talks with angels and spirits.

The other led straight to godlessness, atheism, and materialism, where, as in Hermeticism, God was only a sun, a spirit of Light, a spiritual heat vivifying the body. To these latter he represented his doctrine as being that of the Egyptians and the Magi, and these adepts went whole-hearted for the Revolution as restoring to man his primitive Equality and Liberty.

In England alone he had 20,000 such followers in 1780,—who looked for the Revolution to overthrow all other beliefs; Swedenborg's God was to be the only King left! In Avignon he had many adepts who mingled with the Martinists, being known as illuminated Theosophists, and among these were found the same vows in favour of an anti-social, anti-religious Revolution.

In a Foreword to one of Emanuel Swedenborg's books on *The Doctrine of the New Church* — the New Jerusalem, translated in 1797, from the Latin of the Amsterdam edition of 1769, it is said in explanation of this doctrine:

> "To be at the same time in the natural world and in the spiritual world, to live in the former in the society of men, and find oneself in the latter in the society of the angels, to see them, to speak with them, to hear them, to move in a kingdom of spiritual substances; here, doubtless, is more than is needed to disconcert the materialistic understanding of the wise men of to-day."

It is, therefore, not surprising that de Luchet considered that "Theosophists, Swedenborgians, Magnetisers and Illumines were a national danger."

TEMPLARS

As the French Revolution approached, the ground, it was found, was being mined and prepared for the sinister upheaval of 1789 by, among others, the still active power of the former Order of the Templars. Eliphas Levi informs us that, although outwardly Catholics, the secret cult of the Templars was Johannism, and their secret aim was to rebuild the Temple of Solomon on the model of the vision of Ezekiel — the arms of the Masons of the Temple, quarterly a lion, ox, man, and eagle, were the banners of the four leading Hebrew tribes. The Johannites, who were cabalists and gnostics, adopted part of the Jewish traditions and Talmudic accounts; they regarded the facts of the Gospels as allegories of which St. John had the key; their Grand Pontiffs assumed the title of Christ. In time the Templars became a danger to Church and State, menacing the entire world with a gigantic revolution, and they were eventually suppressed. As the high Mason Albert Pike wrote, in *Morals and Dogmas:*

> "The Order disappeared at once... Nevertheless it lived under other names and governed by Unknown Chiefs, revealing itself only to those who in passing through a series of degrees had proven themselves worthy to be entrusted with the dangerous secret... The secret movers of the French Revolution had sworn to overturn the Throne and Altar upon the tomb of Jacques de Molai."

According to Louis Blanc, in his *History of the French Revolution,* 1848, Cagliostro was initiated at Frankfort, 1781, under the authority of "the Grand Masters of the Templars," the Illuminati of Weishaupt, from whom he received instructions and funds to carry out their diabolical intrigues against Marie Antoinette in preparation for the later seizure of power through the illuminised Grand Orient Lodges. Speaking of Weishaupt's projects, Louis Blanc wrote:

> "By the sole attraction of mystery, by the sole power of association, to subject to the same will, to animate with the same breath thousands of men in every country in the world... to make new beings of these men by means of slow gradual education, to render them, even to the point of frenzy or death, obedient to invisible and Unknown Chiefs; with such a legion to secretly weigh upon the Court, to surround the sovereigns, unbeknown to direct Governments, and to lead Europe to that point where all superstition is annihilated, all monarchies brought down, all privileges of birth declared unjust, the right even of property abolished; such was the gigantic plan of the founders of Illuminism."

In *Orthodoxie Maçonnique,* 1853, the Jew and Masonic authority, J. M. Ragon, gives details of the two grades of the Order "Juges Philosophes Inconnus," a Templar regime. He places these as belonging, probably, to the "Order of Christ," an Order which, after the suppression of the Templars, was constituted in Portugal by King Denis, and into which reformed Templars were admitted, without, however, their former immunities and entirely dependent on the Head of the State. It is admitted that modern Templars have used the veil of Masonry as being better for spreading their ideas, but it is Masonic only in form. The jewel of the adept is a dagger and his work is vengeance. The Novice grade of these "Philosophes Inconnus" is the first in the last grade of Masonry-Kadosch, 30th degree — the brother must be at least Rose-Croix (18th degree) and already instructed in the royal art. The President addresses him:

> "You were for long the object of our observation and our study ... as soon as you have taken your new obligation you will cease to belong to yourself; your life, even, will have become the property of the Order. The most absolute obedience, the entire abnegation of your will, the prompt execution, without reflection, of the orders which will be transmitted to you on the part of the Supreme Power, such will be your principal duties. The most terrible punishments are reserved for perjurers ... and who is a perjurer in the eyes of the Order? He who even in the lightest thing infringes the orders which he has received from the Chief or refuses to execute them, for nothing is unimportant in our sublime Order... Your employment in the future will be to form men... You must learn here how the feet and hands of those who usurp the rights of men can be bound; you must learn to govern men and dominate them, not by fear, but by virtue *[sic]*. You must consecrate yourself entirely to the Order which has undertaken to re-establish man in his primitive dignity... The secret Government, but not less powerful, must lead other Governments towards this noble aim. without, however, allowing itself to be perceived except through the universal opinion and assent of society. There exists a considerable number of our brothers; we are spread throughout most distant lands, all led by an invisible force... If you desire only to be a perjurer and a false brother, do not pledge yourself among us, you will be cursed and unhappy; our vengeance will reach you everywhere."

If he hesitates, he is blindfolded and led out; if he consents, he takes the obligation and is received. After three years of study and preparation the final grade, Juge-Commandeur, may be given. He then takes another obligation, in which he promises and swears to work for the propagation of the Order and its safety, to obey his Superiors in all ways, whether they are known to him or not. Finally, it is said to him:

> "You swear and promise to keep inviolable the secrets I am going to confide to you; never to pardon traitors, and to subject them to the fate that the Order reserves for them... To guard yourself from the excesses of wine, the table, and women, the ordinary causes of indiscretion and Weakness" [in case of betraying Order secrets!].

At the end of both grades a portion of an abridged history of the destruction of the Knight Templars is read to the adept. And of their Order it was said:

> "It can no longer be denied that in early times we have never recognised more than five degrees of knowledge; the number twenty-five or thirty-three degrees which form the frame of Scottish Masonry is the result of the love of innovations or the product of self-esteem; for it is certain that of the thirty-three degrees practised to-day there are twenty-eight apocryphal which merit no confidence."

In their regulations, Article 32 says:

> "The penalties against the brothers who have been guilty of any offence whatsoever are: reprimand, expulsion, and even graver penalties if the crime compromises the Society. Sentences of the last nature cannot be executed without confirmation of judgment by the Supreme Power."

In his final discourse upon the unhappy fate of the Templars, the Chief of the Philosophes Inconnus said:

> "... Now as the number of Templars escaped from the murderous sword of persecution was very small, also as, in order to avenge the unheard-of crime of which they had been victims, it was necessary to repair their losses, they admitted into their Order men of recognised merit, whom they sought for and found among the Masons... They offered them initiation into their Order, which was eagerly accepted, and in exchange the Templars were initiated into the Masonic mysteries."

In conclusion we give two passages from Le Couteulx de Canteleu, who in his well-documented book refers to the trial of the Templars:

> "Certainly, far be it from me the thought to defend the cruel procedure followed against several members of the Order and the torture applied during interrogations; far from me the thought to believe all the absurdities of which they were accused. But in the midst of all these cruelties and all these infamies, the foundation of the accusation was true; they knew it, and that was what made more than 300 members, not yet subjected to torture, admit facts which appeared to us so extraordinary, but which were understood when one knew the foundation of their doctrine, revived from Egyptian and Hebraic initiations, also their affiliation to the Freemasons of the East (the Assassins), and the vices that the Grand Masters had permitted to be introduced into the Order, so as, probably, to increase their power."

He also regarded as positive that the Templar Guillaume de Monthard received Masonic initiation from the Old Man of the Mountain in a cave in Lebanon, and that the Assassins held some of the beliefs of the Ophites, serpent or dual-sex worshippers, hence, he says, Baphomet! Again he said that Pope Clement V was slow to believe in this formidable heresy:

> "It was only after having seventy-two Knights interrogated in his presence, as a man interested in finding them innocent, exacting no other oath from them but to reply to the questions asked; it was only after their admissions, given in the presence of notaries, that he was forced to recognise their guilt and revoke the suspension (previously ordered) of the Bishops, allowing them to pursue the arrangements made by Philippe le Bel in order to come to a judgment."

CHAPTER IV

WEISHAUPT'S ILLUMINATI AND THE FRENCH REVOLUTION

WRITING of the Illuminati in his *Essai sur la secte des Illuminés,* published in 1789, the Mason de Luchet says:

"There are a certain number of people who have arrived at the highest degree of imposture. They have conceived the project of reigning over opinions, and of conquering, not kingdoms, nor provinces, but the human mind. This project is gigantic, and has something of madness in it, which causes neither a arm nor uneasiness; but when we descend to details, when we regard what passes before our eyes of the hidden principles, when we perceive a sudden revolution in favour of ignorance and incapacity, we must look for the cause of it; and if we find that a revealed and known system explains all the phenomena which succeed each other with terrifying rapidity, how can we not believe it?... Observe that the members of the Mystical Confederation are numerous enough in themselves, but not relatively so to the men they must deceive... Indeed, to realise this proportion one must get a just idea of the force of combined man (was not Mazzini's cry, 'Associate, Associate'?). A thread cannot raise a pound's weight, a thousand threads will raise the anchor of a ship... also man is a feeble being, imperfect ... but if several men mix together half-qualities they temper and strengthen each other ... the weak yield to the stronger, the most skilful draw from each what he can supply. Some watch whilst others act, and this formidable ensemble arrives at its goal, whatever it may be... It was according to this that the sect of the Illuminati was formed. One cannot, it is true, either name its founders or prove the epochs of its existence, or mark the steps of its growth, for its essence is the secret; its acts take place in darkness, its evasive Grand Priests are lost in the crowd. However, it has penetrated sufficient things to astonish and draw the attention of observers, friends of humanity, to the mysterious steps of the sectaries."

Jean Adam Weishaupt, founder of the Order of the Illuminati, was born at Ingolstadt, Bavaria, 6 February 1748, according to R. le Forestier's book, *Les Illuminés de Bavière et la Franc-Maçonnerie Allemande*, 1914, from which we take the following details: His father, who was then professor at the University there, had married a niece of Mme Ickstatt, whose husband was Curator of the same University. In 1756 Baron Ickstatt secured a scholarship for their son Adam, at the Jesuit College, Ingolstadt, who when fifteen entered the University as a student of Law, steeping himself at the same time in the literature of the atheist philosophers of the day. The electors of Bavaria were firm supporters of the Catholic faith, and Ingolstadt gradually became a stronghold of Jesuit teaching from 1556 until they were suppressed by Clement XIV in 1773; even then, for want of other qualified men, they were retained in the chairs of Theology. The University of Ingolstadt and all equivalent to secondary schools in Bavaria had been placed in the hands of the Jesuits. It was in 1775 that Weishaupt, then Professor of Canon Law at Ingolstadt, "formed the plan of an association of which he would be the head … which would oppose to the united forces of superstition and lies (religion) groups more and more numerous of libre-pensée and progress."

He and his collaborators believed "that the adversaries of all progress, intellectual and moral, were the priests and monks … desiring to fight against the State religion, and, above all, the most vigilant soldiers of Catholicism, the Jesuits, it was necessary to conceal the existence of the Order… Historians who have seen in the Order of the Illuminati a war-machine invented by a former pupil of the Jesuits in order to fight them with their own weapons, are, therefore, not far wrong." René Fülöp-Miller, in his book *The Power and Secret of the Jesuits*, 1930, supports this opinion. He tells us that the *Encyclopaedists* "made use of many of the ideas of the Jesuits in order to build from them a revolutionary philosophy inimical to all the beliefs of the Church." And again he says:

"Besides the Freemasons, there rose up a kindred association, the 'Order of the Illuminati,' which from the very beginning, was intended as an anti-Jesuit organisation. Its founder, Weishaupt, a professor of Ingolstadt, heartily hated the Jesuits, and formed his league of Illuminati with the express intention 'of using for good ends the means which the Jesuit order had employed for bad'; this means consisted mainly in the introduction of an obligation of unconditional obedience, reminiscent of Loyola's *Constitutions;* of a far-reaching mutual surveillance among the membership of the order; and a kind of auricular confession, which every inferior had to make to his superior."

Of the Jewish power in these secret societies, Bernard Lazare, in *L'Antisémitisme,* 1894, writes:

"It is certain that there were Jews at the cradle of Freemasonry-cabalistic Jews, as is proved by certain existing rites; very probably during the years which preceded the French Revolution they entered in still greater numbers into the councils of the society, and themselves founded secret societies. There were Jews around Weishaupt; and Martinez Paschalis, a Jew of Portuguese origin, organised numerous groups of Illuminés in France;"

In a number of *La Vieille France,* 31 March — 6 April, 1921, it was stated that five Jews were concerned in the organisation and inspiration of the Illuminati—Wessely, Moses Mendelssohn, and the bankers, Itzig, Friedlander and Meyer. Further it is curious to find that the important Illuminatus Mirabeau, under the influence of Mendelssohn's disciples, wrote a book, *On Moses Mendelssohn; on the Political, Reform of the Jews,* 1787.

Freemasonry ended in playing a considerable role in the Order of the Illuminati. Weishaupt was affiliated to it in 1777, and in 1778 decided to link his Order with Freemasonry. In the Greater Mysteries two grades were extremely important, those of Priest and Regent. "The College of Priests should constitute in the order a seminary of atheists … the grade of Regent corresponded in politics to that of Priest in religion." "Weishaupt, however, considered it as "incomparably less important than the latter." At the summit of the hierarchy was the Supreme College of the Areopagites, held, according to Weishaupt, at Munich, being composed of seven members, three of whom were principals.

Further, Weishaupt, among other regulations, stated that without special permission, "Jews, pagans, women, monks, and members of other societies were excluded from the Order." As regards Jews, Louis Daste speaks of documents showing that, although early English Masonic Lodges admitted all religions, later the secret chiefs of Masonry in Holland, Germany, and France, because of transitory obstacles, reserved their lodges for Christians only. But at the Wilhelmsbad Congress, 1782, it was resolved that Jews should no longer be excluded from the Lodges. There is a mass, however, of evidence to prove the Jew influence upon and behind all secret societies, and as Disraeli said in *Lothair* in 1870:

> "If you mean by political freedom the schemes of the Illuminati and the Freemasons which perpetually torture the Continent, all the dark conspiracies of the secret societies, then I admit the Church is in antagonism with such aspirations after liberty... The civil powers have separated from the Church.

> ... It is not their choice: they are urged on by an invisible power that is anti-Christian, and which is the true, natural, and implacable enemy of the one visible and Universal Church."

In *Marie-Antoinette et le Complot Maçonnique*, 1910[2], Louis Daste quotes a rare brochure, *The Role of Freemasonry in the XVIIIth Century,* by F.·. Brunellière, which says:

> "Weishaupt aimed at nothing less than the complete overthrow of authority, nationality, and the whole social system, in a word, the suppression of property, etc... As to his principle, it was absolute and blind obedience, universal espionage, the end justifies the means. This system of conspiracy so strongly organised which would have upheaved the world, spread through Germany, where it seized almost all the Masonic Lodges. Weishaupt sent to France Joseph Balsamo, so-called Comte Cagliostro, to illuminise French Masonry. Finally he assembled a Congress at Wilhelmsbad in 1782, to which he convoked all German and foreign lodges... In 1785 the Illuminati were revealed to the Bavarian Government, who, terrified, appealed to all Governments, but the Protestant Princes showed little haste in suppressing it. Weishaupt found refuge with

---

[2] Published by Omnia Veritas Ltd, www.omnia-veritas.com.

the Prince de Saxe-Gotha. He had for the rest taken great care not to tell everything to the Princes, or even to many of his initiates; he had hidden from them the appeal to the force of the masses; he had hidden from them the Revolution" (Masonic report, *l'Ordre de Nantes*, 23 April, 1883).

The Bavarian Government's suspicions, according to le Forestier, were seriously aroused, and by continued search Zwack's papers connected with the Order, and those held by Bassus, were found and seized on two separate occasions. These were ordered by the Elector to be published as follows:

1. On 26 March, 1787:

> "Some original writings of the Order of the Illuminati found at the house of Zwack, former Government Councillor, during a perquisition made at Landshut, 11 and 12 October, 1786, and published by order of his Electoral Highness."

The Preface invited all those who doubted the authenticity of the documents to go to the Privy Archives where the original documents would be shown to them.

> 2. "Supplement to the original writings concerning in general the Sect of the Illuminati and in particular its founder, Adam Weishaupt, former professor at Ingolstadt, documents found in the Castle of Baron Bassus at Sandersdorf during the perquisition carried out in this celebrated den of the Illuminati, published immediately by order of the Elector and deposited in the Privy Archives to be examined by all those who showed the desire to do so." (Two Parts, Munich 1787.)

Outwardly finished, the Illuminati still continued their underground mining.

As told by Crétineau-Joly, Cardinal Caprara, in a confidential memoire, October 1787, said: "The danger approaches, for from all these mad dreams of Illuminism, Swedenborgianism and Freemasonry, there must evolve a terrifying reality. The visionaries have their day, the revolution which they forebode will have its day."

It was into the lodges of the *Amis réunis* that Mirabeau and Bonneville introduced Weishaupt's Illuminati. One of its chiefs was the famous revolutionary Savalette de Langes, Keeper of the

Royal Treasure, but secretly deep in every mystery and lodge, and all plots against religion and Royalty. They called themselves *Philalèthes* — seekers of Truth; it was a form of Martinism, and, according to Clavel, led to the deification of man, being a mixture of the dogmas of Swedenborg and de Pasqualis. To cover his intrigues, Savalette de Langes at times gave up the common Lodge to adepts, brothers, and sisters of high rank, who danced and sang of equality and liberty, while unknown to them, in the upper Lodge, was the secret committee guarded above and below by two *frères terribles*. Among the principal members of this committee were Willermoz, Chappe de la Heuziére, Mirabeau, Comte de Gebelin, and Bonneville. There the codified correspondence of the Grand Orient was received by Savalette de Langes and dealt with by the Committee, To be admitted to these councils they had to swear, as *Chevalier du Soleil*, hatred to Christianity and, as *Chevalier kadosch*, hatred to Crowns and Papacy. They had a branch in Paris, and this was frequented by Saint-Germain, Raymond, Cagliostro, Condorcet, Dietrich, brothers of Avignon, and students of Swedenborg and Saint-Martin. Outside they passed as charlatans, visionaries, evoking spirits and working prodigies, while secretly searching out accomplices in the Masonic Lodges.

Consorting with the chief disciples of Weishaupt, Mirabeau was initiated in Brunswick into the final Mysteries of Illuminism. Already he knew the value of Masonry in revolution, and on his return to France he introduced these mysteries among the *Philalèthes*. It was then decided to illuminise all the lodges of France; for this purpose the Illuminati, Bode, or *Aurelius*, and Baron de Busche or *Bayard*, pupil of Knigge, were deputed to assist. After much discussion it was resolved to adopt the Bavarian mysteries without changing the old forms of the lodges, to illuminise them without revealing the name of the sect from whom the mysteries were received, and only to use Weishaupt's code in so far as it would hasten the revolution (Le Couteulx de Canteleu).

From then the political aim was accentuated, a new grade was added, preserving Masonic emblems and rites, and this was passed on to the provinces. The closest alliance was concluded, and a general Convent of Masons in France and abroad was convoked by. the secret committee for 15 February, 1785. Savalette de Langes was elected president, and among the deputies were: Saint-Germain, Saint-Martin, Etrilla, Mesmer, Cagliostro, Mirabeau and Talleyrand, Bode, Dalberg, Baron de Gleichen, Lavater, Prince Louis de Hesse, and also deputies from the Grand Orients of Poland and Lithuania. The Duc d'Orléans was then Grand Master of the Grand Orient of France, and ·his committee had under its jurisdiction and orders lodges of 282 towns in France and abroad (Mirabeau). At this Congress the French Revolution and its propagation throughout Europe was resolved upon even to the decree of regicide. The part, according to Mirabeau, to be taken by the people is thus described in his Memoires by Marmontel:

> "Have we to fear the great part of the nation which knows not our projects, and would not be disposed to lend us their support?
>
> ... If they disapprove of them, it will be only timidly, without clamour. For the rest, does the nation know what it wants? We will make it want and say what it has never thought of... The nation is a large herd which thinks only of browsing, and which, with good dogs, the shepherds lead at will... One will have to impose upon the bourgeoisie who sees nothing to lose, but all to gain by the change. To stir it up one has the most powerful motives: poverty, hunger, money, rumours of alarm and fear, the frenzy of terror and rage with which we will strike their minds... What will we do with all this people while muzzling their principles of honesty and justice? Good men are feeble and timid; it is the blackguards who are determined. It is advantageous to people during revolutions to have no morals... there is not a single one of our old virtues which can serve us... All that is necessary for revolution, all that is useful to it is just — that is the great principle."

About the beginning of the revolution a manifesto was issued from the committee of the Grand Orient addressed to all Masonic Lodges and Councils, to be used throughout Europe. By it

> "all the lodges were summoned to league together to unite their efforts for the maintenance of the Revolution, everywhere to seek followers, friends, and protectors, to propagate its flame, to stir up its spirit, to excite zeal and ardour for it in all countries and by all means in their power."

After the receipt of this manifesto anti-Monarchy and Republican ideas everywhere became dominant, and anti-religious ideas were used only to undermine nationalities (Deschamps, *Les Sociétès Secrètes et la Société*, vol. ii). .

The Jew and high Mason, Crémieux, founder and president of *L'Alliance-israélite-universelle,* said in his manifesto, 1860:

"The net which Israel now casts over the terrestrial globe enlarges and extends... Our power is immense; learn to turn that power to our cause. The day is not far distant when all the riches, all the treasures of the earth, will become the property of the children of Israel."

In his book *Marie-Antoinette et le complot maçonnique,* Louis Dasté shows how that net was spread before and after the French Revolution of 1789. He writes: "From 1774 to 1783 we have seen Masonry unceasingly cover Marie-Antoinette with the mud of its pamphlets. The hour approached when the sect was to strike the blow from which the Queen died."

It was the Affair of the Necklace which was, according to G. Bord, "organised by the *Stricte Observance* and the *Amis réunis* of Paris." "The Jew Cagliostro," said ex-Mason Doinel 33°, "was the contemptible agent of this intrigue in which the popularity of the Queen foundered and the prestige of the unfortunate Louis XVI was ruined." Further, Louis Blanc wrote, 1848:

"His initiation took place a short distance from Frankfort in a subterranean vault, (he was shown) a manuscript book in the first page of which could be read: We Grand Masters of the Templars; followed by an oath formula traced in blood. The book... maintained that Illuminism was a conspiracy plotted against thrones, that the first blows would fall on France; that after the fall of the French Monarchy they would attack Rome. Cagliostro learnt from his initiators that the secret society to which he henceforth belonged possessed a mass of money scattered in the banks of Amsterdam, Rotterdam, London, Genoa, and Venice.

... As for himself, he handled a huge sum destined for the expenses of propaganda, received instructions from the Sect and went to Strasbourg."

On the seals of the lodge founded by him at Lyons were the three letters *L.P.D.* — *Lilia pedibus destrue,* trample the (Bourbon) lilies underfoot (see Bernard Picard, ritual, 1809). This, then, was his diabolical mission. When, therefore, Cagliostro arrived in Strasbourg, 1781, his first care was to control and set his tools in motion. The Cardinal Prince de Rohan, his dupe, and the Comtesse de la Motte, his accomplice, were made known to each other; the latter being in reduced circumstances, the Cardinal advised her to apply direct to the Queen, at the same time confiding to her his ambitions and his bitterness because of the Queen's refusal to see him. From then Mme de la Motte, pretending to be in touch with the Queen, under instructions from Cagliostro, acted as intermediary in a correspondence between the Queen, whose name was forged, and the Cardinal, which was nominally to bring about his restoration to the Royal favour and the realisation of his ambitions, but was eventually to besmirch and compromise the unwitting Queen. Nothing was done without consulting Cagliostro. In May, June, July 1784, the forged letters multiplied, written by Retaux de Villette and dictated by Mme de la Motte. Then at midnight, II August, came the brief pretended interview in the park at Versailles between the Queen and the Cardinal. Nicole d'Oliva dressed as the Queen strongly resembled her; the Cardinal believed he had seen and spoken with Marie-Antoinette. When, therefore, further forged letters twice asked him to find 60,000 livres for the Queen's bounties, both sums were willingly borrowed by the Cardinal from the Jew Cerfbeer. The money was retained by Mme de la Motte!

In December, having come into touch with the Court jeweller, Boehmer, who was anxious to dispose of a diamond necklace worth 1,800,000 livres, she quickly planned to acquire it, in the same way, for herself. More forged letters from the Queen, along with advice from his oracle Cagliostro, reassured the Cardinal, and on 1 February, 1785, the negotiations with Boehmer were completed; the necklace passed into the possession of Mme de la Motte, and the finest stones were sold in London by her husband. Failing to receive the first payment of 100,000 écus which fell due on 30 July, Boehmer realised the fraud; the indignant Queen was informed of everything, and in August the Cardinal, Mme de la Motte, and Cagliostro were arrested, but not before most of the compromising letters were secretly burnt. The Cardinal refused the King's offer to act as judge; they were, therefore, tried by Parliament, which was largely Masonised. The Cardinal and Cagliostro were acquitted, Mme de la Motte was condemned to be branded as a thief, whipped, and shut up, but was later secretly assisted to escape.

From London she waged her campaign of calumny against Marie-Antoinette; in 1788 her *Mémoire justificatif* was published, formed, said de Nolhac, of rage and lies, dragging the Queen through infamous mud. It was almost wholly retouched by M. de Calonne in a ferment of hatred against the Queen, whom he blamed for his disgrace from Ministerial office. In 1789 appeared the *Second mémoire justificatif,* again attributed to but repudiated by Mme de la Motte, and which outdid the first in filth and venom. Then followed an avalanche of indecent pamphlets, all based on the *Mémoire* with the double object of vilifying the Queen and besmirching minds with filthy pictures, killing in advance all pity in the hearts of the people and of her executioners — *Lilia pedibus destrue.* But Cagliostro was finished, the Secret Power, fearing disclosures, mercilessly broke him; forced to leave London, hunted through Europe, he was finally arrested in Rome by the Pontifical Police. After a long trial, recorded in *Vie de Joseph Balsamo,* 1791, he was condemned to death, commuted to imprisonment for life, and died in 1795. In a wretched garret in London, 1791, Mme de la Motte ended her life in terrible suffering, deserted by all. The Secret Power having no use for broken tools, had ceased to protect them.

In *La Revue,* 1 March, 1909, the editor wrote of an indecent pamphlet, *O Marquez de Bacalhoa,* published February 1908, a month before the assassination of Don Carlos:

> "It is published in the form of the romances which appeared about 1780 on the private life of Louis XVI and Marie-Antoinette.

> ... It smothered the King in mud and did not spare Queen Amelia... The pages consecrated to the Queen were a mere tissue of infamous lies..."

And the Portuguese Revolution of 1910 was the work of Jews of *l'Alliance-israélite-universelle* united to Freemasonry. Again we have Proudhon writing:

"What mysteries of iniquity would be revealed if the Jews, like the mole, did not make a point of working in the dark."

FRENCH FREEMASONRY

Freemasonry, originating and organised in England, where the Judaising cabalists of the Rose-Croix had grafted it on to the old Corporations of Mason-workers, was introduced everywhere into Europe from 1725 to 1730. And as de Poncins writes: "In France, where minds were in open ferment, Freemasonry found a favourable soil and under the double influence of the *Encyclopaedists* and the Illuminati of Bavaria it evolved quickly to the point of being one of the preponderant elements of the great revolutionary movements of 1789." And in a report of a meeting of the Lodges *Paix et Union* and *La Libre Conscience*, at the Orient of Nantes, 23 April, 1883, it was said: "It was from 1772 to 1789 that Masonry elaborated the great Revolution which was to change the face of the world... It was then the Freemasons vulgarised the ideas they had absorbed in their Lodges" (see Dasté). Dasté adds: "It was in fact on 23 December, 1772, that the formation of the Grand Orient of France was proclaimed. On this day was carried out the concentration of all Masonic arms for the assault to be made on France." And Ragon, the Jewish Masonic authority, tells us that on that date it was "solemnly declared that the former Grand Lodge of France ceased to exist, that it was replaced by a new National Grand Lodge which would be an integral part of a new body which would administer the Order, under the name of Grand Orient of France" (*Orthodoxie maçonnique*, 1853).

And in *Vérité-Israélite*, 1861, it was written: "The spirit of Masonry is the spirit of Judaism in its most fundamental beliefs."

"It is, therefore," — writes Freiherr von Stolzinger, 1930 — "perfectly understandable that Judaism early turned towards Freemasonry, and that, thanks to its remarkable powers of adaptation, it became an increasing influence within it. One is hardly mistaken in affirming that to-day the greater number of the Lodges are subject to Jewish influence, and that they form the spiritual storm-troops of Judaism."

Finally, as explained in the *Freimaurer-Zeitung*, 15 December, 1866:

> "In a lecture on the religious element of Freemasonry... F. Charles de Gagern made the following statement: 'I am firmly convinced that the time will, and must, arrive when atheism will be the general opinion of all humanity, and when the latter will consider deism as a past phase, just as deist-Freemasons are above religious divisions. We must not only place ourselves above different religions, but above all belief in any God whatsoever.'"

BLUE MASONRY

Below we give a short account of the most important grades in Grand Orient Masonry, that is: Blue Masonry, Rose-Croix, and Kadosch degrees as practised in France. In these will be found the same pantheistic and nature ideas as expressed in their symbolism.

According to Bazot, Secretary-General of the Grand Orient, 1812:

> "Masonry is merely the primitive cult of man discovered after his first wants are satisfied. The Brahmans and Egyptian priests transmitted its mysteries to Solomon. Jerusalem, victim of revolutions, having been destroyed, the Jewish people being dispersed, this Masonry spread with them all over the earth."

And man's place in this cult is thus expressed in an official Dutch Masonic document: "A sacred unity reigns and governs in the vast firmament. There is only one mission, one moral, one God ... we, men, form a whole with the Great Being. All ends in this revelation: *We are God!*" Here we find the pantheistic idea of Judaism, its race, its God Yahveh. As Claudio Jannet and Louis d'Estampes wrote in *La Franc-Maçonnerie et la Révolution*, 1884:

> "This deification of humanity is not at first openly stated by Freemasonry, but is insinuated in all its rites and expressed in all its symbols. A vast temple is to be built, apprentices, fellow-craftsmen, and masters work at it; Hiram or Adonhiram, one of these masters, is killed by three craftsmen in order to obtain the word of Master; the body of this Master, hidden in the earth, has to be found and replaced and his death avenged; the building of the temple is

resumed and is to be finished; such is the fundamental and universal allegory, basis and essence of Freemasonry and all secret societies. Thus do all their rites and manuals, their most authorised orators and interpreters teach it. This allegory is indicated in the grades of Apprentice and Fellow-craft, is developed at length in that of Master, is completed and explained in the grades of Rose-Croix and Kadosch, and in the last grades of the Misraim rite it reaches its final development."

The three assassins to be pursued and exterminated are: superstitions, prejudices, and tyranny; that is, religion, moral control, monarchy and all authority, family, property, and nationality.

As we have already shown, French Masonry was captured, just before the French Revolution of 1789, by Weishaupt, and secretly illuminised by certain of his high adepts. He thus gained direction of all the lodges, and to-day, even, the taint of his pernicious system still remains amongst them, and among all those who are in any way linked to them. The fundamental thought of this system is thus expressed by Weishaupt himself:

> "Equality and liberty are the essential rights which man in his original and primitive perfection received from nature. The first attack upon this equality was made by property; the first attack upon liberty was made by political societies or Governments; the sole supports of property and Governments are the religious and civil laws. Therefore, to establish man in his primitive rights of equality and liberty, we must begin by destroying all religion, all civil society, and finish by abolishing property."

To which Claudio Jannet adds: "These few lines indicate the root idea of Masonry and all secret societies; the germ is found in the symbolic grades, it is scientifically developed in the high grades, and brutally realised in the communism of the International and the anarchism of Bakunin and Socialist democracy." And we would add: in the Soviet system in the Russia of to-day, and again attempted in Spain, South America, and elsewhere. Briefly, the three grades represent generation, putrefaction, and regeneration. The Temple, that of nature, is maintained, as Clavel says, by two Pillars, "Boaz and Jakin, the generative principles; the one, light, life, and good, the other darkness, death, and evil; they maintain the equilibrium of the world." It is the dualism of the Gnostics,

Manicheans, the Jewish Magical Cabala, and all ancient mysteries. In each grade an oath of secrecy, etc., is taken. In the first grade, neither clothed nor yet unclothed, the candidate enters as the man of nature who is to receive the light; he is the rough stone upon which he has to work, under the direction of his chiefs, to free himself from prejudices, vices, and superstitions. The Apprentice thus freed passes from the Pillar Jakin to the Pillar Boaz, from natural science to wisdom, as he enters the second grade, Fellow-craft, in which he is to learn to know the letter G, the God of Masonry. Speaking of the consecration of the triangle in the lodges, Ragon writes: "In the centre is the Hebrew letter Yod, life-giving spirit, or fire, generative principle, represented by the letter G, initial of the word God in northern languages, and whose philosophic signification is generation." Further, according to Ragon, the grade of Master allegorically represents the death of the Light-God, solar, philosophic, or physical putrefaction, for the life is withdrawn, as expressed in the grade word *Macbenac* — the flesh leaves the bones, and out of which arises the regenerated form. Finally, as Ragon explains:

> "The entire triangle has always signified God or nature, and the allegories of the truths, foundation of the early mysteries, the successive and eternal acts of nature: (I) that all is formed by generation; (2) that destruction follows generation in all its works; (3) and that generation re-establishes under other forms the actions of destruction."

In revolutionary Masonry and secret societies this pantheistic and cabalistic creed is applied to all aspects of life; old ideas and opinions are destroyed, others, new and subversive, are insinuated and more or less unconsciously absorbed and established; Christian beliefs are perverted and nullified; man, illuminised, apparently becomes his own redeemer, and God, though in truth enslaved to the invisible hierarchy — according to some the kundalini is man's redeemer! Kings are dethroned and replaced by some form of disintegrating republic or socialist democracy. It is death to all old traditions and civilisations, and out of inevitable chaos and putrefaction is to arise the "New Heaven and New Earth," the Universal Brotherhood of all these subversive and Judaic sects.

ROSE-CROIX

As Gaston Martin tells us: "All Freemasons of the three obediences in friendly relations, belong to what in politics is called 'the Left.' The shades in doctrine are not such as to prevent accord reigning amongst all the members." These three obediences are: the Grand Orient, the Grand Lodge, and the Droit Humain.

> "As the three grades of ordinary Masonry [said Louis Blanc] include a great number of men opposed by position and principles to every project of social subversion, the innovators multiplied the degrees of the mystic ladder to be climbed; they created secret lodges reserved for ardent souls; they instituted the high grades of *élus, chevalier du soleil, Rose-Croix, stricte observance,* of *Kadosch* or regenerated man, mysterious sanctuaries whose doors only open to the adept after a long series of tests, calculated to establish the progress of his revolutionary education, to prove the firmness of his faith, to try the temper of his heart. There was, in the midst of a crowd of practices, sometimes puerile, sometimes sinister, nothing which related to the ideas of freedom or equality" *(History of French Revolution).*

In the Rose-Croix grade, when holding Chapter the lodge should be hung with red, and in the East a triangular altar, one face turned to the West. On this altar should be a great transparent picture representing a Calvary; two crosses at the side (good and evil, light and darkness, of the Manicheans), and on that in the centre is a rose and interlaced drapery, above being the inscription I.N.R.I. Below, in front of the picture, there are broken pillars, on the ruins of which are the sleeping watchmen; in the midst of them is a kind of tomb whose upper stone has been moved and out of which comes a shroud. When there is a reception the hangings, transparency, and altar should be covered with black sown with tears. There should be three great triangular pillars above which are the three virtues, Faith, Hope, and Charity, or as Ragon suggests: active, passive, and manifestation of the Creative Principle.

At the opening of the Lodge the "Très-sage" is seated on the third of the seven steps of the altar, his head supported by his hand. After the first orders, he says: "My brother, you see me overwhelmed with sadness; all has changed; the veil of the temple is rent, the pillars of masonry are broken, the cubic stone sweats blood and water, the Word is lost, *et consummatum est.*" The first and second chevaliers are requested, with the help of other worthy chevaliers, to look on the pillars and find the lost Word. Each brother gives the Word, whispered in the ear — the lost Word is found, and, paying homage to the Supreme Architect, all rise and, turning to the East, make sign and bow with one knee on the ground. In the East is the Flaming Star, the Delta and the letter G or J, signs of fire. The Chapter is opened.

The prepared candidate is led into the lodge, now hung with black, and when questioned, replies that he was born of noble parents of the Tribe of Judah, his country is Judea, and he professes the art of Masonry. He is then told that the Word is lost, and they hope to find it through his courage; was he willing to use it for that purpose? Consenting, he takes the oath, and finally, in the lodge, now hung with red, he replies to questions again, that he comes from Judea, passing through Nazareth, led by Raphael, and he is of the Tribe of Judah. Uniting the initials of these four names, he makes I.N.R.I. — he has found the lost Word. The candidate then kneels at the foot of the altar, and the "Très-sage" places his naked sword on the head and admits, receives, and constitutes him now. and for ever, *Chevalier prince de l'aigle et du pélican, perfect free Mason of Hérédon, under the sovereign title of Rose-Croix.* He is then raised, given the sash, word, sign, and grip; the Word is I.N.R.I. *(Recueil précieux, Avignon,* 1810; Teissier, *Manuel,* 1854). Such is the grade of *Rose-Croix* of the Scottish Rite. The French rite only differs in the drawing up of formulae and accessories. It is on Good Friday that the Rose-Croix hold their Chapters and have their receptions (Deschamps, 1881).

A few explanations of the symbolism as given by the Jewish writer, Ragon, "sacred" Grand Orient authority, in his *Cours philosophique,* etc., 1841, are enlightening:

> "Three major events should fix the attention of the Rose Croix: the creation of the world (generation), the deluge of Noah (destruction), and the redemption of mankind (regeneration). The triple consideration should be, in fact, ever present in the mind of all

Freemasons, since the royal art has, like the ancient mysteries, no other aim than the knowledge of nature, where all are born, die, and regenerate themselves... This regeneration of man was and will always be the work of the philosophy practised in the mysteries ... the eagle is liberty, the Rose-Croix, humanity, symbolised by the pelican... The rose was also the emblem of the woman, and as the cross or triple phallus symbolised virility or the sun in all its force, the combination of these two emblems offers one more meaning expressing, as the Indian *lingam*, the union of the two sexes, symbol of universal generation.

Fire (or vital energy) is concealed everywhere, it embraces all nature, it produces, it renews, it divides, it consumes, it maintains the whole body ... heat and light are but its modifications, fecundity, movement, and life the effects (of the letters I.N.R.I., he says). Their combination formed a mysterious meaning long before Christianity and the sages of antiquity had attached to it one of the greatest secrets of nature; that of universal regeneration."

Thus they express it: *Igne Natura Renovatur Integra*, entire nature is renewed by fire.

Finally, there is the supper:

"All ancient mystagogies were terminated by all breaking bread and tasting the wine from a common cup, to recall among themselves the community of goods and that initiates have nothing of their own. The bread and wine are consecrated. This mystic nourishment, which should feed body and soul, was an emblem of immortality"

active and passive forces!

Thus we see that this Rose-Croix grade is a complete perversion of Christian symbolism and sacred beliefs, it is the cult of nature by whose forces, generation, destruction, and regeneration the adept, under the mask of deification or development of latent powers, is led to the slavery of illuminism, whereby he becomes a willing instrument in the hands of some powerful and unscrupulous but unknown leaders, who profess as their goal the emancipation of humanity, through whom they hope to rule the world.

KADOSCH

In the *Tuileur de l'ecossisme*, 1821, it is said:

"30th degree, grand inquisitor, grand élu, chevalier Kadosch, also called White and Black Eagle. Although the Scottish, they say, never confer this grade except by communication, and that it occupies, in the ancient rite, only the thirtieth degree, it must be considered as the final, the real aim of the Scottish Rite, just as it is the *nec plus ultra* of the Templar Masonry. In it they commemorate the abolition of the Order of the Templars by Philippe le Bel and Pope Clement V, and the punishment of the first Grand Master Jacques Molay, who perished in the flames, 11 March, 1314."

As Deschamps writes, 1881:

"In vain they repeat with complaisance that the Kadosch of France is purely philosophic... War to the throne and the altar is the grand cry of the Order. The fierce *Nekam Adonai* (Vengeance Lord!) has produced the Illuminati and the Carbonari. In the hands of fanatical men, aided by favourable circumstances, it constantly gives similar results."

According to the manuals of Willaume and Teissier, authorised by the Grand Orient, the cry, when making the sign of the grade, is *Nekam Adonai,* and the three passwords for entry into the Supreme Council all begin with Nekam — Vengeance!

Ragon further writes:

"The more or less development, extension, or application given to vengeance introduces into the Kadosch a multitude of variants, or rather, makes it like so many different grades (some he admits are horrible). One finds in very old manuscripts of English Masonry that the Kadosch is called *Killer.*"

It apparently belongs to all rites, among others: 30th degree Scottish Rite, 66th Egyptian or Misraim Rite, 25th Hérédon Rite or Perfection Rite or Order of the Temple, believed to be its source, 10th degree Rite of Saint-Martin, also in the Lyons Lodge, which served later as the cradle of French Illuminism under the name of *chevaliers bienfaisants de la sainte cité,* 1743 (Deschamps). Again, in his *Cours d'initiations,* 1842, Ragon writes of this grade:

"It bears with reason the title *nec plus ultra;* the three degrees above are merely administrative... The Kadosch is not only the Mason of the Lodges, the Mason of the Chapters, but admitted to the third sanctuary, it is to him that these two precepts of ancient initiation will be addressed. Give·yourself to the science of nature, study politics for the good of your fellow-creatures. Penetrate the secrets of religion and of high sciences, and communicate your ideas with prudence ... the initiate, therefore, studied politics and religion."

He then tells us that there are four apartments in the grade, and the initiation is accomplished in the fourth. He says: "The Hebrew word *Kadosch* signifies *saint,* consecrated, purified. It must not be thought by that that the Knights of the White and Black Eagle have any pretensions to sanctity, they wish to express by this word that they alone are the elect, men *par excellence,* purified of all the dregs of Prejudices."

In the fourth room, which is hung with red, sits the Supreme Council.

"Reaching this divine sanctuary the candidate learns the pledges that he contracts. There is a cross in this sanctuary, a three-headed serpent wearing, the first a crown, the second a tiara, and the third a sword; they give him a dagger with a black and white blade. The cross, says Ragon, is the phallic Tau. The serpent represents the evil principle; its three heads are the emblem of the abuses or evil which has entered into the three high classes of society. The head of the serpent which wears a crown indicates the *sovereigns,* that which wears a tiara or key indicates the *Popes,* that which carries a sword the *Army."*

The dagger, Mithraic or the sickle of Saturn,

"morally recalls to the grand elect that he must continually work to fight against and destroy prejudices, ignorance, and superstition, or that which is upon the three heads of the serpent."

Finally, the new grand elect Kadosch is told:

"... Thou knowest thyself; never forget that there exists no degree of good fortune to which the man who enters again into his primitive rights could not aspire to. Forget not that thou hast within thyself the precious thread (kundalini) by aid of which thou art able to come out of the labyrinth of material things... Reintegrated (by illuminism) to-day into thy natural (or primitive) rights, behold thyself for ever freed from the yoke of prejudices; apply thyself without ceasing to deliver thy fellow creatures from it" (Ragon; Willaume; and Teissier).

In the *Morning Post,* 14 July, 1920, *Cause of the World Unrest,* speaking of this revolutionary Masonry, it said: "When at length the candidate is admitted into the 30th grade, and after going through terrifying ordeals to test his obedience and secrecy, becomes a Knight Kadosh, he learns that it is no longer Adoniram or Hiram whose death cries for vengeance." And their catechism says:

> "Do you fully understand that this degree is not, like much of so-called Masonry, a sham that means nothing and amounts to nothing... that what you are now engaged in is *real,* will require the performance of *duty,* will exact *sacrifice,* will expose you to *danger,* and that this Order means to deal with the affairs of nations, and be once more a *Power* in the world."

WOMEN IN MASONRY

And the women too were drawn into the Masonic net. Minos, one of Weishaupt's chiefs, wrote: "Women exercise too great an influence over men for us to hope to reform the world if they themselves are not reformed... but they will need something which directs and stimulates them: an order, meetings for reception, secrets etc..." According to Albert Lantoine, the Masonic writer: of the Grand Lodge of France, the Anderson Constitution, 1723, says: "Slaves, women, immoral and dishonoured persons cannot be admitted, but only men of good reputation." However, Clavel informs us that Freemasonry for women was first instituted, 1730, in France, but until after 1760 the forms varied in name·and ritual, and it was only recognised and sanctioned by the Grand Orient in 1774, on condition that meetings were held by officers of regular lodges. Later they were attached to a masculine lodge, receiving its name, that is to say, "Loge d'adoption." In 1743 the sisters of the Order of the *Félicitaires,* in imagination, sailed under the pilotage of the brothers to the Isle of Felicity, and in 1747 was instituted the Order of the *Fendeurs,* or woodcutters, copied from the coterie of the Charbonniers. The lodge was the Chantier or woodyard, the members were cousins and cousines. Still another was the

Order of the *Chevaliers and Nymphes de la Rose*. These were frequented by men and women of the Court, and clothed as peasants, they joined in all the rowdyism of popular gaiety.

Later these were succeeded by others more closely akin to ordinary Masonry, and about 1760, and later, the most famous were the Lodges, *des Neuf soeurs,* presided over by Mme Helvétius, the *Contrat social,* with the Princess de Lamballe as President, and the Duchesse de Chartres as Grand Mistress (or Master!), and *La Candeur.* In *The Power and Secret of the Jesuits,* 1930, Fülöp-Miller writes:

> "The leaders, of the Enlightenment *(Encyclopedists),* Montesquieu, d'Alembert, Diderot, Lamettrie, Helvétius, La Chalotais, and shortly before his death, Voltaire, were members of the Parisian Lodge 'At the Nine Sisters.'... The success of the great *Encyclopedists* was to a considerable extent due to the initiative and support of the Parisian Grand Lodge."

And yet they could not save the Princess de Lamballe from her horrible death at the hands of the revolutionaries! The fêtes and balls of these women's lodges were frequented by all that was most brilliant in literature, art, and nobility; the whole Court was infatuated by Freemasonry. But as Ragon says, although frivolous in appearance, these societies were powerful agents for sowing in the minds of members the germs of the Masonic principles of equality.

The Masonry of adoption, says Teissier, consists of five principal grades, of which three are obligatory: Apprentice, Fellow-craft, Master; the others were Perfect Master and S*ouveraine illustré écossaise.* This last grade was political, and a Florence journal, *Vera buona nouvella,* gives the speech of the Grand Master before the reception. After the oath of secrecy he says, "... An arduous but sublime task is henceforth imposed upon you. The first of your obligations will be to incense the people against kings and priests, in cafe, theatre, and evening entertainment work with this sacrosanct intention" (Deschamp). This infatuation persisted during the Empire, Restoration, and following régimes.

MISRAIM RITE

At the beginning of the nineteenth century the Masonry of Cagliostro reappeared, combined with the so-called French and Scottish grades under the name of Misraim or Egyptian Rite. It had 90 degrees. As Clavel writes:

> "This system to which great antiquity is attributed, is divided into four classes, called: symbolic, philosophic, mystic, and cabalistic. The degrees of instruction were borrowed from Scottish Rite, Martinism, Hermetic Masonry, and various reforms formerly in force in Germany and France and whose text-books are now found only in the archives of connoisseurs. At first postulants could only attain to the 87th degree. The other three, which complete the system, were reserved for the Unknown Superiors, and even the names of these degrees were hidden from the brothers in the lower grades. Thus organised the Misraim Rite spread, in the second French invasion of the first Empire, into the Kingdom of Italy and Naples... It was brought back to France in 1814 and propagated later in Belgium, Ireland, and Switzerland."

According to Ragon, in his *Cours Philosophique des Initiations, 1841,* their solemn feasts were held at the Equinoxes; during the vernal under the name of *awakening of nature;* during the autumnal under the name of *repose of nature.* Further he writes:

> "The 87th degree has three apartments. The first is hung in black and represents *chaos;* it is lighted by a single light. The second is lighted by three lights and hung with green, symbolising *hope.* The third is lighted by 72 candles and on the entrance door is a transparency of a Jehovah on a throne — sign of eternal creation and the vital fire of nature."

Now, according to Eliphas Levi

> "The name Jehovah resolves into *72* names, called *Shemahamphoras.* The art of employing these 72 names and discovering therein the key of universal science is called by the cabalists the Keys of Solomon... by the aid of these signs and their infinite combinations it is possible to arrive at the natural and mathematical revelation of all secrets of nature."

Here again, as in all such grades, it is the eternal Pan with his seven-voiced flute!

CHAPTER V

CARBONARI, MAZZINI, L'ALLIANCE-ISRAELITE-UNIVERSELLE AND KARL MARX

IN a prefatory letter to George Pitt-Rivers's *World Significance of the Russian Revolution,* 1920, the Jew, Dr. Oscar Levy, wrote:

> "There is no race in the world more enigmatic, more fatal, and, therefore, more interesting than the Jews. Every writer who, like yourself, is oppressed by the aspect of the present and embarrassed by his anxieties for the future must try to elucidate the Jewish question and its bearing upon our age. For the question of the Jews and their influence on the world, past and present, cuts to the root of all things."

One of the most powerful instruments of Jewish universality of the last century was the *Carbonaro* and its affiliations, of which it is said both Mme Blavatsky, 1856, and later Dr. Steiner, were members. Two of the most formidable leaders of the Haute-Vente, known, except to the few, only by their pseudonyms, were *Nubius* and his Jew colleague, *Petit-Tigre* or *Piccolo-Tigre;* and their sinister methods of enticing the unwary into their universal net have been exposed by the latter in the following letter of instructions sent by him to the superior agents of the Piedmontese Vente, 18 January, 1822:

> "It is essential to isolate the man from his family and cause him to lose his morals... He loves the long talks of the café, the idleness of the shows. Entice him, draw him away, give him any kind of importance, teach him discreetly to tire of his daily work, and in this way ... after having shown him how tiresome all duties are, inculcate in him the desire for another existence. Man is born a rebel. Stir up his desire for rebellion as far as the fire, but let not the

conflagration burst out! It is a preparation for the great work which you must begin. When you have insinuated in several minds the distaste of family and religion, let drop certain words which will incite the desire to become affiliated to the nearest lodge. This vanity of the bourgeois to identify himself with Freemasonry has something so banal and so universal that I am ever in admiration before human stupidity…"

Both des Mousseaux and Crétineau-Joly tell how Nubius, this formidable chief of occultism, gained the confidence of the Prince de Metternich, Prime Minister of Austria, and thus drew from him most political secrets of Europe. *Gaetano*, the pseudonym of a Lombard noble named V—, member of the Haute-Vente, was placed near Metternich, at Vienna, there to spy, observe, and report to Nubius. In one such report, 23 January, 1844, he confessed to fears and doubts:

"… We aspire to corrupt in order to attain to govern… We have corrupted too much… I begin to fear that we will not be able to stem the torrent we have let loose. There are insatiable passions of which I did not guess, *unknown appetites, savage hatreds* which ferment around and under us… It has been very easy to pervert; will it also always be easy to muzzle the perverts?… I am disturbed, for I am getting old, I have lost my illusions, I do not wish, poor and denuded of everything, to assist as a theatrical supernumerary in the triumph which I have created and which would repudiate me by confiscating my fortune and taking off my head. We have gone too much to the extreme in many things. We have taken from the people all the gods of heaven and earth which had their homage. We have torn from them their religious faith, their faith in monarchy, their honesty and their family virtues, and we hear in the distance their sinister roarings. We tremble, for the monster may devour us… The world is launched on the declivity of democracy, and for some time for me democracy has meant demagogy. Our twenty years of intrigues run the risk of being wiped out by babblers who would flatter the people, pull the legs off the nobility, after having machine-gunned the clergy… I have as yet no remorse, but I am agitated with fears, and in your place, as I perceive the spirit in Europe, I should not wish to take upon my head a responsibility which might lead Joseph Mazzini to the Capitol. Mazzini at the Capitol! Nubius on the Tarpeian rock or in oblivion!… Does this dream smile upon you, O Nubius!"

In 1849 Metternich, at last realising the truth, exclaimed:

"... In Germany the Jews occupy the principal rôles and are first-rate revolutionaries. They are writers, philosophers, poets, orators, publicists, and bankers, and on their heads and in their hearts all the weight of ancient ignominy! They will one day be terrible for Germany ... *probably followed by a morrow terrible for them*" (Rougeyron, 1861).

And this 'consummate scoundrel' Nubius, according to des Mousseaux, "was poisoned by one of his own followers after having done marvels in favour of anti-Christian revolution." Again des Mousseaux writes:

"But whence comes this sinister marvel (the progressive Judaic power)? It comes from the failing of the Christian faith ... from the progress of secret societies, filled with apostate Christians who desire what the Jew desires; that is to say, Judaic civilisation as given to us by our teacher and master, the philosophic Jew, the Jew of the 'Alliance universelle.'"

Carbonarism was a forcing-ground for the propagation and building-up of the Universal Republic, and Domenico Anghera, writing in 1864, tells us that about 1820-21 the work of the Carbonari was directed by the Masonic lodges and conducted by their adepts. But all Masons were not carbonari, only those definitely Republican. These secret societies have been agents in all insurrections and revolutions in Italy, Spain, and France. In Italy they were known as *Carbonarism,* in France as *Charbonnerie,* and in Spain as *Communeros,* and they were all bound together by an occult direction, forming the irresistible weight of public opinion influencing elections. The Haute-Vente was composed of some corrupt grand seigneurs and of Jews, and was the continuation of the *Inner Order* constituted before the revolution of 1789. In the last grade, which few attained to,

"one learns that the aim of the Carbonari is entirely the same as that of the Illuminati... The initiate swears the ruin of all religion and of all positive government, whether it is despotic or democratic. All means for the execution of their plans are allowed, murder, poison, perjury, all are at their disposal."

So we are told by Jean Witt in his *Les Sociétés Secrétes de France et d'Italie,* 1830.

In their organisation all precaution was taken to prevent police penetration of the whole. Therefore Carbonarism consisted of the sovereign authority, the Haute-Vente, of Central Ventes, and under them again individual Ventes, both of unlimited number, the latter communicating with the Supreme Vente (Paris) only through the deputies of the Central Ventes, each member being again forbidden, on pain of death, to try to enter any other Vente but his own. To penetrate the army they had the legion, cohorts, centuries, and manipules. Members were called "bons cousins," and had each a pseudonym and a special number.

Their work has been thus described by the Jew carbonaro, *Piccolo-Tigre,* to his colleague Nubius, 5 January, 1846:

> "... Everywhere I found minds much inclined to exaltation. All feel that the old world is cracking, and that kings are finished... The harvest made should fructify... The fall of thrones makes it no longer doubtful to me, who have come from studying the work of our societies in France, Switzerland, and Germany, and even Prussia. The assault which, a few years from now, or perhaps a few months, will be delivered upon the princes of the earth, will bury them under the ruins of their *powerless armies* and their decrepit monarchies. *Everywhere there is enthusiasm among our people and apathy and indifference among the enemy* (as we see to-day!). It is a certain and infallible sign of success... In order to kill surely the old world we have believed it necessary to stifle the Catholic and Christian germ... This brave Mazzini, whom I have met at various times, has always his humanitarian dream in his brain and in his mouth. But, apart from his small failings and his methods of assassinations, he has good in him. With his mysticism he strikes the attention of the masses who understand nothing of his grand airs of prophet or his discourses of a cosmopolitan Illuminatus..."

Mazzini, however, by his activity and audacity which recoiled from no means, succeeded in making himself a kind of supreme director over all that was most young and most democratic in the lodges, ventes, and clandestine clubs; in 1832 he founded at Marseilles the journal and society of *Jeune-Italie,* and from end to end Italy was soon as on a volcano. Among their articles of adherence were: "Art. 2.-Having recognised the horrible evils of absolute power, and those still greater of constitutional monarchies, we must work to found a republic one and indivisible. Art. 30.-Those who will not obey the order of the secret societies, or who reveal the mysteries, will be mercilessly stabbed. The same punishment for traitors. Art. 31.-The Secret Tribunal will pronounce the sentence, and will appoint one or two affiliates for its immediate execution. Art. 32.-Whoever shall refuse to execute the order will be reputed a perjurer, and as such killed at once..." The *Jeune-Allemagne,* largely dominated by Jews, was working for the 1848 revolution; and, as Eckert wrote: "Mazzini was head of Jeune-Europe and of the warrior power of Masonry." The Universal Republic prepared by Mazzini and Jeune-Europe appeared as if it would triumph everywhere but it was premature!

Much later, in 1865, he founded the *Alliance-républicaine-universelle* in America, and in January 1867 issued an appeal, hoping thereby to spread his idea in that vast country. Its organisation was in reality a League of Nations:

> "The association should be composed of distinct sections... These sections will be so many representatives of future republics, whilst their delegates, united in a Central Council, will represent the solidarity of republics, realisation of which is the supreme aim proposed for the work of the Alliance. The Central Council should be composed of a president, secretary of finance, secretary of records, and as many secretaries as there shall be nationalities represented in the Council. Each secretary, representing thus a republic, present or future, will be the accredited member of his own section and intermediary for it... The proceedings of the Central Council will be secret... General orders and regulations will emanate from the Central Council. Special agents nominated by the Central Council for all affairs necessary for the organisation or extension of the *Alliance-républicaine-universelle*..." (Deschamps, 1881).

Further, we find the Jew Freemason Crémieux, founder and president of the *Alliance-israélite-universelle,* proclaiming in the name of the Provisional Government, 1848: "The Republic will do what Masonry does, it will become the splendid pledge of the union of peoples over all points of the globe on all sides of our triangle. Citizens and brothers of Freemasonry! Long live the Republic!"

Finally Mazzini, dreamer of this Universal Republic, in his instructions to his followers, 1 November, 1846, said:

"Associate, associate, associate! Everything is in that word. Secret Societies give an irresistible force to the party that can invoke them. Do not be afraid to see them divide; the more they divide the better it will be; all move towards the same end by different roads... The secret is necessary to give security to the members, but a certain transparency is needed to inspire fear in those who stand still. When a great number of associates receive orders to spread an idea and form public opinion, and can for a moment work together they will find the old edifice penetrated in all parts and falling as by a miracle at the least breath of Progress. They will be astonished to see kings, nobles, the rich and the priests, who form the carcass of the old social edifice, fly before the sole power of opinion. Courage, therefore, and perseverance!"

To know, to dare, to will, to keep silence! Such is the system common to all occult, subversive, and secret societies, always apparently controlled by some Unknown Superiors working for the Universal Domination.

L'ALLIANCE-ISRAELITE-UNIVERSELLE

In 1869, in his book *Le Juif,* the Chevalier Gougenot des Mousseaux wrote:

"The anti-religious but, above all, anti-Christian efforts which distinguish the present epoch have a character of concentration and *universality* which marks the stamp of the Jew, the supreme patron of the unification of peoples, because he is the cosmopolitan people *par excellence;* because the Jew prepares by the licence of the *libre-pensée,* the era called by him 'Messianic' — the day of his universal triumph. He attributes its near realisation to the principles spread by the philosophers of the eighteenth century; the men at once unbelievers and cabalists, whose work prepared the Judaising of the world. The character of *universality* will be noted in *L'Alliance-israélite universelle,* in the *Universal Association of Freemasonry,* and in the more recent auxiliaries, *L'Alliance-universelle-religieuse,* open to those who are still frightened off by the name of Israelite and finally in the *Ligue-universelle de l'enseignement...*"

L'Alliance-israélite-universelle, that vast revolutionary association of defence, attack, and propaganda, with its astonishing diversity of membership, was founded by the Jew Adolphe Cremieux, who, according to the *Archives israélites,* was "elected in 1869, Sovereign Grand Master of the Scottish Rite of Freemasonry, the highest dignity of the Masonic Order in France." The Alliance arose out of the slackening of the Jewish religion and the spread of the revolutionary reformed *libre-pensée* movement, and its dogmas were those of Freemasonry and Occultism. In 1861, the same Jewish journal wrote:

> "*L'Alliance-israélite-universelle...* addresses itself to all religions... It desires to penetrate into all religions as it has penetrated into all countries. How many nations have disappeared? How many religions will in turn vanish? *Israel will not cease to exist* ... the religion of Israel will not perish; it is the unity of God."

From Edouard Drumont's *La France Juive,* 1886, we draw the following information about this same Alliance. As we know, Cremieux, its founder, was an important leader of French democracy, and he more than any other gave a strictly Jewish character to the French revolutionary movement; "He prepared and loudly proclaimed, during the last years of his life, the Messianic reign, the time so long expected when all nations will be subject to Israel and all men will work for the representatives of the race blessed by Jehovah." The Alliance was founded in 1860, and its first General Assembly took place, 30 May, 1861. "In reality it had already functioned secretly for many years, but certain Jews, sure of victory, felt the need of an official power, an effective representative of their nation which could speak to Europe in its name."

The constitution of the Alliance is apparently very simple. Any Jew, by paying a yearly subscription of six francs, could belong to it. It is governed by a Central Committee in Paris, composed at first of forty members and later of sixty, elected for nine years by the vote of all members of the Alliance. From among themselves the Central Committee elected every year a bureau consisting of a President, two Vice-Presidents, a Treasurer, and a Secretary-General. A committee could be constituted wherever the society had ten adherents, and a Regional Committee could be constituted in any country where there were several local committees. In local and regional matters these committees acted on their own responsibility, but in matters concerning the Association they acted on communications received from the

Central Committee. Subscriptions were collected and remitted to the Central body. In 1886 the members were about 28,000, and the budget of the Association was about a million francs, but their real resources were almost unlimited.

Among the societies attached to it were: The Anglo-Jewish Association, the Union of American Hebrew Congregations, the B'nai B'rith of America, etc. Controlling by money most of the big European Press and acting through them upon the peoples, the Israelites had nevertheless numerous journals addressed solely to the Jews, such as *Archives israélites, l'Univers israélite* of Paris, the *Jewish Chronicle,* the *Jewish World* of London, the *Jewish Messenger* of New York, etc. As Crémieux said: "L'Alliance is not a French, German, or English Alliance; it is Jewish, it is universal. That is why it progresses, why it succeeds." The Alliance was treated on an equality by the Powers; it sent notes, protests, and even ultimata which were received and considered by the Sovereigns, as for example, the question of Roumania in 1867-68, and the oppression of its people by the Jew usurers. Cremieux successfully intervened in favour of the Jews.

The dogmas of *l'Alliance-israélite-universelle* are those of reformed Judaism, which, according to the rationalist Kluber, "were prepared by Moise Mendelssohn — friend of Mirabeau — ... [and] would in all probability lead to a pure Deism or natural religion whose followers need not belong to the Judaic race." It hopes to Judaise the world and open the way for Judaic expansion and development, penetrating all religions and all nations. According to Leon de Poncins, 1928, the Jewish Masonic Order B'nai B'rith was founded in New York in 1843:

> "It divides the world into eleven districts, of which seven are in the United States. The number of Lodges is about 500, with nearly 100,000 adherents... According to well-informed sources, there is in the B'nai B'rith a super-position of secret societies ending in a single governing power. Above the B'nai B'rith are the B'nai Moshé, then the B'nai Zion, and finally the hidden centre of supreme command."

He makes the last statement without proof.

In this same book, *The Secret Powers behind Revolution*, de Poncins tells us that the League of Nations was largely due to the world-wide influence of *l'Alliance-israélite-universelle*, and was the realisation of a long pursued and persistent Jewish idea and ambition. As for example: In March 1864, the *Archives israelites* published a letter written by a member of the Alliance, Levy Bing, in which he said:

> "if, in a word, it is no longer permitted to give judgment oneself, but rather remit it to judges generally accepted and disinterested in the litigation, is it not natural, necessary, and, above all, important soon to see another tribunal, dealing with great public disputes, with complaints between nations, judging as a final appeal, and whose word would be law? And this word, it is the word of God pronounced by his eldest sons, the Hebrews, and before which all younger sons [nations] will bow with respect, that is to say, the Universality of men, our brothers, our friends, our disciples."

HOLY VEHM

From time to time secret societies have played a great rôle in the life of the Germanic people. There was the "Holy Vehm," a secret society unique in the world whose name had for centuries throughout the German Empire made the powerful and simple alike tremble with fear. It openly admitted itself to be revolutionary, a secret Tribunal issuing and executing decrees, and during the Middle Ages acting in the name of the Emperor even when opposed to him. In the fourteenth and fifteenth centuries its number was estimated at 100,000. It differed essentially from the Masonic type of secret society, although its members qualified themselves as "seers" and "illuminés," that is, *Wissend*, while describing outsiders of all ranks by saying they "had not received the light."

The Mason Clavel, in his *Histoire Pittoresque de la Franc-maçonnerie et des Sociétés Secrètes*, 1843, gives a long and interesting account of the "Holy Vehm," linking it also, in its general aim, with the Assassins. He says:

> "What, in its beginnings, had an appearance of equity and salutary result degenerated later into a crying abuse. The association no longer used its power to protect the feeble against the oppression of

the strong; it employed it to satisfy personal vengeance;... [having ended by losing the support of the people] it was forced to succumb under the weight of the universal reprobation it had stirred up."

He gives the oath taken at a reception; receptions were always held in a cave or in the solitary depths of some forest, under a hawthorn tree:

"I swear to be faithful to the secret Tribunal, to defend it against myself, against water, sun, moon, stars, foliage of trees, all living beings, all that God has created between heaven and earth; against father, mother, brothers, sisters, wife, children, finally all men, the head of the Empire alone excepted [the Emperor was as a rule a *Wissend*]; to uphold the judgment of the secret Tribunal, to aid in its executions and denounce to the present or any other secret Tribunal all misdemeanours against its jurisdiction, which may come to my knowledge ... so that the culprit should be judged as by law or judgment be suspended with the assent of the accusor. [No one and nothing created by God] will be able to persuade me to break this oath... So help me God and his saints."

Further, Le Couteulx de Canteleu writes of this terrible Tribunal:

"In the old acts, still retained at Dortmund, the members of these tribunals were often designated under the name of Rose-Croix; there were three degrees of initiation: the Francs-juges, the real Francs-juges who executed the sentences of the first, and the Saints-juges of the secret Tribunal, whose duty it was to observe, to scour the country, and report on what went on."

They had signs and words for recognition. In 1371, after the Peace of Westphalia, they, reinforced by the wandering and proscribed Templars, according to Clavel, established themselves throughout the whole of eastern Germany, the Red Country, and the principal seat of the Holy Vehm was then at Dortmund and Westphalia. Although the abuses became so great and their power so formidable, it was only about the seventeenth century that their power was broken. As Baron de Bock says in his *Histoire du Tribunal Secret*, 1801: "These Tribunals, according to some, were never formally abolished by the laws of the Empire; they were only brought back to their original destination and circumscribed to the districts where they had the right to exercise their jurisdiction," which was ultimately public and very limited.

Jews were not admitted into the "Holy Vehm," and until the sixteenth century were not punishable under the Tribunals. Whether it still existed or not in some secret organism, the old Vehmic spirit strongly marked the first Masonic lodges created in Germany during the eighteenth century, approved of and supported by Frederick the Great and his successors. His policy was to break the Franco-Austrian Alliance of 1756, and establish a united Germany under Prussian domination.

Again according to Clavel:

> "Frederick the Great was received at Brunswick, 14–15 August, 1738, unknown to his father, the reigning King, who was always opposed to the establishment of the society in the State… Becoming King, the Templar Masonic propaganda met with no further obstacles."

In 1740 he encouraged the foundation, at Berlin, of *La Grande Loge Nationale Aux Trois Globes.* He is said to have organised, in 1762, the 25 degrees of Scottish Masonry superimposed upon the Masonry of Saint-John, bringing it thus into more direct relations with the Templar system. After the apparent dissolution of Weishaupt's Illuminati Fessler, as Eckert says, took upon himself the task of giving an exterior form to the aims and methods of Illuminism. He, therefore, organised in Prussia the *Grande Loge Royal York À l'Amitié,* under the patronage of the Prince Royal, afterwards Frederick-William III, which served as a centre for anti-Christian and anti-social conspiracy. The idea of the reunion of Germany under Prussia never ceased to be the aim of these lodges, and after 1848 Bismarck was the man who grouped all the forces of secret societies under his own direction, and the Jews, allied with him from 1866, were his most active supporters in this unification.

And of recent German Masonry, the *Revue Internationale des Sociétés Secrètes,* 21 June, 1931, and I June, 1933, gave the following information. After the War all German lodges under whatever obedience tended towards denying the classic universalism of Masonry and admitted a Germanism equally strict.

> "It fell back on itself and thought to discover that the world could only be cured by the culture and exaltation of Germanism. And they

dogmatically proclaimed it as being specifically German. Aryan domination, Christian spirituality, the principle of private property, and a Germanism opposed to all outside influence" (Dr. R. Teilhaber — An. *Mac. Uni.,* 1930).

Or as Dr. Steiner, late head of Anthroposophy or "Christian Illuminism," said at Stuttgart, 1918, the only nation in the world that knows right from wrong is the German nation, and Germany must fulfil her mission, otherwise European civilisation will be ruined.

KARL MARX

It has been said with good reason that the origin of Leninism and Bolshevism was firstly the *Encyclopaedists,* and secondly, Marxist and other Socialist systems. The first were the atheists, *philosophes,* and *economistes* of the Hôtel d'Holbach, a lodge or literary academy founded about 1769, of which Voltaire was honorary and permanent president, having d'Alembert, Condorcet, Diderot, La Harpe, and others as members. Most books and pamphlets against religion, morals, and the Government were written and controlled by them; in this lodge they were revised, added to, cut, and corrected to suit their revolutionary propaganda, creating the mental, moral, and political outlook which brought about the French Revolution of 1789. Further, we have shown how Freemasonry, Carbonarism, and Martinism spread their cankers, secretly initiating the ideas which eventually led in part to the Russian Revolution of 1917. Out of this secret Masonry was built up the simpler outside manifestations, the Marxist and other Socialist systems, which in Russia culminated in the present Soviet regime of collectivism, slavery, immorality, and atheism. Their aim was that of Weishaupt — liberty and equality of the forests, upon the ruins of religion and property.

In 1850 several towns of Germany possessed workers' associations called *communes.* The heads of this conspiracy were Engels and Marx, and at the head of their manifesto, 1851, was written: "Proletarians of all countries unite!" In 1862 the association developed immensely under the name of the *International Association of Workers,* and finally in 1864, at an assembly of workers in London, a committee was nominated of fifty members, who elaborated the statutes. Mazzini's manifesto and statutes were rejected and those of Marx unanimously adopted and ratified later at the Congress of Geneva in 1866. The International had two characteristics: the simple, non-political Socialists, and the political Jacobin Socialists; it is also curious to note that the latter almost inevitably eliminated or absorbed the former. Each year the all-supreme Congress indicated the seat of the General Council and nominated its members. This seat was at first in London, but in 1873 it was transferred to New York.

From 1864 to 1870 the International continued to develop; at its congresses the most revolutionary motions were heard and applauded, and in 1870 it was the promoter of the short-lived Paris *Commune*. Everywhere it was felt; the poison of its doctrines ate into the social life of all countries. As Dupont said at the Brussels Congress: "We no longer want Governments, for Governments crush us with taxes … we no longer want armies, for armies massacre us; we no longer want religion, for religion stifles the intelligence." And at a meeting of Internationals in London, 1869, Vezinier said: "The negation of Divinity is to affirm man in his strength and liberty. As for the family, we repudiate it with all our force in the name of the emancipation of mankind…"

Besides the proletarian International and the universal republican International, there was that of *L'Alliance Internationale de la democratie-socialiste,* organised by Bakunin, 1850-60, which published its manifesto in 1868. It aimed at complete levelling of all men, it declared itself atheist, it desired the abolition of cults, the substitution of science for faith, and human justice for Divine justice. The workers' International inscribed on its banner: "Community of Property"; the republicans' International: "Community of Power"; the democrats' International: "Community of Property, Power, Women, and war against God."

This last was more terrible because of its advanced negations. In 1860 this Socialist-Democrats' International was affiliated to the International of the Workers, retaining a secret organisation, becoming a state within a state. Trouble arose, and the alliance was dissolved, but was soon reorganised by Bakunin as the

Fédération jurassienne, and was excommunicated later by the International Congress at The Hague. Of these *anarchists* the Nihilist Kropotkin wrote: "Two great currents of ideas were found, the popular State and Anarchy — 'anarchy,' that is to say, complete abolition of States and organisation of free federation of popular forces, production, and consumption."

In Russia the Nihilists were what the Socialist Democrats, or the *Fédération jurassienne,* were elsewhere, only they increased to the utmost the principles of anarchy and destruction. Their dogma, which has given them their name, is that all is nothingness, zero, such as we find among the Manicheans and Martinists; they profess gross materialism, a return to nature. As Winterer wrote: "Nihilism is not a system, it is a negation of all religious, moral, political, and social order." It spread like the canker it was throughout Russia, and deeply attacked all organs of the social body; it included all ranks of Russian society-nobility, clergy, bourgeois, and officials, but few peasants. Its most valuable members were the cultured women of the universities. The heads of Nihilism were not in Russia, but in Western Europe, chiefly Switzerland. As Winterer continued:

> "If Nihilism could for a short time only have at its disposal the enormous resources of the immense Empire, we would see a devastating torrent such as the world has never seen before precipitate itself from east to west, carrying upon the entire continent its terrible ravages."

The creators of theoretic Marxism were Jews, or of Jewish family, from Karl Marx to Trotsky and his band. The Jew, Dr. Angelo Rappoport, member of the Bund and of the Poale Sion, in his book, *The Pioneers of the Russian Revolution,* 1918, wrote:

> "The Bund, or General Union of the Jewish Workers, was founded in 1897. It is a political and economic association of the proletarian Jews... It carried on active propaganda in Yiddish ... [it] served as model to those who fought for liberty and were pioneers of the Russian Revolution. There was not a political organisation in the vast Empire which was not influenced by the Jews or directed by them — the Social-Democrats, the Revolutionary Socialist parties, and the Polish Socialist Party, all had Jews among their directors..."

Moreover, the *Jewish World*, 25 June, 1931, said: "The real author of the Five-Years' Plan, Kaganovitz, is a Jew, and what is more, a great favourite of Stalin."

Are we not, in Bolshevism, witnessing that devastating torrent, feared by Winterer, having at its disposal the enormous resources of the immense Empire, pouring its ravages—economic, social, religious, and political into the life of all countries, working for this Jewish World Revolution and World Domination?

In his book, *Le Temps de la Colère*, 1932, R. Vallery-Radot writes: "It is well to observe that in April 1917, the Judaeo-Mason and financier of Wall Street, Jacob Schiff, head of the firm of Kuhn Loeb and Co., had publicly boasted of having had a share in the Russian Revolution." And of the Bolshevik philosophy, M. Pierre Dominique, brilliant editor of *La République*, says:

> "The Bolshevists have ·therefore a philosophy. Let us ask from whence have they got it? To be frank, they have drawn this philosophy from *L'Encyclopédie*, which was a vast enterprise of atheism and which, politically speaking—, expressed itself in a precise way at the end of the eighteenth century by the French Revolution. They are attached to a philosophy which we find at the root of all socialist systems propagated during the nineteenth century, and particularly at the root of the Marx system. Thus its early source: *L'Encyclopédie;* later source and very diverse: the series of contemporaneous socialist systems… Such are the deep origins of Leninism and of the Soviet revolution."

Further, both Bolshevism and Judaeo-Masonry work for a Universal Republic by World Revolution.

In his famous *Catechism*, as given in the *Revue des Deux Mondes*, on June, 1880, Bakunin thus describes the revolutionary tool:

> "The revolutionary is a man *dedicated*. He must have neither personal interests, business, sentiments, nor property. He must be absolutely absorbed in a single exclusive interest, a single thought, a single passion, *revolution*. He despises and hates actual morals; for him all is moral which favours the triumph of revolution, and immoral and criminal which impedes it. Between him and society there is a fight to the death, incessant and irreconcilable. He must be prepared to die, to endure torture, to put to death with his own hands

all those who are obstacles to revolution. So much the worse for him if he has in this world links of family, friendship, or love. He is not a true revolutionary if his attachments stop his arm. Nevertheless, he must live in the midst of society feigning to be what he is not. He must penetrate everywhere, among the upper classes as among the middle, in the shop, the Church, the Army, the literary world, the secret police, and even the Imperial parlour. He must consider his subordinates as part of the revolutionary capital placed at his disposal, and he must dispose of it economically so as to draw all possible profit from it."

Further one reads in the statutes of *L'Alliance humanitaire universelle:*

"Kings, nobles, the aristocracy of money, employees of the police or of the administration, priests, and permanent armies are the enemies of mankind. Against them one has every right and every duty. All is permitted to annihilate them: violence, ruse, shot and shell, poison, and the dagger; the end sanctifies the means."

To-day the Masonic review *L'Accacia,* writes:

"Between Church and Freemasonry it is a war to the death, without mercy." And comparing this Judaeo Masonry and Revolution, M, Xavier Vallat aptly explains: "Therefore we have on one side an organisation in appearance essentially anti-religious, Freemasonry, and it is found that in addition it follows a revolutionary, social, and political aim! On the other side a Revolution in appearance political and social, to-day unveils itself as being profoundly atheistical! This singular meeting behind the mask of violent antagonism is of a nature to cause awakened minds to think" *(R.I.S.S.,* 1 January, 1933).

The revolutionary means of propaganda differs from that of yesterday only in its increased and extended field and facilities, including such international intercommunications as press, wireless, cinemas, etc. We have also our modern *Encyclopaedists,* not a whit less powerful or persistent than those of the eighteenth century. Writing of that century in his *Paroles d'un révolté,* the noted Nihilist Kropotkin said:

"The brochure placed within reach of the masses the ideas of the *philosophes* and economists, precursors of the Revolution; pamphlets and leaflets stirred up agitation by attacking the three principal enemies: the King and his court, the aristocracy, the clergy.

They did not theorise, they derided ... the police in vain raided the libraries and arrested colporteurs; the unknown authors escaped to continue their work... Placards printed or written by hand appeared on every occasion when something happened to interest the public... It awakened in the hearts of the peasants, workers, and bourgeois hatred against their enemies, it announced the day of liberation and vengeance... It overran the villages and prepared minds."

To-day in every country the Moscow-directed Communists have their centres of activity, their pamphlets, and their journals of revolt against capital, civil, and religious authority; their single thought, their single passion, the creation of a Soviet machine working for World Revolution which would bring in, not as they think, the reign of democracy, but that of unknown taskmasters whose slaves they would eventually become. And to quote M. R. Vallery-Radot again:

"Having exiled the gods from the City, the modem world seeks for something to replace them, they know not what, which exists nowhere... As on the eve of the Revolution, we perceive on the surface a diffused odour of heresy: the same treachery of words, the same confusion of principles ... strange apostles try to reconcile with Christianity the Masonic ideologies of Democracy, Humanity, Society, Progress, Pacifism, and Internationalism; by unavoidable but unilateral endosmose their dogmas dilute themselves into abstractions, their mysteries into politics."

Again:

"It is, that the Peace, whose fruits we are tasting to-day, should have nothing in common with former Treaties. It would accomplish the great Masonic plan sketched in 1789, taken up again in 1830, then in 1848 and in 1870, by proclaiming the coming of Universal Democracy."

What was said by Disraeli in 1876 might still be applied to present world conditions: ·

"The Governments of this country have to deal, not only with Governments, emperors, kings, and ministers, but also with secret societies, elements which must be taken into account, which at the last moment can bring all plans to naught, which have agents everywhere, agents without scruples, who incite assassinations and can, if necessary, lead a massacre."

And according to Disraeli men of Jewish race were found at the head of every such political secret society. George Sand also wrote: "There are moments when the history of Empires only nominally exists, and when there is nothing really alive but the sects hidden within them." The mother of all these secret societies is Judaeo Masonry, whose principles are identical with those realised with Revolution. As Claudio Jannet says:

> "It extends itself throughout the entire world, covering itself with mystery, acting in all parts of the social body ... binding within it, by secret links, individual societies apparently most different. Its doctrines are everywhere the same; its unity, its universality thus explains the unity and universality of Revolution."

As to the directing power, in the report of the Third Congress at Nancy, 1882, the orator, Knight Kadosch, believed that the last degrees carried on an International Masonic work of very great penetration, and that probably from there came those mysterious words which in the midst of uprisings passed at times through the crowds, setting them on fire "for the good of humanity." This secret hierarchy was also said to be Rosicrucian, a kind of Third Order, such as the "Hidden Chiefs" of the Stella Matutina.

René Guénon, orientalist, moreover explains in the *Voile d'Isis*, January 1933:

> "Even if certain of these organisations, among the most outside, find themselves in opposition to each other, that will in no way prevent the effective existence of unity of direction. To sum up, there is something comparable to the role played by different actors in the same play in a theatre, and who, although opposed to each other none the less agree in the progress of the whole; each organisation also plays the role to which it is destined; and this can extend also to the esoteric domain where the elements which fight against one another none the less all obey, although quite unconsciously and involuntarily, a single direction whose existence they do not even suspect."

And as Henri Misley, who took an active part in Italy's revolutions about 1830, said:

> "I know the world a little, and I know that in all this great future that is being prepared, there are only four or five who hold the cards. A

greater number believe they hold them, but they deceive themselves."

Again, in the Congress at Nancy, 1882, it was said:

"What force will not Masonry have upon the outside world, when around each lodge will exist a crowd of societies whose members, ten or fifteen times more numerous than the Masons, will receive inspiration and aim from the Masons, and will unite their efforts with ours for the great work which we pursue. Within this circle once founded, one must perpetuate with care a nucleus of young Masons in such a way that the young people of the schools will find themselves directly subjected to Masonic influences."

In the Convent, Grand Orient of France, 1923, was resolved:

"An active propaganda is urgent, so that Freemasonry shall again become the inspirer, the mistress of the ideas through which democracy is to be brought to perfection... To influence social elements by spreading widely the teaching received within the institution." Some of these elements were "sports societies, boy scouts, art circles, choral and instrumental groups. All organisations which attract Republican youth to works of education, physical and intellectual." But as Mazzini exclaimed: "The difficulty is not to convince people, some great words, liberty, rights of man, progress, equality, fraternity, despotism, privilege, tyranny and slavery, are sufficient for that; the difficulty is to unite them. The day when they are united will be the day of the new era."

In *La Temps de la Colère*, M. Vallery-Radot, 1932, further elucidates the methods:

"What has been called the conquest of revolution is in reality only an implacable dogma affirmed by one party to the exclusion of all others ... this party has known how to extend its conquests with admirable method, sometimes subterranean, as under the First Empire; sometimes combining infiltration with violent demonstration, as under the Restoration, the July Monarchy, the Republic of 1848; then again taking up its hidden intrigue under the Second Empire, and, finally, frankly unveiling its game under the Third Republic... This intangible general Will revealed to the world by a half-fool as the sacred emanation of an autonomous humanity, who has to render account to no one but itself, this general Will calls itself Democracy, Progress, Revolution, Republic, Humanity, Laicity, but it is always the same Power, which shares it with none, jealously guarded by its priests and doctors."

And showing what may happen in the world if the nations do not awaken and realise the secret undermining force which is seeking the destruction of Christian civilisation, he says:

> "There are in the tropics houses which appear solid, although slowly and surely the white ants are busy gnawing the internal structure. One day the inhabitants sit on the chairs, the chairs fall into dust; they lean against the walls, and the walls crumble away. Thus it is with our civilisation, of which we are so proud."

The following is taken from an article by de Fremond, in the *Revue Internationale des Sociétés Secretes*, 1 July, 1932:

> 'Now, let us not forget, even in the opinion of the most optimistic, the people themselves are almost entirely de-Christianised... *(Mercure de France*, 1 April, 1932).

> "And according to Cardinal Verdier: "Every day we see the number of Pagans increase."...

> "The causes...

> "Without going back to the Renaissance or even to the Reform, which have both prepared the ground, we find as first cause the Revolution, called French, but in reality European, world even; the Revolution everywhere spreading nationalistic ideas and applying, more apparent than real, the false principles of the 'Rights of Man': *Liberty, Equality,* and *Fraternity...* Let us not omit the Regency, which preceded by so little the Revolution. The great crisis, says Demolins in his *Histoire de France*, 1880, *à propos* the system of law, has had deplorable consequences: it developed above all in the higher classes, cupidity, craving for material powers, love of speculation; it displaced fortunes and rendered them unstable by detaching them from real estate in order to found them on the money-changing operations of the Bourse; it produced also in the organisation of property and public fortune an upset which should soon contribute to the entire collapse of society.

> "Where are we a half-century later?

> "The enormous material progress realised, thanks to the great discoveries of the nineteenth century and the leap they have still more made in the twentieth by bringing these discoveries to perfection; the new facilities of existence which flow from them instead of keeping people in admiration of such marvels, by reasonable use of them, in gratitude in short towards the Creator, upon whom they depend and who dispenses them to us, the people

have, on the contrary, turned their backs upon religious practices and even on belief.

"Does this movement act of itself spontaneously and because of human passions of pleasure and pride, etc.? Not for the first part, a power has intervened which has pushed the wheel more and more: that which, systematically, credits all to man, his sagacity, his power to bring to perfection, and thus substitutes him, gradually and almost imperceptibly, in place of the Divine Creator, suppressing at the same time all obligation towards Him. First indifference, then unbelief. The mixture of rationalist and materialist ideas...

"It places all religions on the same equality: that is to say, recognises no religion... What is the result? A society unbalanced and demoralised, where crimes abound, all the more so that the provocation of the Press more often remains unpunished, where general materialisation accentuates itself day by day... From top to bottom of the social ladder there is no longer any but one motive, pleasure, but one agent, money..."

Is it not "the greater Judaism, gradually casting non-Jewish thoughts and systems into Jewish moulds," as described by the *Jewish World* of 9 February, 1883?

CHAPTER VI

THE JEWISH QUESTION

I N order to illustrate the history of the Jewish people from its earliest beginnings down through the ages to the present day, as seen and depicted by the Jewish mind itself, we give the following account of a Jewish pageant, details of which were received from a friend who witnessed it in Chicago, and also from the *Chicago Tribune*, 4 July, 1933.

This marvellous, impressive, and spectacular pageant of "The Romance of a People," tracing the history of the Jewish race through the past forty centuries, was given on the Jewish Day in the Soldier Field, Chicago, 3–4 July, 1933. It was listened to almost in silence by 125,000 people, the vast majority being Jews. Most of the performers, 3,500 actors and 2,500 choristers, were amateurs, but with their race's inborn gift for vivid drama, and to their rabbis and cantors, deeply learned in centuries of Hebrew ritual, much of the authoritative music and pantomime was due. "Take the curious placing of thumb to thumb and forefinger to forefinger by the High Priest when he lifted his hands, palms outwards, to bless the multitude... Much of the drama's text was from the Old Testament and orthodox ritual of Judaism." A Hebrew chant in unison, soft and low, was at once taken up with magical effect by many in the audience, and orthodox Jews joined in many of the chants and some of the spoken rituals.

The story as shown in the pageant was imparted to the audience by hidden voices, almost perfectly amplified the drama of the Egyptian bondage, the shame of idolatry, the woes of exile, the bitterness of defeat and desolation by the Legions of Rome. The return to monotheism, the joy and triumphs of temple-building and nation-building. Everywhere were seen the interlaced triangles of the six-pointed star and the white flag of Palestine with the two blue bars and this same star in between. As Dr. Chaim Weizmann stated, there were now about 200,000 Jews in Palestine, and it was proposed to get 250,000 more out of Germany into Palestine. But what of the rights of the Arabs!

Our correspondent quotes from the official programme, with its Foreword, and *The Visionary on the Mountain Top,* and in these will be found the hidden significance of the whole imposing pageant. "It was the largest Jewish assemblage since Temple days," and as the *Visionary* says:

> "Within all the cross currents within Jewish life, amidst the inner divisions which bore witness alike to the weakness of the Jew and to the strength of the Jewish convictions, one truth asserted itself, with a power which silenced all doubts: the Jewish people *lived...* In number, superior to any Jewish generation of the past, in the caliber of its human material, as powerful as ever, in self-consciousness, more alert and more proud than it had been for centuries, it was entering, not on a decline, but on a new efflorescence."

It is a racial dream, not a religious spectacle, and possibly meant to be "prophetic" of coming world power.

According to the official programme, the Jew is found in trouble under Alexander of Macedon, under Assyria, Persia, Rome, in Spain, Russia, Ancient England, Poland, Roumania, and now in Germany. Why? Our correspondent concludes: "I think the secret of it is found in the *imperium in imperio* matter and in the common programme towards which each *imperium in imperio* moves, and has been moving for forty centuries." As the *Visionary* says:

> "Those who stand too close to the canvas of history while it is being woven will err in their estimate of forces. Minor set-backs will take on the aspects of decisive defeats, minor advances the aspects of major victories. Only in the perspective of all our history — the longest perspective of which any people can boast — shall we be able to estimate the significance of recent events. To-day the hearts of the Jews are oppressed by the bitter events in Germany; let them, while they extend help to the victims of a cruel régime, recall that governments and rulers change, the Jewish people remains. In other

lands than Germany then smoulders still a dangerous threat against Jewish life. Let the Jews be prepared... Let their fears be tempered by an understanding of their long past, and their hopes be rendered sober by an appreciation of the long future before them. Let them measure all tasks, all difficulties, and all prospects by the standard of a world-wide outlook."

Again our correspondent notes:

"As I looked upon that spectacle, as I saw the flags of the nations carried to their places before the reproduction of the Jewish Temple in Jerusalem, and as I saw the six-pointed star, the illuminated interlaced triangles, shining above all the flags of all the peoples of all the world, my mind turned back to what Judge Harry M. Fisher, Chairman of the Jewish Day Committee, said in advance as to the whole idea of this pageant: "The idea summarised by the prophet Isaiah — At the end of days all peoples shall be coming to the mountain of the Lord — will be portrayed."

But all reference to the Founder of Christianity was omitted in the Pageant.

With regard to the significance of the symbols and the Jewish unity of race and purpose — the High Priest joining thumbs and forefingers in blessing the people, thereby represented the Hebrew Divine Triangle, the Trinity in Unity of the Ineffable Name — Yod, He, Vau — the Creative Principle which becomes manifest and powerful in the final He, the material basis in and through which it acts. It is Yahveh, the Tetragrammaton, a symbol of creation or generation, the mysterious union of their God with his creatures and which is said to be all-powerful in working miracles or magic. This Ineffable Name was looked upon by the Jews as too holy and sacred to be spoken, but so that it might not be lost the High Priest uttered it once a year in the temple at the great feast of Atonement. Further, they hold that the true name will be revealed at the coming of their Messiah; and *to many the Messiah means the race!*

Of the interlaced triangles or Solomon's Seal, it is said in the *Lesser Assembly,* par 720: "So also here, when the Male is joined to the Female, they both constitute one complete body, and all the universe is in a state of happiness because all things receive blessing from their perfect body. And this is an arcanum." It is the star of the Macrocosm, the dual forces in all nature, the sign of a power which nothing can resist. It constitutes the secret power of the Jew through which he dominates the mind and actions of men and nations. It is the Hebrew talisman of power and illuminism.

Turning to *Nomades* by the Jewish writer Kadmi Cohen, 1929, we read:

> "The perfect Semite is positive and impassioned. The two elements exercise a reciprocal influence, each moderating what is too excessive and therefore unlikely to live in the other, creating a being apart who easily arrives at domination, for nothing can stop such a man... It is the eternal opposition of Shylock and Jessica. It is the illogical and monstrous mixture of the rarest qualities with the most abject defects, mixture of irresistible force and of irremediable weakness."

And of their race-idea of God, Kadmi Cohen says:

> "The Jews are not a part of a vast Whole which they reintegrate in dying, but they are a Whole in themselves, defying space, time, life, and death. Can God be outside the Whole? If he exists, necessarily he confounds himself with this Whole... Thus Divinity in Judaism is contained in the exaltation of the entity represented by the Race-passional entity, eternal flame, it is the Divine essence. It must be preserved and perpetuated, therefore the idea of pure and impure was created."

It is pantheistic and cabalistic.

We might, therefore, conclude that *The Romance of a People* represents this Jewish Divinity, the eternity and unity of the Race and its everliving hope of bringing all nations under the influence of the uniting and illuminising power of these interlaced triangles. Hence the many illuminising sects and cults of to-day, some of which are nominally Christian, but in reality all are cabalistic, gnostic, pantheistic, and instruments of Judaism.

In *Nomades,* which is an essay on the Jewish soul, we find many interesting and enlightening ideas on the place, as the author sees it, of the Jew in the world. Socialist, Communist, revolutionary, passional, utilitarian, unitarist, the Jew is yet a fixed solidarity, undifferentiated. Kadmi Cohen writes: *"I am that I am,"* said the

Eternal. The Eternal — it is the race. One in substance-undifferentiated. One in time — stable and eternal."

From a psychological point of view there are two kinds of Jews: *Hassidim*, the passionals, the Mediterranean mystics, cabalists, sorcerers, poets, orators, frenetics, dreamers, voluptuaries, prophets; and the *Mithnagdim*, the Utilitarians, the Nordics, cold, reasoners, egoists, positives, and on the extreme left, the vulgar elements, keen on gain, without scruples, arrivists, merciless. The "Passionalism" of the Semites is characterised by

> "a nervous excitability, a chronic exaltation of the passion, in which commingle the interior life of the individual and its exterior manifestations, a state in which sentiment, idea, and will are confounded together, where for the lack of the powerful corrective of logic, the flights of imagination know no bounds, where life and human activity are deprived of a regulator, and move outside of material and concrete factors, by the sole interior force of the soul."

A condition which apparently corresponds to the unbalanced psychic visions of Illuminism!

> "It is not only this fervent 'Passionalism' which conditions the attitude of the Jews in the political and social order... They always experience the need to seek unity. Because of that they are sentimentally led to reject in a more or less absolute fashion all which is contradictory to this unity. For them, what is differentiation is an attack on the principle of unity; injustice and inequality are differentiations. They must be rejected or lessened... Thus is explained the Socialist and Communist tendencies of which they are reproached. It is in what is called business that the Jewish soul, by utilitarianism with which he is so strongly impregnated, finds a liberal career: commerce, trade, banks, finance, and industries. It is this same characteristic which in all times and in all places has brought upon the traditional Jew sarcasms and reprobations, often enough, let us recognise it, justified."

The Jewish role in world Socialism

> "is so important that it is not possible to pass it over in silence. Is it not sufficient to recall the names of the great revolutionaries of the nineteenth century and twentieth, the Karl Marxes, Lassalles, Kurt Eiseners, Bela Kuhns, Trotskys, and Léon Blumes, in order to find thus mentioned the names of all theorists of modern Socialism?... Further, in Europe in the same years, the rôle played by the Jews in

all revolutionary movements was considerable...
"Revolutionarism" exacts, at least technically, a very strong dose of
passionalism together with the *esprit de masse* of the crowd. The
different individuals, in principle autonomous, blend even to
disappearing in the whole, and the "magma" thus created takes on
an aspect entirely different from the individual figures, however
characteristic each may be, of which it was primarily composed. "

Again:

"The same basis of a State: opposing interests balanced by
combating each other, is wanting. In its place passions animating
popular masses, passions deprived of the corrective of the
consideration of realities, passions let loose at the will of mere
psychic factors ... these factors which agitate the masses muting
their material power of reason, which those who take no account of
imponderables will find mysterious. Like a compass needle,
influenced by a magnetic storm, imperceptible to our senses,
becomes erratic, sending astray the vessel which trusts to its
indications, losing it in the mysterious ways of the ocean...

"In a general way, almost everywhere, the Jews are Republicans.
The Republic tending towards levelling has always been one of their
most cherished aspirations. Not the Republic which affirms and
consolidates the privileges of the possessors, but a Republic...
whose theoretic mission is to make most ·social inequalities
disappear. For them the Republic is not crystallised in a
constitutional formula: it is a constant progress, a slow but sure
march towards the meeting of the heights and abysses, unification,
individual, social, and political equalisation...

"Finally, a phenomenon of contradiction attests to the existence of
the Semite concept of unity: it is that of anti-Semitism.

... An *anti* ... *ism* shows the reality of the thing, the system. We do
not mean that vulgar anti-Semitism, fermentation of hate and
calumnies, composed of errors and absurdities, factor of injustice
and crimes... We speak of that anti-Semitism which is untroubled
by passion, a particular form of judgment, claiming logic, reasoned
and rational. Such an anti-Semitism has its own contention, its
intrinsic value, its force of ideas and action. Qualified
representative, champion of a determined order of thought, of
sentiments, beliefs, and results, it has, thanks to the powerful
extension of Christianity... established a mode of civilisation
almost universal. If it is opposed to the Semite concept of unity in
almost all domains, if it rises up against it on almost every ground,

it does not ignore it, it does not deny it: it affirms by contrast the substance, the consistence, and constance of this concept."

Showing the two opposing factors, Kadmi Cohen continues:

"To national anti-Semitism, produced by the recent genius of peoples, is opposed the age-old genius of the race (nationalities and a race identical in itself)... To intellectual anti-Semitism, produced by the claims of reason, constructed on the solid basis of logic, is opposed a form of thought, troubled, incoherent, passional. To social anti-Semitism, produced by the exigencies of the most conservative principles — sustained by the force of order and hierarchism — opposed by a spirit of innate indiscipline, revolt and unitarism. To economic anti-Semitism produced by the existence and dominance of the right of property, a conception resists and attacks which refuses to that right all necessity and virtue..."

Thus certain of these Jews became inevitably the ferment of all revolutions, and even Bakunin, Social-Democrat, anarchist and nihilist, came up against the power of this Jewish unity. In his *Study of the German Jews,* 1869, he wrote:

"I know in expressing with this frankness my ultimate opinion of the Jews, I expose myself to enormous danger. Many people share it, but very few dare to express it publicly, for the Jewish sect ... constitutes to-day a veritable power in Europe. It reigns despotically in commerce, in the banks, and it has invaded three-quarters of German journalism, and a very considerable portion of the journalism of other countries. Woe, then, to him who has the clumsiness to displease it!"

He was not a Jew hater or detractor, but the Jew saw to it that his *Study* lay unpublished for over thirty years.

In a recent book, *Israël aux mystérieux destins,* by A. Cavalier and P. d'Halterive, we find the following useful statements on anti-Semitism by various eminent Jews. *The Jewish State,* by Theodore Herzl, the celebrated initiator of Zionism, an essay on the modern solution of the Jewish question, appeared in 1895, creating a great sensation in the Israelite world. In it he writes:

"The Jewish question exists wherever the Jews live, however small their number. Where it does not exist it is imported by Jew immigrants. We naturally go where we are not persecuted, and, still persecution is the result of our appearance... By persecution we cannot be exterminated... the strong Jews turn proudly to their race when persecution bursts out. Entire branches of Judaism may disappear, break away; the tree lives."

Again:

"I believe I understand anti-Semitism which is a very complex movement. I see it as a Jew, but without hatred or fear. I recognise what in anti-Semitism is rude jesting, vulgar jealousy of métier, hereditary prejudice; but also what can be considered as *in fact legitimate defence.*"

Those who foresee its disappearance in the development of universal love or human brotherhood are, according to Herzl, "soft dreamers" or "sentimental dotards."

Further he says:

"We incessantly produce average intelligences who remain without outlet, and who, because of that, constitute a social danger.

... The cultivated Jews without fortune naturally all tend to-day towards Socialism... Among the peoples anti-Semitism grows from day to day, from hour to hour, and must continue to grow, for the causes continue to exist and cannot be suppressed... At the bottom we become revolutionaries by proletarising ourselves, and we form the inferior officers of all subversive parties. At the top, at the same time, grows our formidable financial power."

Herzl had understood and proclaimed the failure of assimilation. In the *Jewish Chronicle*, 28 April, 1911, M. Schindler, an American Rabbi, wrote:

"For fifty years I have been a resolute partisan of assimilation of the Jews, and have believed in it. To-day I confess my error. The American melting-pot will never produce the fusion of one Jew. Fifty years ago we were near to assimilating ourselves to the Americans. But since then two millions of our brothers (or three) have arrived from the East, keeping their ancient traditions, bringing with them their old ideal. This army has submerged us. It is the hand of God. The Jew must differentiate himself from his neighbour; he must know it; he must be conscious of it; he must be proud of it."

But as Isaac Blumchen said in *Le Droit de la Race Supérieure:*

"We are hostile strangers, guests in all countries, and at the same time we find ourselves at home in all countries when we are masters there."

"I do not intend," declares Herzl, "to provoke a softening of opinion in our favour. It would be idle, and would lack dignity. I am content to ask the Jews if, in the countries where we are numerous, it is true that the position of advocates, doctors, engineers, professors, and employees of all kinds, belonging to our race, is becoming more and more intolerable."

And as the Israelite Cerfberr de Medelsheim said in *Les Juifs*, 1847:

"[The Jews] fill in proportion, thanks to their insistence, more posts than the other communities, Catholic and Protestant. Their disastrous influence makes itself felt above all in affairs which have most weight in the fortune of the country; there is no enterprise in which the Jews have not their large share, no public loan which they do not monopolise, no disaster which they have not prepared and by which they do not profit. It is, therefore, ill-considered to complain, as they always do, they who have all the favours and who make all the profits!"

(Quoted also by Gougenot des Mousseaux in *Le Juif*, 1869.)

With regard to the influence of the Jews in the various revolutions of the nineteenth century, we quote another Jewish writer, Bernard Lazare, in *L'Antisémitisme*, 1894:

"During the second revolutionary period which began in 1830 they showed even more fervour than during the first. They were moreover directly concerned, for, in the majority of European states, they did not enjoy full civic rights. Even those among them who were not revolutionaries by reason or by temperament were such by self-interest; in working for the triumph of liberalism they were working for themselves. There is no doubt that by their gold, their energy, their ability, they supported and assisted the European revolution... During those years their bankers, their industrial magnates, their poets, their writers, their demagogues, prompted by very different ideas moreover, strive for the same end ... we find them taking part in the movement of Young Germany: they were numerous in the secret societies which formed the ranks of the militant revolution, in the Masonic lodges, in the groups of Carbonaria, in the Roman Haute-Vente, everywhere, in France, in Germany, in Switzerland, in Austria, in Italy."

(Quoted by Leon de Poncins in *The Secret Powers behind Revolution*, 1929.)

Again, Bernard Lazare writes:

> "What virtues and what vices brought upon the Jew this universal enmity? Why was he in turn equally maltreated and hated by the Alexandrians and the Romans, by the Persians and the Arabs, by the Turks and by the Christian nation? Because everywhere and up to the present day the Jew was an unsociable being.

> "Why was he unsociable? Because he was exclusive, and his exclusiveness was at the same time political and religious or, in other words, he kept to his political, religious cult and his law... This faith in their predestination, in their election, developed in the Jews an immense pride; they came to look upon non-Jews with contempt and often hatred, when patriotic reasons were added to theological ones."

As de Poncins has justly said, the secret forces of subversion which must be fought and overcome in order to return to world sanity are: "Freemasonry, Judaism, and Occultism, whose alliance and reciprocal interpretation no longer require demonstration." By means of these the mentality of the Western world has been for long and still is being Judaised in all departments of life, producing Socialism, Communism, and Bolshevism, which if successful would inevitably lead to Jewish domination and the destruction of Western and Christian civilisation.

In *Le Problème Juif,* 1921, Georges Batault tells us that when studying Greek civilisation —

> "arrived at the Hellenic period I saw the Jewish people surging before me armed with its strange and powerful religion, which throws itself into the conquest of the world. I saw arising face to face with Hellenism in its splendour, but already declining, Judaism insinuating, tenacious, and mysterious, which grew and extended itself over the ancient world like a pernicious evil which spreads to the detriment of the body it invades. As the success and then the victory of the Judaic conceptions have marked the decline and then the ruin of the ancient world, we are fully justified in maintaining that the Jews brought absolutely nothing to ancient civilisation except the most powerful ferment of dissolution."

And the chief cause of this destructive ferment of Judaism lies in its "exclusivism," out of which has arisen its eternal spirit of revolt.

To quote Georges Batault:

> "There is no people in history so narrowly and so ferociously conservative and traditionalist as the People of Israel, and its national traditions are all religious; we find ourselves in the presence of this unique, strange, and bizarre composition — a *people-religion* and a *religion-people*, the two ideas are inseparable".

As the Jewish historian Graetz wrote:

> "The Talmud has been the banner which has served as a rallying sign to the Jews, dispersed in diverse countries; it has maintained the unity of Judaism."

Batault continues:

> "Humanity changes, empires arise and fall, ideals spring up, become resplendent, and are extinguished, the Jew remains, Judaism remains clothed in its fierce exclusivism, hoping all from the future, indefatigable, superhuman, inhuman... A people without land, wandering nation, dispersed race, they preserve a country — their religion... ever pursuing the mirage of a golden age, a new era, a messianic time when the world would live in joy and peace, subject to Yahveh, serving his Law under the rule of the sacerdotal people, who had been prepared by trials for the attainment of this hour... [This] the most conservative among peoples is justly reputed as being possessed by a spirit of inextinguishable revolt ... they are eternally unadaptable, and can only hope for subversion..."

From the time of Alexander the Great the Jews of Alexandria, both numerous and powerful, were continually working sedition and rising in revolt, and these revolts were religious, not social, due to exclusivism, not humanitarianism. Realising their power they used the menace of revolt to gain privileges. Little is known of the influence and power of the Jews in Rome towards the end of the Republic, except for a passage from *Pro Flacco*, by Cicero. Flaccus, praetor of the province of Asia, was accused by the Jews through Lelius of laying hands on the gold which was being sent to Jerusalem by certain Jews; Cicero, in defending him, said to Lelius:

"Thou knowest how numerous this tribe is, how united and how powerful in the assemblies. I will plead in a low voice so that only the judges may hear, for instigators are not lacking to stir up the crowd against me, and against all the best citizens. To scorn, in the interest of the Republic, this multitude of Jews so often turbulent in the assemblies shows a singular strength of mind. The money is in the Treasury; they do not accuse us of theft; they seek to stir up hatreds…"

As Batault added:

"We suddenly learn, not only that there were Jews in Rome in great numbers, but that they had political influence which they exercised to the profit of the popular party against that of Cicero and the Senate."

"Revolutionaries by doctrine, since all messianism declares the destruction of all existing order … the Jews have drawn profit from all revolutionary movements in history since the fall of the Roman Empire. At the Renaissance, a time of perpetual uprisings, they lent money to Princes and merchants, and were well-considered; again at the Reformation they took advantage of religious schisms to further their own beliefs. From the Revolution of 1789 came the emancipation of the Jews in France, and their principal advocate was Mirabeau, largely under the influence of Moise Mendelssohn and Dohm; the revolutions of 1830 and 1848 brought further ameliorations to them."

Coming to the present day Batault continues:

"The sombre destiny of the Russian Empire has profoundly terrified souls and brought trouble into the world. The Bolshevik ideology by its nature and the will of its creatures, is in the first place international; so that it may have a chance to triumph, it is not enough to subjugate Russia, it must also disorganise and subjugate the rest of the world. For this end the Treasury of Russia, fallen into the hands of the Moscow tyrants, is placed at the service of an intense outside propaganda, and the funds are sent into all countries by clever propaganda agents; if threequarters of the Bolshevik staff are Jews, its agents abroad with rare exceptions are all Jews… It appears, therefore, that Bolshevism is one of the most powerful and actual causes of the universal anti-Semite movement."

And of Germany he says:

"In no place so much as in Germany do the Jews [in finance, industries and commerce] hold such an important, almost preponderant part. Therefore it might easily be said that all the newly-rich and war-profiteers were Jews ... the Jew-usurer, the Jew-exploiter, the Jew-profiteer, is an ancient of a thousand years... The immense majority of the influentials in Austrian Socialism were and are still Jews [1921]... Finally, in a certain sense the Jews oppose themselves to non-Jews, above all in the role they play as initiators and actors in the extreme-left parties as internationalism opposed to nationalism."

To conclude:

"More than ever the study of the Jewish problem is a pressing reality, but ... the Jewish question is also more than ever *taboo*; one must not speak of it, still less study it. At most the right to deny its existence is recognised. Those even who should be most interested in finding a solution pretend to solve the problem by abstention or silence which is considered both a sane method and a high humanitarian idea... Judaism in its origins and expansions presents an ensemble of sentiments, notions, and ideas which are the source of veritable systems, religious, political and social; one has the right to discuss and contest these systems."

According to the *Jewish Chronicle,* 4 April, 1919:

"... that the ideals of Bolshevism at many points are consonant with the finest ideals of Judaism."

On 22 April of the same year a letter was made public, signed by ten of the best-known Jews in England, dissociating themselves and other British Jews from the above statement made by the *Jewish Chronicle.*

In *Le Livre Proscrit,* a diary written during the terrors of the Hungarian revolutionary and Bolshevik movements, Cecile Tormay thus describes this spirit of Judaism so closely akin to Bolshevism:

"A bestial tyranny establishes itself over the peoples weakened by the war. The flood-tide carries away, in its endless boilings, cities, nations, and parts of continents. Underground it breaks forth through burst sewers, invading houses, ascending the marble staircase of the banks, unfurling itself in the columns of the journals. At every place where the softened soil appears to yield, it foams, and everywhere it is the same flood-tide."

Speaking of its dissolving effect upon Russia, Hungary, and Bavaria, the author continues:

"So great are the specific differences between the three peoples that the mysterious similitude of events cannot be because of the analogies of race, but solely the work of the fourth race living among the others without mixing with them. Among modern nations the Jewish people is the last representative of ancient oriental civilisation... It weeps over the destroyed ramparts of Jerusalem and unperceived raises new ones. It complains of being isolated, and by mysterious ways it binds together the infinite parts of Jerusalem which cover the entire universe. Everywhere it has connections and links which explain how capital and the Press concentrated in its hands can serve the same plans in all countries in the world... If it glorifies someone, the latter is glorified throughout the whole world; if it wishes to ruin someone, the work of destruction operates as if a single hand directed it... If it teaches revolt and anarchy to others, itself it admirably obeys invisible guides... How did it succeed in dissimulating this world plan? ... They placed in front of them men of the country, blind, volatile, venal, perverse or stupid, who served as screens and knew nothing. They then worked in safety, they the formidable organisers, the sons of the ancient race, who know how to guard a secret."

Moreover, René Fülöp-Miller, in *The Mind and Face of Bolshevism*, 1927, writes of the primitive Gnostic sects, which for long have dominated peasant Russia, and even invaded the intelligentsia. As the *Jewish Encyclopaedia* says, Gnosticism "was Jewish in character long before it became Christian," and both the pantheism and rationalism of Judaism, which so often ends in cabalistic theurgy, are to be found in these sects. Fülöp-Miller informs us:

"Almost all the Russian sects, as they existed in the time of the rule of the Tsars, and still exist in the midst of the Bolshevik world of orthodox materialism" show in their spiritual principles a predominantly religious-rationalist character. It is true that there are also a number of brotherhoods of orgiastic, mystical tendencies; but in their rites, religious worship and articles of faith, a trained psychologist will also recognise, without difficulty, many of the roots and first stages of present-day Bolshevism... If we pass in review all these Russian sects we can... establish a remarkable advance in the form in which they express the idea of communism, which is fundamental in them all, the Molokany and the Dukhobors and all the other rationalist sects confined themselves to proclaiming a community of earthly possessions (to these, we are told, Tolstoi owed his system of social ethics); but among the Khlysty we see an advance: love, marriage and the family have ceased to be a private matter, and with them we find promiscuous sexual intercourse... Finally, if we consider that we can hardly be in error in estimating the number of the members of these sects, before the Revolution, at about one-third of the total population of this enormous country, we are bound to admit that we are here confronted by a phenomenon of truly elemental power, which must be of the greatest significance, not only from the religious, but also from the socio-political point of view. For these rationalistic-chiliastic (millennium) notions of the Russian sects ... soon forced their way into the higher strata of the Russian intelligentsia, and even into the world of ideas of the politicians.

... Linking up these half-mystical notions with the modern principles of Marxist materialism, for it was only by the amalgamation that the soil was prepared for the Bolshevik revolution."

In the same way, and with the same effect, demoralising, de-Christianising, and Judaising, we see a swarm of neo-gnostic, cabalistic, mystic and Illumine sects invading all nations of the Western world, poisoning their mentality from a religious and socio-political point of view, infecting them with pantheism, rationalism, socialism, and communism, preparing the way for domination by this same secret power working behind Bolshevism.

English-speaking peoples are wholly uninformed about the differences of character between the various sections of the more than fifteen millions of Jews dispersed over the earth. Those varied sections of Jewry are, nevertheless, capable of bringing into world movements a marvellous solidarity of racial influence, exercised by means of important political positions held in all countries, and by a far-flung power over the Press and other means of publicity. But it is quite impossible for the British public to understand the movements of Bolshevism and World Revolution, owing to the prevalent ignorance of the dominant part played by revolutionary Jews in all countries. As Thackeray has expressed it:

"Sow a thought and reap an action; sow an action and reap a habit; sow a habit and reap character; sow character and reap destiny."

Thus are revolutions sown and reaped; so also would revolutions be frustrated and brought to naught but for the sinister power which everywhere to-day controls the Press and Publishers.

As far back as 29 June, 1789, Arthur Young, in his *Travels in France and Italy,* writes of this secret Press control:

"Will posterity believe that, while the Press has swarmed with inflammatory productions that tend to prove the blessing of theoretical confusion and speculative licentiousness, not one writer of talent has been employed to refute and confound the fashionable doctrines, nor the least care taken to disseminate works of another complexion."

Further, in *Les Victoires d'Israël,* Roger Lambelin wrote of this same evil:

"What of the big newspapers of all countries, controlled directly or influenced indirectly by the great Jewish capitalists, through intermediaries, editors, information agencies, or publicity! Try to advertise in the big Press, or even in so-called national journals of Paris, London, New York, Vienna or Rome, a publication which clearly shows the action of Israel and its imperialism, and you will see what kind of welcome it will receive."

As an example, the "Anti-Defamation League, Chicago," 13 December, 1933, wrote to publishers of Anglo-Jewish periodicals, concerning a book antagonistic to Jewish interests — *The Conquest of a Continent* by Madison Grant:

"We are interested in stifling the sale of this book. We believe that this can be best accomplished by refusing to be stampeded into giving it publicity... The less discussion there is concerning it the more sales resistance will be created.

We therefore appeal to you to refrain from comment on this book... It is our conviction that a general compliance with this request will sound the warning to other publishing houses against engaging in this type of venture. (Signed) RICHARD E. GUTSTADT, *Director.*"

Speaking of one of his own books Léon de Poncins relates how an American offered to get it translated and published, but advised as follows by her solicitor, negotiations were stopped:

"In my opinion, according to the law of defamation prevalent in this country (U.S.A.), you cannot in any way participate in the publication of the *Forces Secrètes de la Révolution* by de Poncins, without incurring grave legal responsibility with risk of damages... The personalities and associations criticised are so powerful in this country that very costly lawsuits would certainly result from the publication of the book."

Another aspect of this formidable Jewish question is to be seen in Algeria in its relations to the indigenous Arab.

In *Le Péril Juif,* Charles Hagel places before his readers what he considers as the true position of the Algerian Jew and Arab. He writes:

"We look at it objectively with documents and proofs in hand, giving conclusions authorised by fifty years of an attentive life, lived with open eyes in this North Africa, which is, indeed, the most marvellous laboratory and the best ground on which to follow the evolution of the Jew... We live in France under the law of a taboo; that is, of the Jew... Who will say I exaggerate ... in this Algeria where there is no longer a single journal in which the word Jew can be written with a capital J.

... Atheist in the religion of others, international in the country of others, revolutionaries in the society of others, but prodigiously jealous and fiercely conservative in what is their own, their originality, spirit and race, such during half a century have the Jews revealed themselves to my attentive eyes... It is not so much through himself and his deleterious action that the Jew is dangerous, it is by the example he gives, the contagion he exercises, and the spirit he teaches to the unchained masses deprived of direction and too much inclined to imitate... Our anti-Semitism, therefore, is not of violence, disorder or recrimination, but of clairvoyance, of methodical protection; our antisemitism is of the State, regulations, and laws."

In 1830, when Charles X became Regent of Algeria, the Jews lived in special quarters, and were permitted well-defined occupations, and until then formed a group completely isolated and strictly supervised by the Mussulmans, who, when necessary, exercised with energy vengeance and the right of reprisals. About 30,000 in number, divided into communities, the Jews formed a nation, with its chiefs, and authorised cult, council, order, laws, jurisdiction *more Judaico,* and its rights; but above all its charges and duties with regard to its Mussulman master having no right to carry arms, or a light at night in the streets, wearing black robes distinctively marked, forbidden entry into certain towns or to pass in front of Mosques or approach wells, and could not be called as a witness. They had no real status, and could not possess property.

In the Mussulman they were up against a primitive man who had no fear of death, a fierce and formidable warrior whose life was rudimentary and poor, but whose force in former times created Empires. From 1830 to 1870 the Jews were judicially and administratively assimilated before being legally and politically incorporated. Covered by French authority and defended by French soldiers, they gave themselves up to their national industry of usury. The Jew was the tempter who brought to the Mussulman, this impulsive, improvident man eager for pleasure, the money to satisfy his passions and pleasures.

In 1848 the Jew Cremieux, member of the Provisional Government of France, Minister of Justice, and later President of *L'Alliance-israélite-universelle,* prepared a decree and tried to accelerate the civil, political, and administrative incorporation of the Jew of Algeria, but the *coup d'état* of 1851 stopped him. Nevertheless, the Jews rapidly prospered, and in 1861 a magistrate declared: "That the Israelites possess a great part of the properties, that the fortunes of the Arabs pass into their hands, and that in the town of Algiers alone one could value their landed worth at more than 12,000,000 francs." Taking advantage of distracted and despairing France after its defeat by the Germans in 1870, the Crémieux decree for Algerian Jews was voted by an overwhelming majority and without debate.

The Jews of Algeria became French citizens, and all that France gained was the hatred of her Arab subjects, the only element of value upon which she could count for populating and economically developing the colony. The Jews placed in superiority over them! The Arabs could not accept the insult! Towns, villages, farms were pillaged, nationals' throats cut, and establishments were ruined. But the Jews did not appreciate the required conscription! The Arab chief Mokrani was killed, and the others laid down their arms. The Kabulia lost its autonomy, and the insurgents had to, pay 32,000,000 francs and 500,000 hectares of their land was confiscated. From time to time other riots and pillages took place, and that of 1898, more severe than the others, was rigorously suppressed by the Jew-dominated France.

> "In a general way, if one cannot attribute to the Jew the whole responsibility of the situation, economic, political, and social, by which Algeria is being strangled, it is no exaggeration to recognise him as morally guilty, for the great part of his role here, still more than elsewhere, has consisted in corrupting, degrading, and disintegrating."

In 1934 the author puts the number of Jews at 120,000 to 150,000 and the Arabs at 6,000,000, of whom three-quarters are permanently underfed from earliest years.

> "Reduced to its own resources since France ... gave it financial autonomy and this Colonial Parliament, at first consultative and then deliberative, of the Financial Delegations... Algeria is incapable of assuring by its own resources the crushing expense of the first establishment of administration and upkeep which falls upon it. The economic equipment is too heavy because of the immensity of its territory and the insignificance of its population.
>
> ... At present the fellah has no longer anything but his dried skin stretched upon his bones, and he must pay the contracts, the banks, and above all the Jew."

In Algeria the Jew has powerfully contributed to the disorder of the public mind. Demoralised by him, a quarter of the citizens in large towns openly trade "their rights," selling their vote for from 20 to 500 francs or more. The lists are cooked: "At each election ... the postal service· returns to the Mayors thousands of electors" cards marked unknown; gone, no address; dead. The Jews 'exercise in Algerian economy a submergence of which it can be affirmed that it will destroy all the élite, eliminate all competition, and place at the discretion of this ethnical group, unassimilable and eternally a stranger, the direction of all the affairs of this country.'

We have Wickham Steed, in his book *The Hapsburg Monarchy*, quoting a letter from a half-Jew writing in 1905 of Hungary:

"There is a Jewish question, and this terrible race means, not only to master one of the greatest warrior nations in the world, but it means, and is consciously striving to enter the lists against the other great race of the north (Russians), the only one that has hitherto stood between it and its goal of world power. Am I wrong? Tell me. For already England and France are, if not exactly dominated by Jews, very nearly so, while the United States, by the hands of those whose grip they are ignorant of, are slowly but surely yielding to that international and insidious hegemony. Remember that I am half a Jew by blood, but that in all I have power to be, I am not."

As we know, Hungary was, in 1918, fast in the grip of Bela Kuhn and other red Jews, all tools of the Bolshevik Government. In *An Outlaw's Diary*, Cecile de Tormay, Hungarian patriot and writer, depicts preparatory conditions:

"Then Karolyi came and prepared the way for Bolshevism in the education of Hungary's younger generation. The mass appointment of Jewish Masonic professors and teachers; the Bolshevik reform of school books; the destruction of the souls of the children; the degradation of parental authority; the systematic destruction of moral and patriotic principles; the revelation of sexual matters; all these were the work of Karolyi's Government."

Further, in explanation of the rôle played by Judeo-Masonry in Hungary, we take the following documented information from Leon de Poncin's book *La Dictature des Puissances Occultes*. The history of this Masonry in Hungary is of special interest, because after the fall of the Bela Kuhn Bolshevik revolution, the Government of Hungary dissolved the Masonic Lodges, seized and published their archives, and these clearly showed the connection of the Jew-dominated Masonry with the revolutionary movement of 1918. He reproduces an open letter on this subject sent by the Deputy Julius Gombos (Prime Minister of Hungary) to Comte Paul Teleki, President of the Hungarian Council, in which we read:

"The Royal Government of Hungary has, as the whole world knows, dissolved Hungarian Freemasonry because some of the members of this organisation have taken part in the preparation of the October revolution and the work of systematic destruction which has taken place against the interests of the people and State of Hungary. There were, according to the investigators, among these people men who, in this country, were representatives or agents of Jewish tendencies having in view universal domination, and who have dreamed in the silence of secrecy to lull to sleep national sentiment so as to make an anti-national doctrine triumph, which is foreign to us but dear to them... Although the decision on the fate of Hungarian Masonry is the business of the Interior order, in my opinion, Your Excellency would render a great service to the country by enlightening the foreigner on this question, and another, connected with it, the Jewish question, so that the foreigner does not form erroneous ideas on the measures taken in view of the defence of the religion and morality of the people and nation."

As to Judaism in Soviet Russia to-day we would quote *L'Univers-israélite*, 7–14 September, 1934, which writes:

"In the U.S.S.R. Judaism and Christianity have been buried together. They sleep in the common grave reserved for all religions. The Communists have made no difference between cults.

... Their philosophy was scientific materialism, they denied the value of all religion, thus they struck at Judaism as at all religions. It is forbidden to give religious instruction to children under eighteen. At school it is explained to the pupils that they will betray the revolution if they put foot within the church or synagogue. With the result that the synagogues are empty... Zionism is banned. To the Communist Zionism is doubly reprehensible, first because they believe it to be in the service of British Imperialism... Whoever defends the cause of Zionism is severely punished; Zionists have been imprisoned, exiled, and even shot. The suppression of Zionism and of religion [continues the editor] was a great tragedy for the Jewish spirit... The children, victorious, pursue their object [communism] with the certainty of having chosen a superior mode of Life."

Finally, a Jewish correspondent of the *Patriot*, who is a close observer of all facts that escape from the Bolshevik political chaos, remarks:

"The fact that anti-Semitism was made a criminal offence in Bolshevia does not prove philo-Semitism; on the contrary, one might reason logically thus: Jew-hatred is so rampant in the country that the authorities were compelled to put the offence in the same category as counter-revolution, which is the most severely punished crime in Soviet Russia, for otherwise they would be unable to suppress the tendency."

He continues:

"Some years ago a Jewish financier was reproached for pouring millions of dollars into Soviet Russia. "Have you," he tersely retorted, "ever visualised in your mind what would happen to our brethren in Russia should — God forbid — the Soviet regime collapse? the retaliatory measures would be terrible, apart from the outbursts of the vengeful populace." The fact remains that in Russia anti-Semitism obtains now in the same degree as in the Czarist days with the sole difference that now it is driven underground, which aggravates the malady."

Again the same writer concludes:

"It is quite evident that the key of the solution of this hoary problem lies in finding ways how to overcome the obstacles of the formidable, both numerically and energetically, revolutionary section of Jewry."

CHAPTER VII

CONTINENTAL FREEMASONRY

GUSTAVE BORD, writing in *La Franc-maçonnerie en France*, 1908, says:

> "Freemasonry stood at the beginning as a defender of natural religion: belief in the beyond, in the existence of God, and the immortality of the soul based solely on the ideas of Reason. But gradually this natural religion was transformed into mere social morals based on the immortality of matter, and after having passed through Pantheism it ended in the negation of the Divinity."

As we have previously explained, there is a curious book *Long Livers,* by Robert Sambers, dedicated to the Grand Lodge of London, 1722, and referred to by Masonic historians such as Mackay, Whytehead, Yarker, etc., in which the author indicates a mysterious *Illumination* and equally mysterious hierarchy working through the higher grades of Masonry, the language used being that of alchemy and Rose-Croix. It is in this secret illumination of the higher grades from some unknown source, common to all theosophical and occult groups, that lies the canker which stirs up revolutions and aims at the destruction of Western and Christian civilisation. As J. Marquès-Rivière justly writes in *La Trahison Spirituelle de la F.˙. M.˙.:*

> "One could easily conclude the existence in Freemasonry of two currents which appear contradictory, and which are merely complementary — the rationalists and the Illuminés. What unites and binds them together is the ritual... The rationalist politicians have inspirers: these are the occultists of the lodges... Freemasonry is the place from whence the diverse sects draw their elements; it is for them a preparatory school, a filter, a discipline. The Martinists demand that their members should be Master Masons. The best recruits of other groups are issues of Freemasonry ... inversely the

opinions, the dreams, the elucubrations of these pseudo-mystic chapels, of these dens of folly, penetrate into the great body of Freemasonry through their members... Theosophy, occultism, Freemasonry, secret sects or mystico-civilisers have but one common aim: to assure the liberation of man, to withdraw from him all traditional moral sense in order to be able to enslave him for the good of the interests aimed at, which they call freeing him... There exists a counter-Church, with its scriptures, its dogmas, its priests, and Freemasonry is one of its visible aspects. This false dogmatism must be exposed, this pseudo-mysticism which attracts more souls than is believable, whose dangers are as real as hidden... This mysticism is indeed the great Masonic Secret, the Supreme Initiation... It is old as is this old world."

RUSSIA

At the Congress of Verona, 1822, Prince de Metternich, Prime Minister of Austria, addressed a *mémoire* on secret societies to Emperor Alexander of Russia, in which he said:

"Dupes of their own disordered imagination, dupes of whoever wishes to make use of their mania for their own diverse purposes, these men [vague mystics] have constantly been as a nursery of adepts for secret societies... these societies are a malady which eats into the social body in its noblest parts, the evil has already thrust out deep and extended roots; if Governments do not take efficacious measures... Europe runs the risk of succumbing to attacks upon it ceaselessly repeated by these associations... absolute monarchies, constitutional monarchies, republics, all are threatened by the Levellers."

Later, Metternich recognised the Jews as one of the most terrible elements of revolution. A brief sketch of Masonry in Russia will confirm his opinion. We take it largely from a book by Georgios Michalof, 1877 (see *Document K, Deschamps*, vol. ii).

During the early years of Catherine II's reign, the lodges multiplied greatly in Russian high society, and Saint-Martin, through the Polish Count Grabianka and the Russian Admiral Pleschischejev, propagated his doctrines in the lodges. He spread his ideas by means of a *Société typographique* which published the writings of Boehme and all French works and translations marked with the moral religiosity of the sect, and soon the literature of the country was impregnated with them (an orientation as with our own pacifists and internationalists). The soul of the society was Novikof, Grand Master and Director of Russian Masonry. All talent was drawn into the net, and Martinist lodges also penetrated the Church by means of the high dignitaries, using it largely as a mask for their political aims and in order to deceive the Empress.

Catherine at first declared herself Protector of Masonry, and in 1784 the Imperial Lodge was formed in Petersburg. However, after the Revolution in 1792, having found that Novikof, unknown to her, had initiated the Grand Duke, later Paul I, Novikof was thrown into the Fortress Schlusselburg and the Princes Leopuchin, Troubetskoi, and Turgenjef were exiled to their estates; still Masonry worked in secret. Paul I favoured Masonry and released Novikof, but in 1797 closed the lodges and exiled most of the dangerous initiates, Alexander I, through Bober Counsellor of State and Grand Master of the Russian Grand Orient, revoked Paul's ordinance, and in 1803 was made a Mason. The first Grand Lodge, *Vladimir,* was founded in 1811, but was later replaced by two groups, *Astres* and *Provinciale.* In 1822, fearing the result upon the State of such a democratic organisation, the lodges were dissolved by Imperial ukase.

During the campaign against Napoleon, Carbonari lodges were formed in the Army, which was thus gradually infected with the ideas of absolute freedom from all civil and religious authority. It was while the Emperor was preparing a Constitutional reform that Pestel and others, with Novikof at the head, founded their *Alliance du salut,* the first group being formed in the regiment of the Guards, 1813. As outside propaganda he organised the *Société de bien public,* divided into four sections: philanthropic, intellectual and moral civilisation and schools, supervision of Tribunals and officials, and national economy. There was yet another society at Kiev, 1823, the *Slavoniens unis,* having relations with the *Société du sud.* Their rites were those of high Masonry, aiming, with certain independence, to unite the eight Slav countries, Russia, Poland, Bohemia, Moravia, Dalmatia, Hungary (?) with Transylvania, Servia with Moldavia, and Valachia, having a federal and central town — one of the sects' early forms of the United States of Europe! If the conspiracy had succeeded Pestel would have been Dictator. He sought to unite with the Poles, but when he disclosed plans to murder the whole Imperial family and proclaim a Socialistic republic, Prince Jablonowski recoiled in horror, and the Poles were allowed to form their own Government. The rising was dated for 1829, but the sudden death of Alexander hastened the outburst, and December 1825 saw the attempt and failure with the execution of the leaders (1826). In 1857 Alexander II in vain permitted the opening of the lodges, for Masonry, it was said, hated both Russia and Austria.

Under Nicholas II Russia was still a prey to Martinism. Papus and Philippe, the magnetic-healer, created Martinist lodges, and spread the pernicious doctrines, not a little helping to bring trouble upon Court and nobility. Philippe, writes Sokoloff in his *Enquiry*, was introduced to Court by the Jew Manoussevitch Manouilof, Rasputin's sinister adviser, who in 1905, according to Paleologue, instigated the workmen's demonstrations and later helped to prepare the Pogroms of Kiev, Alexandrovsk, and Odessa. As the Jewish writer Dr. Angelo Rappaport, wrote, 1918:

> "There is not a political organisation in the vast Empire which was not influenced by the Jews or directed by them... Plehve was perhaps right when he said that the fight for political emancipation in Russia and the Jewish question were practically identical."

Imperial Russia for the time has been swept away, still Russian Masonry persists. The American *Builder,* June and August 1927, gave an account of four ordinary lodges, a Lodge of Perfection, and a Rose-Croix Chapter then functioning in Paris, in the Russian language, and according to former Russian rites, under the jurisdiction of the Grand Lodge of France, and the Supreme Council, but with complete liberty. The four ordinary lodges are directed by a committee which represents the embryo of the future Grand Lodge of Russia. The Lodge of Perfection works in close relations with the Rose-Croix Chapter, and there exists, conformable to the Congress of Lausanne, 1922, a temporary committee recognised by the Supreme Council of France, which will subsequently become the Supreme Council of the Scottish Rite in Russia. The task will consist: "In restoring to Russia a normal government and in establishing ordinary conditions of economic and political life" (quoted from *R.I.S.S.*, II December, 1927).

Is Masonry, this universal ferment, a fit instrument to restore normal conditions to an immense Empire shattered and corrupted by the secret forces of Jewry?

POLAND

The following is taken from the Polish Nationalist review *Mysl Narodowa*, Nos. 30–33, 1933. The *R.I.S.S.* reproduces it, taking no responsibility, as throwing light on the universal Judaeo-Masonic work of anti-religious destruction and domination. We give a short summary. It was above all during the Great War that Masonry appeared on Polish territory. In Poland, under the Russian Empire, there was the Lodge *Odrodzenie,* dating from before the War, and among its members were officials of the Ministry of Public Instruction and professors at the Polytechnic Institute and the Free University. Some aimed at Masonic infiltration. Already there were a number of Jews belonging to the Grand Orient of France: Litauer, important official in the Ministry of Foreign affairs; Wasserzug, called Wasowski, initiated in Paris before the War, where he published, along with other Masons, the anti-Christian review *Panteon.* Returning to Warsaw, he collaborated in the review *Pravda,* then, at the beginning of the War, in *Widnokreci,* and during the German occupation in the journal *Glos Stolicy,* an organ directed against the Allied Powers, particularly France and England. After the declaration of independence he was removed from the Ministry of Foreign Affairs. He then resumed collaboration with the anti-national and Jewish Press, and founded L'Agence Polonaise Publiciste, still pursuing his Masonic propaganda with an eye to the provincial press. To-day he edits the Warsaw Masonic review *Epolia.*

Another member was the Jew Salomon Posner, of the Grand Orient of France, writer to the Socialist daily *L'Ouvrier,* also President of the *Ligue des Droits de l'Homme* in Poland. Now dead, he was one of the most influential and active ambassadors of Polish Jewry. The Jew Simon Askenazy, one of the most influential Polish Masons, secretly controlled all the strings. Another member was the Jew Léon Chrzanowski, correspondent of the *Courier of Warsaw* at Rome, and later at Geneva. The Provisional Council of State was infested with Masons. The director of Polish Masonry, belonging to the Grand Orient of France, was the Jew Jan Finhelhaus, for long living in Paris as "Jean Finot," where he directed the *Revue des Revues*. He transmitted information to the Jewish families Natanson and Kempner at Warsaw. The former were mostly financiers and industrialists with considerable social influence. The latter were journalists, and ran *La Gazette Nouvelle,* organ of the Radicals and Socialists. These Jews played a great role during the German occupation, and one of them, under the pseudonym A. Kerr, was closely connected with journalistic and literary circles in Berlin. During the War Russian Masonry exercised a certain influence in Poland. The Polish Masons were instructed by the Jew Winawer, member of the Constitutional Democratic Party and Minister in the Kerenski Government. Many of the Polish young men in Russia, subject to Radical and Socialist centres, returned to Poland instructed in Masonic doctrines, and became affiliated to lodges in Poland. Most officials of the Provisional Council of State were nominated by pressure from German, French, and Russian Masons. Masons dominated the League of the Partisans of the Polish State (L.P.P.).

After the death of the Jews Finhelhaus and Kempner, a re-grouping of the lodges took place. In 1920 Italian Masonry instigated the founding of the Grand Lodge of Poland, an affiliation of the lodge "Polonia" at Rome. The *Union of Philalètes,* founded in 1909, was intensely active in independent Poland. Apparently harmless, it had occult directors, and the initiates were Freemasons of a particular rite, who invaded all administrations. To-day it is consolidated and strong, and the Jews in it, although discreet, are influential.

In collaboration with it is the *Polish Association of Libres-Penseurs,* founded in 1921 by four Jews, and directed by Masonry. In relation with that, again, was the *Community of Productivity,* devoted to Bolshevik propaganda, and founded by the Jew Lubecki in 1922. All members are Jews. They renounce all religion, declare war on nationalism and prejudices against Jews, and object to mixed marriages—Jews and Aryans. The Polish Union of professional men of letters is directed by the Jew-Mason Jules Kaden-Bandrowski. Masonry in particular acts upon the women through the Association of Women's Civic Work. One of its prime movers is Mme Kipa, a Jewess and wife of the Grand Secretary of the Grand Lodge of Poland. Finally, the "sexual democracy," which aims at the destruction of religion and family, is led by a Jewish writer supported by Jews and Masonic organisations.

HUNGARY

According to Léon de Poncins in *La Franc-maçonnerie,* 1934, after the Bolshevik revolution of Bela Kuhn in Hungary, the Government ordered the Masonic archives to be seized and published, thus showing the flagrant connection of Masonry with the revolutionary movement. In a résumé of the secret papers found in the lodges of Budapest we find:

"The book on Hungarian Freemasonry which has just been published by the *Union des Sociétés chrétiennes et nationales de Hongrie,* is divided into three parts: (1) The crimes of Freemasonry, by Adorjan Barcsay, contains a great quantity of documents seized when the Lodges were dissolved in 1922. (2) Written by Joseph Palatinus, is called, *The Secrets of a Provincial Lodge,* and exposes the secret work of Masonic destruction which led Hungary to the revolution of October, 1918, and to Communism in 1919. (3) Contains the list of members of the Masonic Lodges in Hungary, which proves to us that 90 *per cent of the Hungarian Masons were Jews.*"

Again:

"The author quotes on this subject a very characteristic preface at the beginning of a book, *La Voie des Juifs,* by Professor Pierre Agoston (one of the commissars of the people who shared the power with Bela Kuhn and whom the Hungarian Tribunal condemned to death in December last). In it he says, among other things: To write the history of the Jews in Hungary is to write the history of the Hungarian Freemasonic movement…"

"With regard to their role in the Communist revolution in Hungary, this book shows that the Freemasons have above all worked through the Press. With patient and persistent labour they have succeeded in gaining over most of the Press organs by the help of which they have sought to diminish the Magyar national sentiment. The daily *Vilag* is very specially responsible for the weakening of discipline in the Hungarian Army; thousands of copies were distributed in the trenches... *Kelet*, official journal of the Hungarian Masons, 14 December, 1910, stated: 'We must gain over the professors and school-masters so as to reach through them the soul of youth and prepare laic teaching. The teachers must be the forerunners of the most advanced ideas.'"

Notwithstanding these and other documented facts, the *Jewish Chronicle,* 20 July, 1934, in writing of *"The Freemasons,"* by the Jew Eugen Lennhof, who founded in Austria *La Ligus Internationale des F.·. M.·.*, informs its readers that inquirers will scan Lennhof's vivid pages in vain for the confirmation of the old absurdity about the revolutionary alliance between Jews and Freemasons. It is not, however, surprising, that Lennhof, himself an International Jew and Freemason, should fight shy of these and many other equally authenticated facts about this Jew-Masonic Alliance. He would whitewash both Jewry and Judaeo-Masonry!

GERMANY

The great fact of the year 1930 was the unexpected triumph of the partisans of Hitler at the September elections. A formidable nationalism suddenly appeared, Prussian and Lutheran, in certain *lodges* — *Grande Loge Nationale des Francs-Maçons d'Allemagne; Grande Loge Mère Aux Trois Globes; Grande Loge Royal York 'À l'Amitié.'* This Prussian Masonry had separated from Universal Masonry in 1924, and, according to Oswald Wirth, had renounced the ideal of the Anderson Constitution to adopt that of uncompromising Germanism. The A.M.I. declared it to be irregular. In 1930 a new obedience was formed, the *Grande Loge Symbolique d'Allemagne,* grouping together eight lodges, dependents of the Supreme Scottish Council of Germany. Their tendencies were pacifist; adopting Anderson's formula in its widest sense they admitted adherents of all religions, including Jews. There were also the humanitarian lodges — the four Grand Lodges of Bayreuth, Darmstadt, Frankfort, and Hamburg. Lastly, the Federation *Au Soleil Levant,* considered suspect and ardently pacifist. It must be recognised that the aims of Prussian Masonry in 1924 have been realised; it has now transformed the lodges into Orders of Chivalry, and all other lodges have been suppressed. We have, they said, transformed the *Grande Loge Mère Nationale Aux Trois Globes,* founded by Frederick the Great in 1740, into the *National Christian Order of Frederick the Great.*

It has broken all existing links with other Masonry; for the members, the obligation is of Germanic racist origin, the secret concerning the ceremony is suppressed, the words "Freemason" and "Lodge" have disappeared, and the constitution is entirely new. The same principles are applied to the other two lodges. *La Grande Loge des Franc-Maçons d'Allemagne* will in future be called *The German Christian Order of the Templars;* the name of the third had not been fixed (July 1933). Their ideal is German-Christianity, having much in common with the old Aryan cult of their ancestors — the cult of Odin! The symbols of the Order are the Light and the Cross; they profess. an ideal of pure Germanic race nationality, whose chosen symbols are the Hammer of Thor and the Sword of the Knight. It is now said that Masonry is entirely suppressed in Germany.

The Hammer of Thor, or Hermetic Cross, is the bolt of whirling flame, a symbol of dynamic strength representing the Fire of the universal generating force cleaving its way through the blackness of matter. In Illuminism, reversed, it is a symbol of that death that leads to Initiation or Illuminism. Further, Frederick the Great was a close friend of Voltaire, who was one of the *Encyclopedists* and president of the atheistic and revolutionary Hotel d'Holbach, precursor of the French Revolution of 1789.

SPAIN

Deschamps in *Les Sociétés Secrètes et La Société,* 1881, writes of Spain:

"The revolutions which since 1812 have succeeded each other in this country have been caused for the most part by the rivalries of the different Masonic factions which always unite in order to fight Christian social order."

A letter, 15 January, 1728, shows that Spanish Masonry began by a delegation from the English Grand Master; the lodge was called *Matritense*. The introduction of the Scottish Rite in Spain was due to Comte de Tilly authorised by his relative, Comte de Grasse-Tilly, who shortly before had introduced the regularised rite from Charleston into France. This rite was a simple evolution of philosophical Masonry. Seville was the first centre, and in 1808 Tilly, along with the Liberal members of the Government, took part in its Supreme Council. This Scottish rite, introducing the high grades, was more democratic, whilst Masonry of the three grades was, under Montijo, the defender of aristocracy and absolutism. Later the two Masonries united, and a Chamber of Rites was created under Montijo's direction *(Monde Maçonnique*, June 1875).

One of the first lodges, under the Grand Lodge of England, was formed at Madrid, 1731, and, when Charles III came from Naples to the Throne of Spain, among his courtiers were several Masons; very soon the lodge at Madrid began to exercise serious influence over the Government. In 1766, through Count Aranda, the Jesuits were driven from Spain and Spanish possessions; Jansenist, Masonic, *Encyclopedist*, and even Illuminé doctrines infected Episcopal seats, chapters, and universities, and under Charles IV the sect unsuccessfully planned to establish the Jews in Spain.

During Napoleon's invasion French officers and officials formed the *Afrançesados*, lodges favourable to French rule. But there were also purely Spanish lodges which sought to realise their plans through the Constituent Cortes of Cadiz, from which nobility and clergy were excluded. Those who represented the provinces occupied by the French, Spaniards originally from these provinces, but settled in Cadiz, were called *suppléants*. From 1753 there was a lodge in Cadiz of 500 affiliates, wealthy and of good position, most of the *suppléants* belonged to it, and it and its adepts formed the majority of the Cortes; a Liberal Press dominated the Assembly and the command of the Army in favour of Masonry. The Catholic and Royalist minority were known as *Serviles,* and the majority took the name of *Liberals,* and later *Jacobinos.* They promulgated a Constitution, 19 March, 1812, maintaining Monarchy as a form, declaring the sovereignty of the people, but the real power lay with the Cortes. When Ferdinand VII returned after Napoleon's fall, influenced by popular sentiment, he repudiated this Constitution, and later exercised personal despotism.

In 1814 Masonry was interdicted, but openly continued its propaganda. Many Spanish prisoners in France became affiliates, 5000 officers, and a greater number of subordinates, who thus gave a powerful impetus to Liberal projects, plotted in secret the annihilation of existing political and religious institutions. A Grand Lodge was established in Granada with Montijo as Grand Master, and many lodges were formed in the Army; this lodge became so active that finally some were arrested, others fled, and Montijo was ordered to Madrid, June 1817; but the Grand Lodge followed him, and there continued its intrigues. According to Thomas Frost, the historian, all moderate constitutionalists were Freemasons, and made use of Masonic organisation to consult secretly on the movement which ended in the revolution of 1820. The extreme party, the *Communeros,* formed a similar organisation, *Confédération,* which was divided into *communes,* each of which consisted of unlimited local groups or *tours.* Their receptions, password, and oath were copied from Masonry: absolute secrecy, obedience, and submission to vengeance if unfaithful as with the Carbonari. It had only one grade, offices were elective, and the *Supreme Assembly* was over all. They were closely linked to the Jew-dominated Haute-Vente of Paris; the *fédéralistes* were their successors.

On 29 March, 1830, the Salic Law was abolished, and Isabella became heir to the throne in place of the King's brother, Don Carlos; when Ferdinand died, Freemasons and Liberals already held all civil and military positions..! The lodges continued their intrigues throughout the Regency and the reign of Isabella, and took active part in the progressivist movement of 1854. The revolution of 1868 was made by Masonry in opposition to Isabella, who in the end was deposed and fled to France. Further intrigues led to the reign of Amadeo, and later a republic; but recognising that Spain was not ready for a republic, the Grand Chiefs decided on a Constitutional Monarchy — always assuring revolutionary propaganda — and to this end supported young Alphonse XII, 1874. The lodges continued to increase, and in 1881 the Grand Lodge of Spain had 154 lodges; the Grand Orient of Spain had 162, plus 30 chapters; the Grand Orient Lusitanien had 40 under its jurisdiction, and all three are now united as obedience-members of the *Association Maçonnique Internationale* (A.M.I., 1933). Thus Nationalism has become Internationalism (Deschamps and Claudio Jannet)!

Much has been written on the present Spanish Judaeo-Masonic manifestation — the Revolution and Republic of 1931 —·and the following speech, made by Mateo Barroso, Grand Chancellor of the Supreme Council of Spain at the Convent of the Grand Lodge of France, 1931, shows the power that was behind the new régime:

> "I bring you the cordial and fraternal greetings of the Supreme Council of Spain... We have now the Republic. We have ... six Mason Ministers, about twenty Mason high officials, and more than 120 Mason deputies in the Constituent Chamber. You therefore see that this weak Masonry has succeeded in creating a democratic and republican conscience... Spanish Masonry works for Universal Peace, it associates itself with the task which the League of Nations has taken up... It is the Masons who must create this universal conscience" (quoted by *R.I.S.S.,* 15 December, 1932).

Again, in the *Boletin oficial y Revisto masonica del Supremo Consejo del Grado* 33, June 1931, we read:

> "The Republic is our patrimony... It can be called the perfect image modelled by the gentle hands of our doctrines and principles. It will be impossible to realise another example of a *political revolution more perfectly Masonic than the Spanish Revolution...*"

Further, the Grand Lodge of Spain, in its *Bulletin,* thus addressed the new Republic:

> "With the eclipse, in the setting, of the splendour of Royalty, came to an end the last personal power of Majesty... As Spaniards and Freemasons, who see lawfully erected the Liberal structure of a new

State engendered by the immortal principles which shine in the Orient, we can but consider ourselves satisfied.

... To Freemasons who compose the Provisional Government, to the higher personnel, also composed in a majority of Freemasons, go out our aspirations. May they be loyal guardians of the moral treasures confided to them and through the Republic may they accomplish the destiny of Spain" (quoted in *R.I.S.S.*, 8 November, 1931).

PORTUGAL

According to the *R.I.S.S.*, 24 May, 1931, Fr. Borges Grainha writes, in his *Histoire de la Maçonnerie en Portugal,* Lisbon, 1912:

"Chance brought into my hands a number of books, until then unknown to me, in which is shown the life of Masonry in Portugal from the middle of the eighteenth century. In examining these books I have noticed that almost all the most noted men in religious, political, and intellectual revolutions of our country, during the last two centuries, were affiliated to Masonry... Several illustrious Portuguese were also Masons, and some even Grand Masters, in the conspiracies and revolutions of 1817, 1820, 1833, 1836, 1842, 1846, 1851, 1868, 1891, and in 1910 almost all the principal personages who took part had been initiated in Masonic lodges... At the end of these researches I was convinced that the history of Masonry in Portugal was absolutely linked with the history of the country."

From the résumé given, and other sources — one, Document G, by F. Chabirand in the *Chaîne d'Union,* 1872-73 — quoted by Deschamp and Claudio Jannet, we have drawn many of the following facts.

Masonry in Portugal goes back to 1735 under Don Joaos V, and since then various foreigners, French, Swiss, Dutch, and English, organised the first lodges. Under the Government of the Marquis de Pombal, Masonry developed in intellectual circles and the Army. He had been diplomat in London and Vienna, and returned penetrated by the philosophy then in vogue in Europe,· and initiated the regime of "enlightened despotism" which was opposed to the Church and had strong "equality" tendencies; he is also said to have established the first regular lodge in Lisbon.

There were certainly Masons among those appointed by him to found the University of Coimbre in 1772, and by 1796 it was permeated with Liberal ideas, becoming in time a recognised and immense instrument for the spread throughout Portugal of the philosophy of Voltaire and Rousseau.

The French Revolution was let loose in Europe, but in Portugal the able director, Pina Manique, for some years kept it in check. It was about 1804 that the first Portuguese Grand Lodge was constituted. The invasions of Napoleon profoundly modified the situation to the profit of Masonry, and the officers of the Portuguese Legion in the armies of Napoleon returned in 1814 largely masonised, and secret societies developed and spread. Just as Halpérine-Kaminsky tells us, it was during the march through Europe after the retreat of Napoleon's army that the Russian officers became imbued with French revolutionary and Liberal ideas, and on their return a secret society was formed in 1816, out of which Paul Pestel finally evolved the Society of the South, advocating the abolition of autocracy and the establishment of a republic. In Portugal at this time F.·. Freire Gomez d'Andrade was Grand Master of the Grand Orient Lusitanien, and had commanded a division of the French Army during the Russian campaign. He, too, became a mover in revolutionary conspiracies, and when the first was discovered in 1817, like Pestel later in 1826, he and others ended their lives on the scaffold. The lodges then closed until about 1824, when Liberal tendencies penetrated the Cortes; along with their Spanish comrades of Cadiz, the Portuguese Masons proposed to proclaim the constitution of an "Iberian Federal Republic," which has ever since remained their secret plan.

In 1834 the Mason Don Pedro IV gave Portugal a new and Liberal constitution, and Freemasonry played a great role in the revolution, lasting some years, which led up to this change. Masonry became powerful, and the desire to use it as a political instrument ended in the formation of as many Orients as there were political parties. In 1840 there were nine authorities, but the Grand Orient Lusitanien in 1859 united most of these under its obedience. Later, in 1863, it was officially recognised by the Grand Orient of France, and finally, 10 August, 1869, it united all Portuguese Masonic groups under the name Grand Orient Lusitanien Uni., with the Comte de Paraty as Grand Master. In 1870 it had under its obedience fifty-six lodges, twenty being in Spain. Since then there has been much Masonic activity culminating in the revolution of 1910, which was planned by the more advanced lodges, such as the "Gremio Mortugua," out of which came the Carbonarios, who decreed the assassination of King Carlos and his elder son, and prepared the Republican Revolution.

According to *The Times,* 28 August, 1931, there have been sixteen revolutions and forty Ministerial changes in Portugal between 1910 and 1926, and although General Carmona's rule has been called a "dictatorship without a dictator," an unsuccessful attempt to depose him was made in 1931. In the same year a revolt broke out, and was suppressed, in Madeira, Portuguese Guinea, and the Azores, and, *The Times* continued:

> "It is currently stated that the agitation was fomented by Portuguese exiles in Paris, and particularly by some preceding chiefs of the Grand Orient of Portugal."

"The Portuguese revolution of 1910," says Dr. Fredrich Wichtl,

> "was brought about by certain leading Jewish families … all related to each other, they were all united by the tie of Freemasonry and… *L'Alliance-israélite-universelle:"* *(Weltfreimauerei,* *Welt Revolution, Welt Republic.)*

Léon de Poncins, after visiting Portugal, where he interviewed several leading Government officials there, wrote an account of "New" Portugal for the French journal *Le Jour,* extracts from which appeared in the *Patriot,* 11–18 July, 1935. He was received by M. José Cabral, instigator of "the law against Freemasonry and secret societies, passed *unanimously* by the National Assembly…" In a few brief sentences M. Cabral summed up the motives which led to the passing of the law against Freemasonry:

> "The new State is an authoritative State guided and limited by the principles of Christian justice, conformable to the historical and spiritual traditions of the country. The openly anti-religious and anti-Christian character of Freemasonry was, therefore, contrary to the spiritual and moral bases of the new State… It subjects its initiates to a rigid discipline, the aims and interests of which are opposed to

those of the nation. The State, charged with the direction and well-being of the country, constantly struck up against mysterious obstacles difficult to surmount, which hindered the progress of national affairs. Freemasonry thus formed a State within a State, a strong occult State behind the feeble apparent State, which reduced the latter to a purely superficial rôle. The new Portuguese State is a strong State which cannot admit a subterranean authority contrary to its own. The hierarchic complexity of Freemasonry indicates that Freemasonry has hidden and complicated plans, aiming at international ends which override those of the National State. Freemasonry thus leads to a great international diplomatic occult action directed probably by a foreign head. Such a submission to foreign international direction is contrary to the patriotic sentiment of the country. Apart from that, the secret which Freemasonry imposes so rigorously upon its adepts allows it to be presumed that what they hide so well is neither insignificant nor beneficial..."

A.M.I.

The *Association maçonnique internationale,* or A.M.I., is neither rite nor obedience, but a confederation formed in an attempt to bring about international unity of all Masonic powers throughout the world, while, nominally, preserving to each full independence. They held, according to the French Mason Albert Lantoine, that "the ancient chain must be soldered again, which, in making the Order more powerful, would allow it to influence, in a humanitarian *[sic]* sense, the politics of rulers."

The first meeting was held in Geneva, 23 October, 1921, and united some eleven obedience-members, including the Grand Lodge of New York; the latter, however, resigned because of the recognition by the A.M.I. of the German Lodge "Au Soleil Levant," which latter was proved irregular, and removed. For some years little advance was made, but in 1932 it had increased in importance, through membership and quality of its adherents as well as through the influence it wielded. At the end of 1930 it grouped together thirty active obedience-members as follows:

Grand Lodge of Vienna.

Grand Orient of Belgium.

Grand Lodge of Bulgaria.

Grand Lodge of Spain.

Grand Orient of Spain.

Grand Orient of France.

Grand Lodge of Luxembourg.

Grand Orient of Greece.

Grand Lodge of Polarstjernen.

Grand Lodge of Poland.

Grand Orient United Lusitanean of Portugal.

Grand Lodge "Alpina" Switzerland.

Grand Lodge National of Tchecoslovak.

Grand Orient of Turkey.

Grand Orient of Brazil.

Grand Lodge of France.

Grand Lodge of Yugoslavia.

Grand Lodge of Panama.

Grand Lodge of Porto Rico.

Grand Lodge Cuscatian San Salvador.

Grand Lodge La Oriental-Peninsular.

Grand Lodge of Chili.

Grand Lodge of Columbia (Baranquilla).

Grand Lodge of the Equator.

Grand Lodge of Paraguay.

Grand Lodge of Venezuela.

Grand Lodge of Haiti.

Grand Lodge of Peru.

Grand Lodge of the Isle of Cuba.

Grand Lodge del Pacifico.

Its president in 1931 was F.·. Raoul Engel, Supreme Grand Master of the Grand Orient of Belgium. The Grand Chancellor was F.·. John Mossaz (Switzerland), who directed it, assisted by an Executive Committee of delegates, which appeared to be a kind of Parliament. Also there was a Consultative Committee composed of a few influential delegates, who apparently prepared decisions and, in fact, exercised authority.. For 1930-32 these were: Charles Magnette, Honorary Grand Master, Belgium; Bernard Wellhoff, former Grand Master, Grand Lodge of France; Arthur Groussier, former President of the Council of the Order, Grand Orient of France; Arthur Mille, of the Council of the Order, Grand Orient of France; and Fritz Brandenberg, former Grand Master of the Grand Lodge "Alpina," Switzerland.

As will be seen, the A.M.I. has spread, above all, in the Latin countries, and includes among its obedience members the great majority of the Ancient and Accepted Scottish Rites, but does not include any English or North American Grand Lodge. Under the influence of the A.M.I., the Grand Orient of France in 1930 annulled the conventions which bound it to the Grand Lodge of France and the mixed International obedience, *Le Droit Humain,* preferring, as it said, to realise unity under the auspices of the A.M.I., in which the Grand Orient of Paris now plays a directing role *(R.I.S.S.)* 20 September, 1931).

In 1877 the Grand Orient of France suppressed from its regulations the name of "The Grand Architect of the Universe" and the belief in the immortality of the soul. Because of this, the Grand Lodge of England, along with others, broke off relations with it, and has never since renewed them. In 1929 the Grand Lodge of England codified eight points as being necessary for recognition by it of any other lodge, among which were:

(2) That a belief in the Grand Architect of the Universe and His revealed will is an essential condition for the admission of candidates. (7) That religious and political discussions are rigorously prohibited in the Lodges (cf. *An. Maç. Uni.,* 1930).

Continental Masonry, on the contrary, is to a great extent anti-religious, political, and largely dominated, directly or indirectly, by Jews, and there are many proofs to show that this Judaeo-

Masonic power has always been, and still is, in the name of Humanity, the secret insidious cause of all revolutionary movements.

The following information concerning the A.M.I. was first published by Leon de Poncins in the *Mercure de France,* 15 August, 1931, and later in *La F∴ M∴,* 1934:

"In 1921 the *Association maçonnique internationale* or A.M.I. was formed at Bâle; its aim is to reinforce the links of International Masonic solidarity. Its reviews give news of Universal Masonry, and its principal books are printed in French, German, and English. The Grand Orient of Paris plays a directing rôle... It edits a public review, *La Paix,* and another secret, *Les Annales maçonniques universelles,* both published at 20 rue Laugier, Paris, under the direction of the Masonic writer and Jew, Edouard Plantagenet. *La Paix* has among its correspondents, Ramsay MacDonald, Ed. Benes... Henri Barbusse, and known Masonic writers such as André Lebey of the Grand Orient, and Albert Lantoine of the Grand Lodge... There is also the Ligue internationale des F∴ M∴, founded in Austria by the Jew Mason and writer, E. Lennhof. The A.M.I. is a union of Masonic Obediences, whilst the Ligue is an individual union of Freemasons."

The author further quotes the engineer, P. Loyer, who, speaking at a conference in Paris, 7 February, 1934, said:

"So long as Democracy has remained confined to the lodges, so long as it has only been a theme for lecture, it has been able to deceive. Mystic Masons were able to believe they could build a livable regime. But Masonry has experienced power, and what has been the result? It has ruled in Russia with Kerensky; it has ruled in Italy with Giolitti and Nitti; it has ruled in Germany with the momentary triumph of the Social-Democrat and the complicity of Bruning; it actually rules in Spain with Largo Caballero, Indalocio Prieto, Rodolpho Llopis, and Alexandre Leroux; it rules still in France..., But everywhere, everywhere without exception, the experience of power has been ill-omened to it... Masonry begins to understand that all its democratic ideology leaves it without resource, and that it can draw not the slightest light from it to solve actual political conflicts. It knows it and it admits it."

TURKEY

The Grand Orient of France reported:

> "International Congress, AM.I., held at Geneva, 21 to 24 August, 1930... The League declares particularly that they aim at no interference in the authority or the central action of the great Masonic bodies. What it desires is individual approachment, good relations, and links of personal friendship between regular Masons, *in order thus to form a chain encircling the globe.*"

Again we find *La Libre Parole*, December and January 1933, writing:

> "The Convent of the A.M.I. took place at Constantinople, September 1932. Notwithstanding the distance, twenty-two countries were represented by the delegates of twenty-four different Masonic obediences. The orators emphasised the importance of this Convent, which for the first time united in the East the representatives of World Masonry... The work of the Convent was opened by the Grand Master Moustafa Hakki... During four days the Convent regulated all administrative questions which had been studied for long months by the Executive Committee. They deplored the financial position, due to the economic crisis, and above all to the laws which, in certain countries, by interdicting the exportation of capital, made payment of subscriptions difficult, if not impossible. The Parliamentary brethren of these countries were invited by the A.M.I. to bring this 'deplorable state of affairs to an end.' A motion in favour of peace — by disarmament — was adopted. F∴ Colaveri ended by declaring: 'In the Assembly the Convent has done important work which affirms the bases of the *Association maçonnique internationale,* and definitely assures its future.'"

In 1922 the Orator of the Grand Lodge of France said:

> "My brother Masons, my hope is that Freemasonry, which has done so much for the emancipation of men, and to which history owes the national revolutions — 1789, 1871 — will also know how to make that greatest revolution, which will be the International Revolution."

According to *The Times* the Turkish *Committee of Union and Progress* was Grand Orient Freemasonry and of the Illuminati. And speaking of Talaat and the Armenian atrocities, the *Daily Telegraph* wrote, 29 May, 1922:

"It was as a humble official in the post office at Salonica that he there became acquainted, at an early date, with the Young Turk Militarists and the politicians of the Grand Orient Freemasonry, the men who were to bring about the revolution of 1908.

... Behaddine Chakir Bey... was after Talaat, Enver and Nazim, the most powerful and sinister figure of the Committee of Union and Progress..."

These, with Dr. Roussouhi Bey and some half-dozen others, formed the all-powerful and secretive executive of this C.U.P., which ruled Turkey for about ten years until 1918. The act which brought Turkey into the Great War, with all its consequences, was theirs. "'The Kemalist reaction set in under the malign influence of the C.U.P. and its Bolshevik allies."

Then came the anti-Kemal plot and trials at Smyrna and Angora, July and August 1926, at which most of the remaining eminent leaders of the "Young Turks" were convicted and hanged. At the trial it was told how Enver and Talaat "got in touch with representatives of the then Irish rebels, and promised to support them, among other oppressed peoples, if they would wage incessant war against Great Britain" *(Daily Telegraph,* 26 August, 1926). Again, in an editorial, 30 August, 1926, the same paper writes:

"Between that 'Young Turk' Party and the Kemalist Nationalism which has succeeded it and stamped it out, there is little to choose as regards their political morals. Both have sought to create and despotically to dominate a New Turkey. Both have upon their record oppression of all kinds and barbarous massacres. These things are easily understood when it is realised that many of the men, including Mustapha Kemal himself, who stand at the head of the Nationalist movement, served their political apprenticeship in the Committee of Union and Progress; and the final assault upon the earlier leaders of revolution represents little more than the determination of the new dictatorship to brook no rivalry or criticism, within the sphere of its authority."

Speaking of the "spirit of revolt and spiritual anarchy" in Freemasonry, J. Marquès-Rivière quotes the Mason Jean Bon, Deputy of the Seine, who declared in the Convent of the Grand Orient of France, 1919: "... We know no limits on the Left. For we ourselves have closed the roads on the Right..." And again at the Convent of the G.O., 1920, the same Mason said:

> "The Society of the Jacobins which was the great author of the French Revolution was only, so to say, the exterior aspect of the Masonic Lodge. What the Jacobins did during the immortal five years of 1789 to 1794 we can and must do again if the danger returns..."

BELGIUM

In three articles in the *R.I.S.S.*, I and 15 February and I March, 1935, Georges Loic gives some useful information about Belgian Masonry, its revolutionary affiliations and activities. Belgian Masonry is subject to three authorities: the Supreme Conseil du Rite Écossais, the Grand Orient, and the Fédération Nationale des Loges Mixtes. The Belgians were the first to join with their French and Spanish brothers in founding the A.M.I. "The principal centres of intrigue, therefore, appear to be the Supreme Councils, the "Ligue Internationale de Francs-Maçons," the A.M.I., the Theosophical Society and its daughter Co-Masonry." The Supreme Councils are all issues of the Supreme Council founded 31 May, 1801, at Charleston, by the Jews Dalcho and Mitchell and by the Comte de Grasse-Tilly. On 19 February, 1922, an alliance was concluded in the Grand Temple of the Droit Humain, Paris, between Co-Masonry and the Grand Orient of France. These links were broken by a decision of the Council of the Grand Orient, 13 September, 1930 (Convent of Grand Orient of France, 1930).

However autonomous the Grand Orient of Belgium was, it felt the need to enter a league of Obediences, the A.M.I., in order to participate in outside current influences. Two Convents of the A.M.I. were held in Brussels, those of 1924 and 1930, and in 1933 the Executive Committee of the A.M.I. was invited to hold the spring session at Brussels in order to take part in the manifestations organised for the centenary of the Grand Orient of Belgium. The place taken in the A.M.I. by the Belgians is therefore definite, and the more so when it is known that in 1925 a Jew of Liège, Max Gottschalk, held office as Administrative Chancellor. He became also Secretary-General of the A.M.I., secretary of the Consultative Committee, financial administrator of the A.M.I., editor of its Bulletin and of other publications. At a special Convocation of *La Parfaite Intelligence et l'Étoile Réunies* of Liège, the following resolution was carried:

> "(1) With regard to the Grand Architect of the Universe, this return to tradition is made from an exclusively symbolic angle, free from all confessional or dogmatic spirit, each being free to interpret the symbol as his conscience, reason, and religious sentiment dictate.

> "(2) With regard to the Book of Moral Law, the Bible being generally considered in Belgium as the sacred Book of the Roman Catholic Church, dominant confession here and hostile to Masonry, to avoid all equivocation the Book of Moral Law will be represented by the Constitution of the Order of 1723 (ancient charges) original text and Masonic precepts. During the workings it will be open on the altar under the Square and Compass." *(Bulletin,* A.M.I., April-June 1930).

The efforts made for over forty years to impose a system of International Arbitration upon States are known. Before the War the F.·. Léon Bourgeois succeeded in founding the International Court of Justice at The Hague. In 1917 a Congress, now celebrated, uniting Latin, some Allies, and Neutral Masonries, met in the hall of the Convents of the G.O. of France, and there the Masons, Andre Lebey and Meoni, laid the foundations of the League of Nations, of which the F.·. Sieyès and the Jacobin Deputy Milhaud already dreamed in 1792. F.·. Magnette in 1930 at Liège, on the occasion of the Convent of the A.M.I., said:

> "This creation of the League of Nations was a manifestation of International solidarity which only scoffing and systematically sceptical minds mocked at or foolishly disparaged... It was the same sentiment which guided the founders of the A.M.I. in 1921; they desired to establish closer relations between the multiple obediences which bore the name of lodges and give to an institution spread over the entire surface of the universe, a rational organisation and a centre of development which would increase its power a hundredfold."

At the same Convent F.·. Henri La Fontaine, vice-president of the Belgian Senate, said:

> "You are not unaware... that Masonry should not occupy itself with politics... But all the same it must not be forgotten that in the past it was in the Lodges that the Great Revolutions were prepared, notably

the French and American Revolutions… In many of our Lodges the batteries end with the words of the French Revolution—Liberty, Equality and Fraternity" *(Bulletin,* A.M.I., July-September 1930).

What Le Couteulx de Canteleu said of Masonry in 1863 might well be said of it to-day:

"Freemasons have contended for the empire of the world as few sovereigns have done, and to what end? To be the point of issue of all follies and all monstrosities; the Cabala, magic, hermetic philosophy, communications with spirits, magnetism, theosophy, deism, atheism, physical and moral regeneration, vengeance, destruction of empires, the Universal Republic; if we exclude these follies, what remains? A few honest citizens playing mournfully in the Chapel of the Tomb of Hiram!"

Georges Loic concludes:

"The Jews who knew the triumph of the Bolshevik Revolution in Russia and in Central Europe are feeling the wind of defeat… The two Socialist Internationals have constituted the Front Unique at Amsterdam to take up the imperilled revolutionary work. Blinded by an absurd mysticism, Freemasonry makes ready to play Kerensky by the side of international Jews. Certainly the forces of Masonry are immense… It is, however, weak, for its principles force it to act through intermediaries, to be only an influence… a machine to form opinion… without outside help-complicity of foreign Governments or international financiers and their troops, the Workers International — it can do little … it is incapable of forming a durable edifice."

THE LEAGUE OF NATIONS

On 28, 29, and 30 June, 1917, the Grand Orient and Grand Lodge of France held a Congress in Paris uniting representatives of Allies and Neutrals Masonries — English excepted. A few extracts from the report of the speeches may, in view of the French proposals at the Disarmament Conference of the League of Nations, be of interest to the general reader. The text of the report is given in *Dans l'Atelier Maçonnique,* by André Lebey, a prominent Mason and orator of the Grand Orient of France; the subject of the discussion was "the preparation of the League of Nations":

"Collective justice which they have desired to make possible by causing it to dominate individual and egotistic justice of State to State... Thus the supreme force of the community of Nations, both material and moral, will know how to overcome the murderous designs of one or several of them. There will then no longer be neutral nations, for none, in an organisation of this order, will be able to isolate itself without defaulting from its agreed duty. Injustice done to one of them will strike them collectively and individually... Neutrals ought therefore to be united among themselves in such a way that they will always be led to lend assistance... ·

"The task which is imposed on our generation, and more especially on you, my FF.·., consists in bringing about a decisive progress towards this International law... This International law is the law of peace... The International law must be armed with sanctions such as will discourage, in advance, those who would be tempted to break their word. United among themselves the nations who wish to live in peace, in the respect of their reciprocal rights, would create an irresistible sovereign force of economic and military action which would prevent the blind masses being drawn into imperialistic conflicts. This union of the different national forces will itself be, in order to realise its defensive task, adapted, arranged, and equipped with a view to its highest efficiency. The Law will thus possess guarantees of continuance. It will become a force by the adherence of the greatest number of States. This force, *through a veritable police of nations,* will maintain universal peace by placing all civilised powers on the side of any nation, whose rights, without provocation, will have been violated by another."

Among the conclusions presented, in the name of the Commission, by F.·. Lebey and adopted by the Congress were:

"The International Parliament associates, in appropriate commissions, for all important questions which facilitate international relations, collaborators chosen by it and ratified by the National Chambers of the different States, so as to regulate collectively and internationally, universal questions of legislation which will draw still closer the links of the peoples...

"The International Parliament will equally form within itself, by means of a member per nation, a judicial power, creating in this way an International Court of Justice, before which will be brought all national conflicts between the nations. Those elected, nominated for three years, according to precedents, are responsible before the

International Parliament and cannot promulgate a sentence unless it is ratified by it.

"No nation has the right to declare war upon another, for war is a crime against the human race. All difference between States ought therefore to be deferred to the International Parliament. The nation who would refuse to do so would thus place itself outside the League of Nations, which would, after having exhausted all other means of convincing it, notably by economic boycott, rupture of all relations, complete blockade by land and sea, and absolute isolation, have the right and duty to constrain it by force to recognise the universal law.

"The International Parliament will itself define the diplomatic, economic and military measures which will be established in order to assure the exercise of its powers. Its aim, properly so-called, is under sufficient guarantees of the autonomy of each nation, the limitation of armaments so as to lead one day to universal disarmament. The International Parliament should support armaments of each country constituting the League of Nations only in so far as shall be necessary to efficaciously counter-balance the armaments of those who would remain outside the League of Nations.

"The International Parliament will itself choose the place of its meetings, the town will become the capital of the world, the territory of which will be internationalised. It will adopt as emblem a banner on which an orange sun will radiate upon a white ground in the midst of yellow stars as numerous as the nations who will adhere to the conventions above."

Such is the Masonic dream of Internationalism, where the most backward and barbarous nation would be on an equality with the great and most civilised Powers — Liberty, Equality, and Fraternity, the slogan of the French Revolution, false as it is subversive!

And when in 1934 the proposal came to admit the Soviet Government — that barbarous regime of tyranny, brutality, and slavery, Jew-dominated and Jew-represented — as an honoured member of this League of Nations, an outcry was raised by at least some of the Press. The *Gazette de Lausanne* of 16 August of that year wrote:

"If Russia is received officially into the League of Nations, we shall have permanently in our country the agents of the Russian Secret

Police, which innocently calls itself "Commissariat of the Interior for the People."... The work of the G.P.U. is military espionage and sapping operations against organisations and persons who oppose the Soviet and Communism in Switzerland. The espionage is also political and industrial, including the constitution of secret 'cells' in industrial enterprises..."

There were also some British papers which made vigorous protests against the admittance of Soviet Russia to the League; for example, the *Sunday Pictorial*, 26 August, 1934, wrote:

"Probably the most interesting story in the world to-day would be the complete revelation of precisely what intrigues are going on to get Russia into the League of Nations. Here is something before which justice, decency, and mercy may well curl up and die. If Russia does get in, then Geneva will, without doubt, be transformed into one of the most sinister and dangerous centres in the world. Behind the cloak of idealism, and all that worthy decency which is supposed to go with the League, we shall have international plotting of purely gangster morality... If Russia breaks into the League we shall be presented with perhaps the greatest irony since history began, the debasement of the great institution formed to make world peace into a laboratory for world disruption, largely via Far Eastern and Indian affairs, but also in many other ways..."

To-day we are witnessing the reaction to this Judaeo Masonic League in the present Italo-Abyssinian crisis, and who can tell what sinister intrigues are at the back of it!

STAVISKY

We cannot leave this question of the power of Judaeo-Masonry without at least touching on the recent Stavisky scandals. So far as we have seen, the best account of what led up to the bursting of the Stavisky bomb is to be found in Léon Daudet's book, *La Police Politique*, 1934, in which he tells us:

"Now there were two rival bands equally powerful as to their political, financial, Masonic, and other relations: the Stavisky band ... and the Levy-Dubois group... The two groups, composed of powerful personalities and banks, attacked each other with violence... Both having need of the complicity of officials, corrupt or corruptible, depended on the Sûreté Générale... The Lévy-

Dubois group was founded in 1927 by three small Jews without fortune ... all three were affiliated to the Lodge *Droit et le Devoir...*"

Their first attempt to manipulate certificates of annuities for war damages and to issue a public loan came to nothing. Then a brilliant idea came, and

> "A law was prepared and voted in July 1933, which permitted financing, by annuities, the liabilities of the State towards Communes and Departments. Through the Lévy-Dubois group they prepared *L'Outillage National*, on the model of what had been done for the liberated regions... But Stavisky intervened. He founded at the same time and on the same model, with the approval of the Quai d'Orsay, the *Caisse autonome...* Suddenly the intervention of the City spoiled everything and set a light to the powder. The Credit Lyonnais forced Levy-Dubois to dissolve *L'Outillage National* and give up the affair..."

This Dubois group, however, exploded the Stavisky scandal by means of pamphlets threatening exposure. The result is known, and how the affair of the "bons de Bayonne" burst.

> "Stavisky, this huge swindler who was at the same time a spy of a certain capacity and a corrupter of genius, had found the means of monopolising a large number of provincial casinos, notably in the region of Biarritz and Saint-Jean-de-Luz, also, with the complicity of the Sûreté Générale's gaming section, some gambling-hells of the Parisian region, giving fruitful returns. In the first rank of the latter was the *Cercle Hippique* or *Frolic's...* in principle the president of Frolic's, a veritable police-trap, was always a police official..." The Stavisky bomb burst, and with it disappeared Stavisky-suicide or murder? Suddenly, on 20 February, fifteen days after the shooting of patriots and ex-Service men on the Place de la Concorde, the Judge Albert Prince, member of the Judiciary Commission to inquire into those responsible for the remissions granted for years by the Parquet to the swindler Stavisky, was found cut to pieces on the railway line some kilometres from Dijon. His portfolio was found nearby, with all papers gone; and it had contained, it was known, two overwhelming documents accusing those responsible for the Stavisky remissions. These were to have been brought up, next day, before the Commission of Inquiry. To further cover those implicated, "suicide" was whispered and suggested."

Stavisky and his Jew accomplices Hayotte and Cohen had swindled the Crédit Municipal de Bayonne of hundreds of millions of francs, and several official personages were directly compromised. Stavisky, a notorious old offender, had been nineteen times found guilty and condemned and nineteen times acquitted, thanks to his Government protectors. In Paris there was an explosion as the Government clearly sought to hush up the affair. The Chamber nominated at the elections of 1932 was very "Left," and composed of a large majority of Freemasons, and although the Government received a vote of confidence in Parliament, owing to public reaction it was forced to resign. It was followed by another, equally permeated by Freemasons, and refused to institute a Commission of Inquiry.

Upon this refusal followed the tragic shootings of 6 February, 1934, when twenty-seven were killed and two thousand wounded. Next day the Government was again forced to resign, and calm was only restored when the President of the Republic called upon the former President Doumergue to save the Parliamentary régime. And what of Freemasonry?

Speaking of Judaeo-Masonry and the Stavisky "affaire," the Editor of the *R.I.S.S.*, 15 March, 1934, gives the names of seven Masons acting on the Commission of Inquiry into the scandals, and six on the Commission of Inquiry into the riots of 6 February, and adds two more names, Masons who were "to aid the Commission of Inquiry to determine in what quarter the guilty and accomplices must be sought." Further, he writes:

> "Thus the existence of Freemasonry queers the pitch of every institution. A secret political power is incompatible with an independent Government. The Commissions of Inquiry are cored by the secret power. The good will of honest members of the Commission strikes up against a permanent conspiracy. It is thus in all workings of the State, the Mason Deputy does not represent his electors: *he represents his Lodge.*

> The Mason-official does not impartially fulfil his duties; *he places his public authority at the service of his secret chiefs.* The Mason-judge is not free; *he is obliged to submit to fraternal pressure.* An independent Government cannot co-exist with a secret Government; it suppresses it or else loses its own independence... What is the exact participation of Freemasonry in the hushing up of the Stavisky Affair?"

The Freemasons themselves were disturbed and certain of them demitted. At the General Assembly of the Spanish Grand Orient, 20 February, 1933, among others, the following decision is all-important, applicable to all Grand Orient Masonry:

> "The Masonic authorities are bound to see to the fulfilment, with necessary frequency, of the duty imposed upon the brethren exercising public employment to renew the oath, to explain and masonically justify their public conduct before their superiors. And as in the exercise of public employment he can fail in his Masonic duties as much by deed as by omission, this signifies that the Mason filling this post will be obliged, not only to explain and justify every action appearing blameable or doubtful, *but also to receive Masonic directions and pay attention to* them…"

Therefore it would appear that these Masons are not free, but subject to their superiors and, under oath, must obey them.

Finally, J. le François, in the *R.I.S.S., 15* September, 1933, gives us the following interesting information. The Grand Lodge of France at its Convent of 1932 reported on the "sickness of contemporary France" as submitted by the lodges and synthesised by F.·. Chaligny. M. le François writes:

> "The report of F.·. Chaligny clearly admits the failure of mystic democracy… In the first place the spirit of revolution has no longer worshippers, enthusiasts, or apostles. The great ancestors have lost face, or rather, their memory has no longer pious adorers among the people. Liberty, Equality, Fraternity, who cares about them? The Rights of Man?… "They have arrived at the period of the abuse of them," said F.·. Chaligny, where the greater part of the members of collectivity or at least the most influential neglect the duties to which they were bound.
>
> … It appears then that the myth has served its day… During 150 years we have lived on the revolutionary myth. Has it been able to realise the infinite hopes that men had placed in the splendid formula, Liberty, Equality, Fraternity"?… We have shown the failure of all institutions which claimed to be inspired by these three prophetic words… It would appear that the principles which they have been accustomed to regard as indispensable to the health of a society are forgotten or trampled underfoot."

Moreover, at the Convent of the Grand Orient, 1920, F.·. Fontenay said:

"Every revolution aims at the assurance of universal happiness. When our ancestors proclaimed as principle, Liberty, Equality, Fraternity, they aimed at realising happiness. After 130 years we see their work; it is not brilliant; of Liberty none remains to us; of Equality there is scarcely any; of Fraternity there has never been any."

Thus vanishes the great Masonic dream!

CHAPTER VIII

THEOSOPHY AND INDIA CO-MASONRY

S PEAKING of the occultism of the nineteenth century as elaborated by the Martinists, Papus, Eliphas Levi, and the Theosophists, which includes the queer ensemble of such things as metaphysical phenomena, spiritism, magic, astrology, hermetic medicine, the Cabala, esoteric numbers, mystic exegesis, and speculations on reincarnation and karma, and above all a doctrinal system presented as the common source from which all religions have been derived, Marcel Lallemand, in *Notes on Occultism,* writes:

"It is in truth an avalanche of pompous words, grandiloquent expressions, apocalyptic phrases, mysterious signs and silences commanded by a pseudo-initiation into the sacred mysteries... Under the influence of Theosophy, it is associated with visions of libraries hidden in the caves of the Himalayas, of fantastic ceremonies in the Egyptian Temples, etc... It is known that the occultists claim to be heirs of the secret traditions going back to the Egyptians and transmitted throughout the Middle Ages by the Rose-Croix, the Templars, etc... Most of these occultists are attached to Freemasonry... This subterranean world works feverishly, and many public events are only comprehensible as a function of the agitation of these occultist-termites, whose activity is one of the least equivocal signs of the spiritual disorder of the Modern World... It would also be legitimate to speak of a *satanisation* (rather than deification) of these obscure aspects of the human soul. It is in this that the danger of occultism lies, which often ends in mental and psychic disorder, leading many of its adepts to founder in sexual perversion, madness, or crime, as shown in the annuals of modern occultism" (quoted by de Poncins).

Further, de Poncins writes:

"Occultism has more important repercussions than one thinks. A wave of occultism preceded and accompanied the two great revolutionary movements of 1789 and 1917. The Theosophists and Illuminés of the eighteenth century, Jacob Boehme, Emmanuel Swedenborg, Martinez de Pasqualis, Cagliostro, the Comte de Saint-Germain, etc., had their counterparts in the numerous Russian sects and in the magi and occultists of the Imperial Court, Philippe, Papus, the Tibetan Badmaev, and above all Rasputin, whose extraordinary influence contributed directly to the unchaining of the revolution."

Looking back over history, it seems to be evident that the spread of secret societies, illuminism, theurgy, and spiritism has always been a sure precursor of revolutions and the fall of Crowns. From its commencement the reign of Nicolas II of Russia was one long succession of mystics, prophets, and Illuminés — instruments of the "Hidden Hand" — who, by their strange practices and sometimes scandalous lives, contributed not a little to bring discredit upon the Court of Russia, eventually led to its downfall, and through death and destruction initiated the Jew-led Soviet rule with its dream of World Revolution and World Domination — the dream of Grand Orient Illuminised Masonry.

The first of these mystery workers of outstanding importance was Maître Philippe, chief of the School of Theurgy at Lyons. He thus described his work: "From the age of thirteen I have performed miraculous cures. I am an unconscious intermediary between *humanity and a Superior Power* who overshadows it. The astonishing results I daily obtain, I admire, but do not understand." In 1900 he was introduced into the Court of Russia by Papus, the well-known Martinist and Illuminé, who looked upon Philippe as his "Master." Gradually he became indispensable to both Emperor and Empress. In 1903, returning to Russia after an enforced absence, he initiated the Empress into the practices of spiritism and theurgy. It was he who inspired the Emperor with the idea of universal peace by general disarmament! He was finally forced to retire to Lyons, and died in August 1905 *(Le Maître Philippe,* by J. Bricaud).

Papus the Martinist and theurgist, whose real name was Dr. Encausse, first appeared in St. Petersburg in 1900, and about then or later introduced Martinism among the Russian aristocracy. In

1905 he was again summoned to Russia in connection with the revolution of that year, his advice being considered valuable at Court. Paleologue, in his *Mémoires*, 1916, tells how, "The very day on which Papus arrived in St. Petersburg a riot spread terror in Moscow and a mysterious syndicate proclaimed a general railway strike." And with regard to the later revolution Papus professed to be able to avert this catastrophe by means of his magic, but only so long as he remained in his physical body. Papus's last visit to Russia was in 1906 and he died, October 1916, in the Great War.

In his book, *Rasputin: The Holy Devil,* Fülöp Miller writes of yet another:

> "One of the most curious phenomena of the Russian Imperial Court was the "doctor of Tibetan medicine," Badmaev... Shamzaran Badmaev affirmed that he had acquired an exact knowledge of the secret doctrines of 'Tibetan magic' and medical science in his father's house (Transbaikalia), as the knowledge was an ancient tradition in the family... There was a time in Russian politics when not only the Court, but the ministers and administrative officials were entirely under the sway of Badmaev.

> ... He established a sanatorium distinguished from all others by its political character. His party affiliations and political views were carefully noted on the chart of every patient at the institution... Badmaev kept up an active correspondence with bis patients after their treatment was over, in which, in addition to medical advice... he also gave them political instructions. In the course of time medicine and politics and "lotus essences" became more and more involved in each other, resulting in a fantastic political sorcery that had its origin in the Badmaev sanatorium, and that decided the destiny of Russia."

According to Paleologue, Protopopov, the Minister of the Interior, was brought into touch with the sinister monk Rasputin by Badmaev, the Mongolian quack. And writing of Rasputin, in his *Inquiry into the Assassination of the Russian Imperial Family,* Nicolas Sokoloff writes that Rasputin was surrounded and directed by three Jews: Ivan Theodorovitch Manoussevitch Manouilof, who had numerous connections both in Russia and abroad and before 1905 was long affiliated to the police in Paris. It was he too who introduced the famous Philippe to the Russian

Court. Secondly, a Jewish banker Dmitri Rubenstein, who was unsuccessfully accused of intrigues with the Germans during the War. Lastly, his secretary, Aron Samouilovitch Simanovitch, a diamond merchant of Petrograd, a Jew by origin and religion. He lived in Rasputin's house and apparently acted for Rasputin without consulting him.

An extraordinary glamour has for long hung around the name of the Comte de Saint-Germain and to-day he is one of the most "sacred" Masters, even to an obsession, of the Theosophical Society. Below we give some varied opinions about this almost legendary character. In a series of articles *The Anatomy of Revolution,* by G. G. or "Dargan," author of the *Nameless Order* (see the *Patriot,* October 1922), he writes:

> "There can be no doubt that a hundred and fifty years ago Grand Orient Masonry and Templar Masonry on the Continent were permeated and used by occult societies with subversive and anti-religious aims. The High Priest and master-mind of this movement in the eighteenth century would seem to have been a brilliant adventurer calling himself 'Count St. Germain' or Ragoczy — believed to have been a Portuguese Jew — an assiduous organiser of revolt, and among whose connections or intimates we find Mirabeau, Weishaupt, Cagliostro and Paschalis (the two last also of Jewish origin), all of whom played their part in preparing the network of secret societies which helped to bring about the French revolution."

Again, in the same series he writes:

> "The origin of all the occult societies of to-day could probably be traced directly back to similar societies of the past... The Theosophical Society, for instance, was founded by Mme Blavatsky, who was employed as an agent of the Carbonari, which she joined in 1856, when under the influence of Mazzini, who appears to have founded a branch of the Carbonari in England, and whose connection with Orient Masonry is well known. Mrs. A. Besant, Mme Blavatsky's disciple and successor, could, therefore, justly claim to be of the line of the prophets of the mystical revolutionary cult which reveres Ragoczy as the 'Master.' Hence it is not surprising to find that in founding Co-Masonry in England the adoration of Ragoczy ... is a cardinal part of the ritual of the higher lodges of that body."

Mrs. Besant, herself, in a pamphlet on "The Masters," 1912, tells us:

> "The last survivor of the Royal House of Rakoczi, known as the Comte de St. Germain in the history of the eighteenth century; as Bacon in the seventeenth century; as Robertus, the monk, in the sixteenth; as Hunyadi Janos in the fifteenth; as Christian Rosencreuz in the fourteenth — to take a few of his incarnations — was disciple through those laborious lives and now has achieved Masterhood, the 'Hungarian Adept' of *The Occult World,* and known to some of us in that Hungarian body."

Another theosophist and occultist, of New York, Mrs. Alice A. Bailey, thus describes him in her book, *Initiation Human and Solar,* 1933. *Master Rakoczi* is a Hungarian, and lives in the Carpathian Mountains. Was known as the Comte de St. Germain, Roger Bacon, and later Francis Bacon. Works with the occult side of affairs in Europe, largely through esoteric ritual and ceremonial, being vitally interested in the effects of the ceremonial of the Freemasons, of various fraternities, and of the Churches. Acts practically in America and Europe as general manager for carrying out the plans of the executive council of the Lodge, which is an inner group of Masters round the three Lords-the latter being, *Manu, Maitreya,* and *Manachohan.*

Then, according to Eliphas Levi, who was a Martinist: St. Germain professed the Catholic religion and conformed to its practices. His family connections were unknown, but he talked as if he had lived for centuries. He chose his own disciples, required passive obedience, and told them that they were called to the royalty of Melchisedek and Solomon which was both an initiation and a priesthood, and he said to them:

> "Be the torch of the world; if your light is that of a planet, you will be nothing in the sight of God. I reserve for you a splendour of which the solar glory is a shadow. You shall guide the course of stars and those who rule empires shall be governed by you."

His principles, according to Eliphas Levi, were those of the Rose-Croix; he was ambassador of the illuminated Theosophists, and he was said to be a skilful physician and chemist. And as Eliphas Levi concludes:

"The Comte Saint-Germain was a fashion for a moment, and as he was an amiable and youthful Methuselah, who knew how to combine the tattle of a roue with the ecstasies of a Theosophist, he was the rage in certain circles, though speedily replaced by other phantasiasts. So goes the world!"

Finally, after the illuminising of the Grand Orient Lodges of France, a General Convent of Masons was convoked by the secret Committee for 15 February, 1785, and among the deputies were: Saint-Germain, Etrilla, Mesmer, Cagliostro, Mirabeau, etc. (Mirabeau). At this Convent the French Revolution and its propagation throughout Europe was resolved upon, even to the decree of regicide. We know that Cagliostro's place in this scheme was to besmirch Marie-Antoinette and so prepare for the fall and death of the King.

Such are the varied accounts of this mysterious "Master Rakoczi," masquerading under the name and cloak of the by-no-means "Holy" Comte de St. Germain, thus enchaining the imaginations and emotions of thousands of worthy but undoubtedly deluded Theosophists, more especially in America, that land of fantastic "isms." Moreover, one can easily understand how important the doctrine of reincarnation is to such sinister Masters, for without it the name "Comte de St. Germain" would be dead and useless as a burnt-out member.

Finally, we would agree with René Guénon, the well-known Orientalist, who accuses Theosophy

"of immediately unbalancing feeble minds who are drawn into these centres; the number of unfortunates led by these things to ruin, madness, and at times even to death is much more considerable than can be imagined by insufficiently informed people.

… It can be said without exaggeration that the diffusion of "Neo-Spiritualism" under all its forms, constitutes a veritable public danger which cannot be too insistently denounced."

M. J. de Boistel, in the *R.I.S.S.*, 15 November, 1934, writes: "It can be said that the occult sects which have formed themselves in the heart of Christianity, and Freemasonry itself, are almost all merely an adaptation, more or less crude, of the Cabalistic and Gnostic errors." He gives the principal dates of the renaissance of this cabalistic gnosticism as: 1855, the revival of Spiritism by

Allan Kardec; 1875, the formation of the Theosophical Society; 1885, the reconstitution of Martinism; 1888, the restoration of the sect of Gnostics; 1912, the foundation of Symbolism; 1919, the opening of the International Metaphysical Institution. In 1888, he tells us, F.·. Jules Doinel, departmental archivist of Loiret and member of the Council of the Grand Orient of France, revived the Gnostic Church, calling himself the First Patriarch, Valentin II. He grouped together high intellectuals, and in 1893 a Synod was constituted, a Hierarchy was established, and several bishops were created. Later F.·. Doinel repudiated these doctrines and returned to the Catholic Church. He was succeeded, as Patriarch, by F.·. Fabre des Essarts, known as Synesius, who founded the review, *La Gnose,* in 1909; in 1907, the rival Patriarch, Jean II (J. Bricaud), founded the review, *Le Réveil Gnostique.*

After his resignation F.·. Doinel wrote:

> "Jewish action, Jewish infiltration, Jewish hatred! How often have I heard Freemasons groan under the domination which the Jews impose upon the Lodges, upon the Philosophic Lodges, upon the Councils of the Grand Orient in all countries, at all points of the Triangle, the whole length of the vast world... Since the Revolution the Jews have invaded the Lodges... To the learned the Cabala; to the ignorant the Jewish spirit. The Cabala dogmatises and makes of metaphysics, the metaphysics of Lucifer. The Jewish spirit directs action."

M. de Boistel notes four characteristics common to all such sects, including Freemasonry: (1) The attempt of a crude adaptation to Christianity. (2) Esotericism, the existence of a secret tradition, and teaching reserved for initiates alone, perpetuated from Antiquity throughout the ages. (3) Esoteric doctrine transmitted only by initiation, necessitating successive phases and corresponding grades. The initiatic organisation has existed in Gnosticism from its origin and was revived by Masonry. (4) Explanation of the World so as to do away with the dogma of creation, leading to the deification of man, necessitating the doctrines of Karma and Reincarnation. Occultists, Gnostics, Theosophists, Martinists, and Rose-Croix join hands in propagating, under varying names, these common errors and speculations.

Therefore, going back to last century we would trace a few links in the occult and subversive chain, so curiously interwoven, which has gradually and insidiously led up to the present International World Revolution, which is to materialise the unity required for their dream of some monstrous World State ruled by invisible "Supermen."

One of the earliest steps in this renewed World Movement appears to be the Theosophical Society, founded in 1875 by the Russian, Mme Blavatsky, a woman, according to Mrs. Besant, "with little education" but a powerful medium. She was an initiate of the Druse Order — a development from the House of Wisdom, Cairo — and was initiated into the Carbonari by Mazzini. The aims of the Alta Vendita, the Supreme Directory of the Carbonari, were identical with those of the Illuminati. In 1880 Weishaupt's Illuminati was reorganised at Dresden by Leopold Engel, under the name of *Ordre Rénové des Illuminati Germaniae,* and played a very suspect political rôle; Steiner, it is believed, belonged to it, but later. Dr. Franz Hartmann, who was born in 1838 at Donauwerth, in Bavaria, along with others, founded the *Ordre de la Rose-Croix Ésotérique,* which was closely linked to the above; he also established in Switzerland, September 1889, a Theosophico-Monastic body called *Fraternitas,* and associated with him in this were Dr. R. Thurmann, Dr. A. Pioda, and the Countess Wachtmeister, the last a friend of Mme Blavatsky. About 1887 he also appears to have belonged to an American branch of the *Golden Dawn* at its centre in Boston.

In 1895 a certain *Ordre des Templiers Orientaux* was founded by Dr. Karl Kellner, and at his death in 1905 was carried on by a Theosophist, Theodore Reuss, and the *Rose-Croix Ésotérique* finally became its "inner circle." Theodore Reuss, who later called himself Reuss-Wilsson, was a German living in London, where for long he held an official position in the "Theosophical Publishing Co." Unable to return to his own country, he, nevertheless, founded a so-called *Grand Orient of the German Empire,* with Franz Hartmann as one of its dignitaries. It was said that Reuss initiated Rudolf Steiner into the O.T.O., and that Crowley's O.T.O. was a branch of the same movement.

John Yarker, who died in 1913, and who has written much on "Arcane Schools," constituted a so-called Swedenborgian Rite, said to be entirely his own invention, and in no way connected with the eighteenth-century Rites inspired by Swedenborg's ideas. Yarker made Papus, the well-known occultist, "Grand Maréchal" of the Supreme Council, and in a list, 1897, Colonel Olcott's name was given as representing the Supreme Council of the Grand Lodge and Temple of Bombay. As we know, the mysterious *Golden Dawn* was launched in London in 1888 by Dr. Wynn Westcott and others, which later became the *Stella Matutina* with its inner Order the R.R. et A.C., when A. E. Waite seceded (1903), taking his followers with him, also the name *Golden Dawn* of which he remained Chief until about 1915, when it went into abeyance. Later he formed another group, calling it the *Order of the Rosy-Cross*. Under Dr. Felkin, who was Chief, from the formation of the *Stella Matutina* until he died in 1926, the Order, and his New Zealand Order were both linked up with Dr. Rudolf Steiner's Anthroposophy, which was a secession from the Theosophical Society, 1913. Theosophy, through its Co-Masonry, was itself linked, for a time, with Grand Orient Masonry. Dr. Wynn Westcott resigned from the *Golden Dawn* in 1897 and Crowley became a member in 1898, but was expelled in 1900. Such are the true facts of this mysterious Order. The present writer was never a member of the *Golden Dawn,* but was initiated into the *Stella Matutina,* under Dr. Felkin, in 1908.

Further, Max Heindel, a former disciple of Dr. Steiner, who disapproved of the demanded secrecy, broke away from Steiner and went to America, where, in 1911, he, without permission, published Steiner's teachings in his book *Rosicrucian Cosmo-Conception.* Steiner soon after published his *Occult Science,* etc. In America Max Heindel founded his *Rosicrucian Fellowship* in order to spread the teaching without the objectionable secrecy. Because of this betrayal of secret teaching the members of R.R. et A.C. were forbidden to work with this Fellowship!

In his book, 1911, Max Heindel writes concerning world changes:

> "The caste system, which was the stronghold of England in India, is crumbling. Instead of being separated into small groups, the people

are uniting in the demand that the oppressor shall depart and leave them to live in freedom under a government of, by, and for the people [Theosophical influence!]. Russia, 1911, is torn by strife for freedom from a dictatorial autocratic government [exchanged for Bolshevik slavery!]. Turkey has awakened and taken a long stride toward liberty [first under the Young Turks of the Grand Orient!] [In America] we are not yet satisfied ... we see that we have still industrial freedom to gain.

... Thus, all over the world the old systems of paternal government are changing. Nations as such have had their day, and are unwittingly working toward Universal Brotherhood in accordance with the design of our invisible leaders, who are none the less potent in shaping events because they are not officially seated in the councils of nations."

As René Guénon says:

"We do not believe, therefore, that Theosophists, any more than occultists or spiritists, have the force to succeed entirely by themselves in such an undertaking; but is there not behind all these movements something much more formidable which even their chiefs perhaps do not know and of which they, in their turn, are merely instruments?"

To again quote G.G. in *The Anatomy of Revolution:*

"Behind every revolutionary movement throughout the world there is always some secret organisation. These revolutionary movements in all countries, whatever the bodies which actually organise them, have always three primary aims: (a) the abolition of existing constitutions, whether Monarchist or Republican; (b) the abolition of private ownership of property; (c) the abolition of established religion. Sometimes the chief aim is camouflaged under a pattern of nationalism or of internationalism; but the attack is always directed ultimately against these foundations of civilisation... The same people often preach nationalism in Ireland, India, Egypt, or South Africa, when the effect is to disintegrate the British Empire... Mr. George Lansbury, the most prominent figure connected with the *Herald* newspaper, and founder of the *Herald* League, is not only a member of the Theosophical Society, and, it is said, of the Co-Masons also, but claims to be of the line of the prophets of revolt. In an article in the *Daily Herald* (24 November, 1921), on the death of Mr. Hyndman, he describes himself as a disciple of that gentleman, who in turn was the disciple of Mazzini. So that here, on his own admission, we can trace once more the political pedigree of a leading revolutionary to the Carbonari of the mid-nineteenth century."

To-day Mr. Lansbury would have us parcel out the British Empire among all nations so as to ensure Peace! The political development of these secret movements is always by gradual stages, culminating in revolution as a preparation for world domination by their hidden directors. Thus Mme Blavatsky, notwithstanding her early adventures in spiritualism and phenomena, firmly established the Theosophical Society, whose influence to-day in one form or another is worldwide. Her *Secret Doctrine,* received, it is said, from the Masters, is to-day the Gospel and binding force among her faithful followers, and thus has she prepared the way. Mrs. Besant, continuing the required development in India, attempted a pseudo-revival of Hinduism and later the establishment of a World-Teacher — mouthpiece of her hidden directors, entirely anti-Christian; further, her social and educational work led inevitably to politics, the disintegrating so-called Nationalism. After a Theosophical Convention in Madras in 1884, the National Congress was initiated by a group of, largely, Indian Theosophists, for the expression of Indian aspirations. In 1885 Mrs. Besant joined the Fabians, and was for fifty years a member of Labour. Much later she drew up her Indian Home Rule Bill, which she brought to England, where it was officially approved of by the Labour Party. Again, in September 1928, this gave place to the Nehru Committee Constitution, supported by Mrs. Besant, demanding Dominion Status. But Gandhi, that fanatical but astute political dreamer, not content to wait, issued an ultimatum demanding a Government decision by the end of 1929; no decision being forthcoming, he thereupon opened his campaign for absolute independence by civil disobedience, leading the country into chaos.

Mrs. Besant joined the Theosophical Society in 1889, and went to India in 1893 in order, as she said, 'to give back to India her ancient freedom... by the revival of ancient philosophical and scientific religions' and by placing 'India as an equal partner in a great Inda-British Commonwealth.' As Sir Valentine Chirol wrote in *Indian Unrest:*

"The advent of the Theosophists, heralded by Mme Blavatsky and Colonel Olcott, gave a fresh impulse to the revival, and certainly no Hindu has done so much to organise and consolidate the movement as Mrs. Annie Besant, who in her Central Hindu College at Benares, and her Theosophical Institution at Adyar, near Madras, has openly proclaimed her faith in the superiority of the whole Hindu system to the vaunted civilisation of the West."

Of the initiation of the National Congress she writes in *India: Bond or Free?:*

"It was significant that, after the Theosophical Convention at Adyar, in 1884, a number of the delegates and members went over to Madras and formed the organising committee of the National Congress to-be, which met in Bombay in 1885, and became the Voice of India; the national self-respect aroused by revived pride in Hinduism, leading to the National Ideal of Self-Government."

Yet in India there are many peoples, many creeds besides Hinduism, and many castes; how could such a Congress claim to be the unified voice of all their opposing ideals, religious and political? She continues:

"Under the influence of those who had made in 1884 the scheme of the National Congress in Madras... the peasants began to discuss their grievances and later to meet in conference among themselves... Thus was the se d in the villages sown which sprang up as the agitation for Home Rule in 1915, when Mr. Gandhi said of myself: 'She has made Home Rule a mantram in every cottage.'... India's intelligentsia worked to educate their countrymen, and the annual meetings of the National Congress, reported in the Indian Press, were as the rain falling on the hidden seed."

And showing the power behind her movement she writes:

"Really, the awakening of India is not only a part of the movement in Asia, stimulated by the aggressiveness of Western peoples, but it is also part of the world movement towards Democracy, which began for the West in the revolt of the American Colonies against the rule of Britain, ending in 1776 in the independence of the Great Republic of the West, and in the French Revolution of 1789."

As we have already shown, secret societies were behind the French Revolution of 1789, and in Mme Blavatsky's book, *Isis Unveiled,* she gives a letter written by Charles Sotheran, corresponding secretary of the New York Liberal Club, high

Mason and initiate of the English Brotherhood of the Rosie Cross, who, writing in January 1877, says:

"In the last century the Illuminati taught "peace with the cottage, war with the palace," throughout the length and breadth of Europe. In the last century the United States was freed from the tyranny of the mother country by the action of the Secret Societies more than is commonly imagined…"

That this same power of secret societies was behind Mrs. Besant she confirms herself in *New India,* 1929:

"Try to perceive the Great Plan as a whole… India is the keynote, India is the centre of that great storm which shall usher in a splendid Peace… No true Theosophist and certainly no one who is working for the *Inner Government of the World* will be careless of India's welfare… Co-Masonry has been given to India that it may be a powerful organised force for India's service."

At every opportunity Mrs. Besant decried the rule of the British Raj, saying: "The masses of the Indian people have been prosperous, free and happy, save during the last hundred and sixty odd years, dating from the time when the East India Company became a ruling power down to the present day." And yet as a leader in *The Morning Post,* 22 September, 1933, said:

"It is the justification of the British occupation that, whereas before it began no invasion of India was ever stopped, since it took place no invasion of India has ever succeeded. Thus the happiness and the very lives of the toiling millions of Hindustan rest upon that power which our complacent reformers are labouring to withdraw."

Lord Sydenham, speaking in the House of Lords, 24 October, 1917, said of Mrs. Besant:

"She wrote a book which contained more reckless defiance of facts than I have ever seen compressed into the same small space, and in her paper *New India,* she said that "India was a perfect Paradise" for 5,000 years before our advent, that it had become 'a perfect Hell' owing to the "brutal British Bureaucracy."… Well might one of these judges point out that this pernicious writing must tend to encourage assassination by removing public detestation of such a crime…"

And as Sir Charles Spencer, retired I.C.S., writing to the *Morning Post,* 11 September, 1933, said:

"... No sane Government can tolerate the presence of anarchical bodies in its midst. Therefore, the only sound policy is to treat the Bengalee terrorists as Government once treated the Thugs. A special department should be formed for tracking and hunting down these pests of societies, and it should be made an offence, punishable with death, to belong to an organisation whose creed is assassination of officials."

For those who do not know the history of the Thugs, the following brief account may be enlightening, showing the real condition of India before the advent of the British, giving the lie to Mrs. Besant's mischievous statement.

According to C. W. Stewart's introduction to the 1916 edition of Meadows Taylor's *Confessions of a Thug*, which was published in 1839, the Thugs were a secret hereditary guild of murderers, who strangled and plundered, under, they said, the protection of the goddess Kalee, and these murders were regarded as a duty and an act of worship. Each gang carried a sacred pickaxe, the original of which was said to be Kalee's tooth, and upon this pickaxe an oath was taken which involved terrible penalties if broken. Kalee also gave her votaries a rib for a knife and the hem of her robe as a strangling cloth. The actual origin of Thuggee is unknown, but Sleeman, in *Rambles and Recollections*, tells of a Thug "saint" living in Delhi at the beginning of the fourteenth century who possessed vast supplies of money. He was regarded as the founder, and Thugs made pilgrimages to his tomb. He came from Persia, where, it has been suggested, he had been a disciple of "the Old Man of the Mountain," the head of the assassins who frequented the shores of the Caspian Sea about 1100. Thuggee existed for at least five centuries in India, but the Company's Government only became aware of the outrages in 1799, and it took thirty years to realise the extent of these practices.

According to Meadows Taylor, so many Army men disappeared on their way to and from their homes in 1810 that the Government issued a warning, and tracked certain of the assassins down in 1812. It was not, however, until 1820, when 'Thuggee Sleeman' was posted in Sagar and Nerbudda territories, that the Government recognised the Thugs to be a distinct criminal class operating simultaneously throughout

India. In 1829 special officers were appointed, a campaign against them began, and many of the gangs were dispersed. In 1840 Sleeman issued a report with a Thug map; much of his information was received through twenty Thugs or professional assassins turned approvers, among others the notorious Feringhea; their statements were verified by the disinterment of the bodies.

This report speaks of gangs of Thugs who ranged the highroads, and under the guise of friendship won the confidence of unsuspecting travellers and, after accompanying them for several stages to some isolated spot or bhil, murdered them by strangulation and plundered their property. Meadows Taylor noted that outside villages and towns the huts and houses of hermits, fakirs, and religious mendicants were used by the Thugs, the fakirs enticing the victims into their gardens or surrounding groves on the plea of giving them rest and shelter.

The difficulty was to convict the murderers, as the victims generally came from great distances, and relatives and other witnesses would not travel so far to the courts near which the murder took place. However, separate courts were formed where each witness gave evidence in his own neighbourhood; this proved a great success. Many leaders and leading members of the old gangs, however, remained at large, and as Sleeman said: 'All these persons would return to their old trade and teach it to their sons or needy and dissolute neighbours, and thus reorganise their gangs should our pressure be relaxed.' From 1831 to 1837, of these gangs 1,059 were transported to Penang, 412 were hanged, 87 imprisoned for life, and 483 turned approvers. ·

The whole matter was warmly taken up by the then Governor-General, Lord William Bentinck, and the Supreme Council, and highly intelligent officers were appointed to superintend the execution of the measures for the suppression of Thuggee. The tracking down was continued until 1860, and up to 1904 there was a Superintendent of Thuggee and Dacoity, after which date it was entrusted to the Central Criminal Intelligence Department.

We might well ask ourselves, do the germs of Thuggee still exist ready to be brought to life by Soviet agents and National

Congressmen in order to further their ambitious political dreams? The position was very clearly stated by Mr. Ashmead Bartlett in the *Daily Telegraph, 20* October, 1930, and seems still to hold good:

> "The situation is infinitely graver than is generally appreciated, and it is rapidly developing into a gigantic race conflict.
>
> ... The Hindu urban intelligentsia are determined to create a complete Hindu "Raj," clearing the British officials, civil and military, out of the country, confiscating British commercial interests, and repudiating public debts contracted under British rule... Afghanistan and Soviet Russia would surely join in the general break up ... once our stranglehold on the North-West Frontier ceases to exist."

In September 1913 a small band of Mrs. Besant's workers created the group known as "The Brothers of Service"; they were to seek freedom under the British Crown, and among other things were asked to promise: to promote union among the workers in the fields of spiritual, educational, social, and political progress, under the headship and direction of the Indian National Congress. On 2 January, 1914, the campaign for Home Rule was definitely begun, when the weekly review, *The Commonweal,* was launched, in which was the declaration:

> "In Political Reform we aim at the building up of complete Self-government, from Village Councils through District and Municipal Boards and Provincial Legislative Assemblies, to a National Parliament, equal in its powers to the legislative bodies of the Self-governing Colonies..."

In the spring of 1914 Mrs. Besant went to England to try to form an Indian Party in Parliament; failing in this, she held a meeting in Queen's Hall, London, with Earl Brassey in the chair, to form an auxiliary Home Rule League for India, and this materialised in 1915. On her return to India she bought a daily paper, published 14 July, 1914, renaming it *New India.* In 1917, after her internment in Ootacamund, she, already Home Rule President, was elected President of the National Congress. In February 1919, the Home Rule League split because Gandhi started "passive resistance" against the Rowlatt Act. That was stopped, only to be followed by his Non-Co-operation movement, April 1920; Gandhi could not control his followers.

At Delhi, 1920, the National Congress carried a resolution demanding: (I) that the principle of Self-determination should be applied to India; (2) the removal of all hindrances to free discussion; (3) an Act of Parliament establishing complete responsible government in India, and that in the reconstruction of Imperial policy, (4) India should be placed on an equality with the Self-governing Dominions. As Mrs. Besant wrote:

> "The second point has been almost carried out; the third and fourth have not. But the Commonwealth of India Bill will carry them out when it becomes an Act. It has been delayed by the breaking up of political parties caused by the Non-Co-operation movement, now dead [1926]."

In Bombay, 28 August, 1924, she said to Sir Michael O'Dwyer:

> "... I think we may fairly say we have made India a burning question in the political life of England. We found the Labour Party entirely with us..."

She therefore looked to the Labour Party to put through the Commonwealth of India Bill. In February 1922, the practical framing of the proposed Constitution for India by Indians was initiated in a discussion in the Political Section of the 1921 Club, Madras, on the method of winning Swaraj. The draft was submitted to the Convention sitting at Cawnpore, April 1925, and finally to a Drafting Committee in Madras, consisting of the Hon. Mr. C. P. Ramaswami Alyar, Messrs. Shiva Rao, Sri Ram, Yadunandan Prasad, and Dr. Annie Besant, who were to see it through the press and publish it in the name of the Convention. In 1925 it was sent to England and was laid before leading members of the Labour Party, backed by them, read a first time in the House of Commons, and ordered to be printed. It then went before the Executive Committee of the Parliamentary Labour Party, and finally passed unanimously. It thus passed into the hands of the future Labour Government, and·was put on the list of Bills balloted for as an official measure.

The following are a few points of this Commonwealth of India Bill as given by Mrs. Besant in the Appendix of her book *India:*

Bond or Free?, 1926, from which we have drawn all the above data concerning the National Congress, etc.:

"India will be placed on an equal footing with the Self-governing Dominions, sharing their responsibilities and their privileges... 'Parliament' shall mean only the Parliament of the Commonwealth of India... *Defence:* There will be a Defence Commission with a majority of Indians thereon, every five years appointed by the Viceroy in consultation with his Cabinet... No revenue of India may be spent on any branch of Defence Forces in which Indians are ineligible for holding commissioned rank. As soon as the Commission recommends favourably, Parliament may pass an Act to undertake the full responsibility of Defence. *Executive:* There will be a Cabinet in the Government of India consisting of the Prime Minister and not less than seven Ministers of State, who will be collectively responsible for the administration of the Commonwealth. The Prime Minister will be appointed by the Viceroy, and the other Ministers on the nomination of the Prime Minister. The Viceroy will be *temporarily* in charge of the Defence Forces. In all matters except Defence the Viceroy will act only upon the advice of the Cabinet... *Secretary of State:* The powers and functions of the Secretary of State and the Secretary of State in Council over the revenues and the administration of India will be transferred to the Commonwealth Executive... *Alteration of the Constitution:* Parliament will have power to alter the Constitution..."

According to the *Chicago Tribune,* 24 August, 1929:

"Dr. Besant, Theosophical leader, came to Chicago for the world congress of Theosophists ... in the Stevens Hotel. Dr. Besant has spent years in India teaching Theosophy [and incidentally politics!]. She said that recently she had been trying to help India obtain political measures by which the country may throw off the 'yoke of England ... if a revolt, she said, were to flare up, the English, with their bombs from the air and their land and water machines of war, would simply cut them down like grain before a scythe'."

In his *Life of Annie Besant,* 1929, Geoffrey West (p. 249) speaks of the meeting held in Queen's Hall, London, 23 July, 1924, in honour of Mrs. Besant's fifty years of public work.

"Among the speakers were George Lansbury, Ben Tillett, Ben Turner, Margaret Bondfield, Mrs. Pethick Lawrence, and John Scurr; messages were read from Lord Haldane, Ramsay

MacDonald, Philip Snowden, and Bernard Shaw and others paid tribute in print to her work, as Socialist, politician, reformer, educationalist, and religious teacher..."

And her work in every aspect was ruled and regulated by her. "Masters" and the mysterious "Inner Government of the World," not for the good of India, but for the fulfilment of their world schemes.

And what do her followers say to-day? In *The Morning Post*, 16 *September*, 1933, we read:

> "At its Lahore session in January 1930, the Congress passed two resolutions: one for establishing Indian independence by severing all connection with Great Britain, and another repudiating India's public debts, especially to the British bondholders. Since 1930 independence has remained the creed of the Congress, and the repudiation of debts is still one of the most important items in the Congress programme."

And as Gandhi said in writing to Jawaharlal Nehru:

> "... The Princes must surrender much of their power and become popular representatives of the people... Nationalism must be consistent with progressive internationalism, so we must range ourselves with the progressive forces of the world."

According to Mrs. Besant: "Shaping their aspirations towards Nationhood as an integral part of the Coming World Empire."

Everywhere we see the spread of this principle of *universality* replacing real patriotism, individual and national initiative by a flaccid international Pacifism, Socialism, unification of all peoples! As another example we have the *Threefold Movement*. Its first European meeting was held in the City Temple, July 1927, although its earliest movement, "The Union of the East and the West," was initiated some twenty years ago. The London Committee included members of the Socialist and Labour Party, International Peace Movement, Free Religious Movements, and the Theosophical Society. At their meeting, 17 July, 1930, their subject was, "World Unity as seen by the representatives of eight religions and seven countries." Their "Anthem of the Universal" ran: "One Cosmic Brotherhood... Race, colour, creed and caste fade in a dreamy past ... all life is one." Bahaism, Buddhism,

Shintoism, Christian, Hindu, and Jew were all represented, and the Jew gave the cabalistic key in saying: "Religion was the symbol by which we endeavoured to understand *Nature*." Their aim was realisation of Peace and Brotherhood to bring about a World Commonwealth. The mainspring of the movement, Charles Frederick Weller, an American, spoke of the Parliament of Religions held in Chicago in 1893 and another proposed for 1933.

In September 1893, on the occasion of the Chicago Exhibition, there was held the famous "Parliament of Religions," to which all religions or pseudo-religions were invited to send delegates. Among those present were Swami Vivekananda, who perverted the Hindu doctrine of the *Vedanta* under pretext of adapting it to Western mentality. He had successes in America and Australia, and was followed by still more daring adapters, such as "the ineffable Swami Yogananda." Mrs. Besant represented Theosophy, and she was accompanied by Chakravarti, founder of the *Yoga Samaj*, who was a Mongolian more or less Hinduised, and was a remarkable hypnotist, whilst Mrs. Besant was said to be a good subject.

Also there was Dharmapala, a Buddhist representing the *Maha Bodhi Samaj* of Colombo, Ceylon (Society of Great Wisdom). Another was Dr. J. D. Buck, one of the most active members of what is now called the *Sadol* Movement in America. Most of the other delegates represented innumerable Protestant sects and various heterogeneous elements. From this an attempt was made to arrange another, "The Congress of Humanity," to be held in Paris in 1900, representing all religions and seekers having as a common aim the progress of humanity, preparing for future unity and peace on earth. Nothing eventuated until 1913, when it met under the name of "Congress of Religious Progress," and there Edouard Schure represented Dr. Steiner's movement, a secession from Mrs. Besant.

The Threefold Movement is the Union of the East and West; League of Neighbours; and Fellowship of Faiths. It stands for the realisation of peace and brotherhood, to hasten the coming of the Commonwealth of the World, to live now and here in the Kingdom (or democracy) of God. The Bahai Movement, which is a strong supporter of the above, is said to unite the streams of Judaism, Christianity, and Islamism, like the Druses. They also claim that their Prophet foreshadowed the League of Nations, a supreme tribunal as follows:

> "About fifty years ago Baha'u'llah commanded the people to establish universal peace, and summoned all the nations to 'the divine banquet of international arbitration' so that the questions of boundaries, of national honour, and property, and of vital interests between nations, might be decided by an arbitral court of justice."

To repeat what the *Archives-israélites* wrote in 1861:

> "*L'Alliance-israélite-universelle...* addresses itself to all religions... It desires to penetrate into all religions as it has penetrated into all countries. How many nations have disappeared! How many religions will in turn vanish! *Israel will not cease to exist...* the religion of Israel will not perish; it is the unity of God."

The second unit of this Threefold Movement, the "League of Neighbours," was founded in the U.S.A. in 1920, by Charles Frederick Weller, a Socialist writer, and its aim is to develop through neighbourly service the new consciousness of human unity. Nevertheless, it was later denied the use of high schools in New York, because of its subversive connections. It was endorsed by President Wilson, President Harding, Rabbi Wise, and many well-known Socialists. We know the part taken both by President Wilson and Rabbi Wise in the establishment of the League of Nations.

It is interesting to note what the Jewish writer, Dr. Alfred Nossig, wrote of Socialism and the League of Nations in his book *Integrates Judentum:*

> "The modern Socialist Movement is in great part a work of the Jews, who impress on it the mark of their brains; it was they who took a preponderating part in the directing of the first Socialist republic, although the controlling Jewish Socialists were mostly far from Judaism... The present world Socialism forms the first step of the accomplishment of Mosaism, the start of the realisation of the future state of the world announced by our prophets. It is not till there shall be a League of Nations; it is not till its allied armies shall be employed in an effective manner for the protection of the feeble that we can hope that the Jews will be able to develop without

impediment in Palestine, their national State; and equally it is only a League of Nations penetrated with the Socialist spirit that will render possible for us the enjoyment of our international necessities as well as our national ones..."

As we know, Mrs. Besant's Co-Masonry was derived from the Mixed Masonry founded in France by Maria Deraismes, supported by Dr. Georges Martin, and which was officially launched in 1894 as the *Droit Humain*. Maria Deraismes had been initiated in 1882, contrary to the constitutions, by the Lodge *Les Libres Penseurs* of Pecq, for which unconstitutional act the Lodge was put into abeyance and the initiation declared null by the *Grande Loge Symbolique Ecossaise*.

In *Etude Abrégée de la Franc-maçonnerie mixte et de son organisation* the French Mason, Dr. Georges Martin, gives a report of a first initiation of several women, 14 March, 1893. They

> "met at 45 rue de Sévres, to constitute a new Masonic obedience in France, under the Presidency of Sister Maria Deraismes, who was initiated Freemason, 14 January, 1882, at the Lodge Symbolique Ecossaise Mixte, *Les Libres Penseurs,* de l'Or ... du Pecq (Seine et Oise). F∴ Georges Martin, who assisted at the Masonic initiation of Sister Maria Deraismes at the Lodge *Les Libres Penseurs,* was present, and desired to help her with his counsels in the creation of the new Masonic Obediente which this Sister would found in France à l'Or ... de Paris."

One of the signed promises required from the postulant was:

> "I promise to reveal nothing whatsoever of the Masonic secrets entrusted to me."

He further tells us:

> "Mixed Masonry has created no new Rite. What distinguishes it from all others is that in place of admitting men only, women are equally admitted; it teaches the methods of recognition of the Ancient and Accepted Scottish Rite, such as were adopted by the Grand Constitutions of I May, 1786, and consecrated by the Universal Convent which met at Lausanne, 22 September, 1875."

Further, he says that with most Masonic powers Mixed Masonry has no relations, the brothers and sisters meet regularly under charter from the *Suprême Conseil Universal Mixte,* constituted in Paris, 11 May, 1899. Albert Lantoine informs us that twice attempts were made to get women recognised by the Grand Orient of France: at the Convent of the Grand Orient, 1900, the voting was 93 for it and 140 against it; in 1901, there were 104 for and 134 against it. According to Lantoine, Dr. Martin was delighted, as complete victory would have ruined his plans, as he wanted to maintain the *Droit Humain,* sincerely believing that the penetration of women into Masonry risked killing it! whilst an obedience apart, but recognised as regular, would consolidate it without compromising it. It was not until 1920 that the General Assembly of the Grand Orient of France recognised the *Droit Humain,* admitting the men into its lodges, but still excluding the women.

At first the *Droit Humain* only practised three degrees, but later introduced the 33 degrees of Scottish Rite. Mixed Masonry was organised according to the general rules of exclusively masculine Freemasonry. There were the four Masonries: (I) Blue Masonry — I to 3 degrees; (2) Red Masonry, the Chapters of the Knights Rose-Croix — 4 to 18 degrees; (3) Black Masonry, the Areopagi of the Knights of Kadosch — 19 to 30 degrees; (4) White Masonry, Administrative — 31, 32, 33 degrees. The Suprême Conseil was the keystone of this Masonry and was recruited only from among the Grand Inspectors-General of the 33rd degree.

This Masonry spread in England, Holland, Switzerland, and the United States, and on 26 September, 1902, the first English Lodge was formed in London under the name of *Human Duty.* In this Mrs. Besant was initiated, and rose rapidly to the highest degrees and offices. Yarker writes in his book, *The Arcane Schools,* 1909:

> "It may be mentioned here that, January 1903, Mrs. Annie Besant established in London a S.G.C., 33rd degree, conferring all degrees from the I[st] to the 33rd indiscriminately upon Men and Women; she received her constitution from India, a S.G.C. which had its authority from a dissension in the S.G.C. of the 33rd degree for France, Tilly's constitution. It has added only to the Ritual a 'Dharma' Lecture, which compares Masonry with secret societies of India and takes the name of Co-Masonry."

She founded the Lodge at Adyar, in India, under the name of *Rising Sun;* became Vice-president of the *Suprême Conseil* in France, and a national delegate for Britain and her dependencies. She then organised the Co-Masonry, and having obtained certain concessions from the *Suprême Conseil,* she, under pretext of adaptation to Anglo-Saxon mentality, made statutes distinctly different from those customary in France. Among others she retained the use of the volume of the Scriptures in the lodges; also the formula, "To the Glory of the Great Architect of the Universe," which had been suppressed by the Grand Orient in 1877 and replaced in French Mixed Masonry by 'To the Glory of Humanity.' In 1913 a Grand Council was appointed as head of British Co-Masonry, with Mrs. Besant as Grand Master, assisted by Ursula Bright, James L. Wedgwood as Grand Secretary, and Francesca Arundale as representative for India. On 21 September, 1909, Mrs. Besant installed the Lodge of Chicago.

In France the Theosophists apparently soon had an assured preponderance, and hoped in time that London would become the central organism of Co-Masonry Universal. On 19 February, 1922, an alliance between the Grand Orient and Co-Masonry was celebrated in the Grand Temple of the *Droit Humain* in Paris, but this link was broken by a decision of the Council of the Grand Orient, 13 September, 1930, according to the Convent of Grand Orient of France, 1930. Mrs. Besant, before she died, was Ire Lieut. G. Commandeur du Supreme Conseil Mixte Internationale du Droit Humain. As their 'World Teacher,' Krishnamurti, taught 'There is no God but yourself,' deification was the aim of Co-Masonry. According to Leadbeater, in *The Hidden Life in Freemasonry,* the aim of Freemasonry is to vivify the force centres in man and awaken the inner senses. Speaking of these force or nerve centres,

he says:

"When quite undeveloped they appear as small circles about two inches in diameter, glowing dully in the ordinary man, but when awakened and vivified they appear as blazing coruscating saucers much increased in size... The seven centres ... are:

(1) the base of the spine;

(2) the spleen;

(3) the navel or solar plexus;

(4) the heart;

(5) the throat;

(6) the space between the eyes;

(7) the top of the head...

When at all in action these centres show signs of rapid rotation, and into each of these centres rushes a force from the higher world (that is, the universal life force which illuminises and is said to awaken the inner senses. It is so-called deification)."

In, his *Results of Initiation*, Steiner, speaking of these same centres or chakras, to develop which is the aim of his *Occult Science*, says: 'When developed permits of intercourse with beings of higher worlds ... white occultists.' No doubt the Great White Brotherhood, the Inner Government of all Illuminised and Theosophical movements. In their official organ, *Freemasonry Universal*, Winter Solstice, 1929, the Co-Masons say:

> "The Holy Royal Arch signifies the awakening of the Kundalini... Freemasonry (exoteric) is the outer shell from which much secret knowledge has been withdrawn... Co-Masonry is leading us to the Light... Through our own intuition [we] make the great discovery of *Ourselves*... The Quest of the Hidden God..."

They look upon the Holy Royal Arch as occult and mystical, "stimulating and arousing the Fire (kundalini) and leading to the discovery of the Divinity within us." Again the cabalistic deified man. According to the Mason, W. L. Wilmshurst, in *The Masonic Initiation*, who writes like an Illuminatus, 'Royal Arch Masonry was introduced into England in 1778 by a Jewish Brother, Moses Michael Hayes.'

Here appears to be the reason why Co-Masonry is to be a force for the so-called service of India, preparing illuminised tools for the 'Inner Government of the World's' Great Plan; and "the Masters have assured her (Mrs. Besant) that Dominion Status for India is part of the Great Plan, and she knows that she will not pass away until that freedom is accomplished" *(Theosophist,* October 1928).

The election of Dr. George Sydney Arundale, June 1934, took place at the Blavatsky Hall, Madras, as President of the Theosophical Society, in succession to the late Dr. Annie Besant, who passed away before the fate of India was decided. He was born in Surrey fifty-five years ago, and was from boyhood under Leadbeater's influence. He was headmaster of the Central Hindu College at Benares, and on 11 January, 1911, he founded the *Order of the Rising Sun,* which a few months later was organised as the *Order of the Star in the East,* with Krishnamurti as head and Mrs. Besant as Protector. Krishnamurti was to be prepared for the manifestation of 'Lord Maitreya,' variously known, according to the Theosophists, as: Orpheus, Hermes, Trismegistus, Vyasa, Krishna, Buddha, Zoroaster, and even Christ." Leadbeater and Arundale were his teachers. In 1913 the latter, as Principal of the College, in a circular letter addressed to a group of teachers and boys, which was published in the Allahabad *Leader,* 13 June, expressed unqualified devotion to Mrs. Besant as one about to become one of the greatest rulers of the world of Gods and men. It was then publicly alleged that the College was not Hindu, but Theosophical. Arundale and some of the teachers and boys resigned in a body, and the Board of Trustees handed the College over to a Committee of the projected Hindu University.

Arundale was also one of those interned during the War along with Mrs. Besant, in Ootacamund, November 1917. In December 1916, Mrs. Besant's Home Rule League had been endorsed at Lucknow by the Congress and the Muslim League, and she said: "I go into enforced silence and imprisonment because I love India and have striven to arouse her before it was too late. I am old, but I believe that I shall see India win Home Rule before I die." As Bishop Arundale, of the Liberal Catholic Church, he was one of the twelve apostles, including his wife, Rukmini Devi, a high-caste Hindu woman, chosen for the "World Teacher." He has also held many services in London. Further, in *Freemasonry Universal,* the official organ of Co-Masonry, Part 3, 1929, we read: Eastern Administration Grand Secretary, The V. Ills. Bro.

G. S. Arundale, 33rd degree, Adyar, Madras, India (including Burma).

From this Co-Masonry there have been two schisms at least: one in 1908, when a number of members, who objected to the introduction of Eastern occultism into Masonry, formed themselves into a separate body under the name of "Ancient Masonry," working only the Craft degrees according to the Grand Lodge of England. This group was for long penetrated by the influence and illuminism of the Stella Matutina and the R.R. et A.C., and as late as 1923-24 not only its Grand Master, Mrs. H—, but several of its members were advanced adepts of that Order and of that of Steiner. From these "Ancient Masons," in turn, a further secession took place, apparently about 1914, adopting the name of "Honourable Fraternity of Ancient Freemasons," exclusively for women and now established at St. Ermins, Westminster. A much later breakaway from Mrs. Besant's Co-Masonry was a group led by Miss Bothwell Gosse, who objected to the Co-Masonic innovations. Eventually she formed the group "Ancient and Accepted Masonry" for Men and Women, apparently working the thirty-three degrees. In her booklet on *The Ancient and Accepted Rite*, she sums up its supposed origins:

> "Thus we find that the nucleus of this Rite arose in France; it was taken to America by Stephen: Morin and established there; Frederick the Great re-organised it and gave it a Constitution; it was lost to Europe by the French Revolution; it was brought back to France by de Grasse-Tilly and reconstituted in Paris; from thence it has spread over the whole world."

As we have shown, most Grand Lodges, except the English Grand Lodge, are represented in the A.M.I., that subversive *Association maçonnique internationale,* and Georges Loïc, in the *R.I.S.S.,* I March, 1933, stated: "The Supreme Councils are all issues of the Supreme Council founded, 31 March, 18o1, at Charleston by the Jews Dalcho and Mitchell and by Comte de Grasse-Tilly."

Much controversy has, from time to time, raged round some of these names; documents and proofs, if not entirely absent, are somewhat rare, leaving in the thoughtful mind a sense of uncertainty and even doubt. The well-known French Grand

Lodge Masonic authority, Albert Lantoine, is perhaps wise when concluding in his book, *La Franc-maçonnerie chez elle,* 1927:

> "In Masonry one must accept such a reasonable opinion as that of the balanced-minded Reghellini de Schio, who, living at the moment when the discussions on Masonic Supremacy were so heated, wrote: 'If one would speak with documents in hand, what Rite or what Supreme Chief of the Order of that Rite could go back to a non-equivocal origin of its power? What Mason, what Rite even, holds the guiding thread to free himself from the labyrinth of all these origins?'"

We read in the *Daily Telegraph,* 26 September, 1933, that the "Honourable Fraternity of Ancient Freemasons," for women alone, a group which seceded from the 'Ancient Masons' in 1914, had removed to new headquarters at St. Ermins, Westminster. The opening and dedication ceremony was conducted by the Grand Master, Mrs. Elizabeth Boswell Reid, who, along with Mrs. Seton Challen, founded the secession; if one might so express it, she was assisted by Mrs. Seton Challen, Deputy Grand Master, and Mrs. Piers Dyer, the Provincial Grand Master. More than 200 members attended from many parts of the country. Other members of the Fraternity were Mrs. Messervy, Mrs. Bank Martin, Mrs. Crawford Munro, and Miss Lata Coventry. They worked the Craft degrees, the Holy Royal Arch, and hoped later to work the Rose-Croix. Its official organ is *The Ray.* Mrs. Boswell Reid died 21 November, 1933, and was succeeded by Mrs. Seton Challen. The former held the titles: the Most Worshipful the Grand Master; the Most Excellent Supreme Grand Zerubbabel; the Most Worshipful Grand Master Mark Masonry. ··

According to the *R.I.S.S.,* I May, 1934, the Occultist Masonic authority F.·. Oswald Wirth, wrote a curious article in *Le Symbolisme.* He evoked the "Honourable Fraternity of Ancient Freemasons" in England. The English women who are not afraid to copy the men have adopted "masculine rites, customs, regulations, insignia and even titles... They work impeccably like men in their own Temple at Westminster, and have economic advantages over the men, as witness the sobriety of their ritualistic feasts." He concludes that the initiation of the woman is more subtle than that of the man, and says:

"Women, learn to be purely and emphatically feminine. So long as you are led by us you will fail in your mission, which is to precede us on the moral road and the realisation of good. You are the priestesses of the cult which Humanity awaits. To prepare you for your civilising work you must have a real initiation developing your feminine nature, therefore entirely contrary to a parody of the masculine rites."

In *Americanism*, the New Order of the Ages, it says: "In this Age woman will rise to her rightful place as the *intuitive spiritual* (psychic) *teacher of the race* and Queen of the home… nor will she usurp male prerogative, but will make the earth a heavenly dwelling place." In other words, she is to be the passive instrument or medium through which the mysterious power behind Masonry rules and directs the world, the man will actively carry out the directions! As Oswald Wirth wrote:

"Many Masons imagine they understand Masonry when they do not even suspect the existence of its mysteries and its esotericism" *(Le Livre de l'apprenti).*

Again, he explains:

"Our two Pillars besides are connected with the ancient cult of generation which was the most universal manifestation of primitive humanity… All that relates to generation remained sacred so long as the religions of life prevailed whose ideal is earthly, but which were supplanted by the religions of death ready to promise happiness beyond the tomb. Now Masonry proceeds from the cults of life whose symbols it has preserved" *(Le Livre du compagnon).*

Further:

"Freemasonry takes great care not to define the Grand Architect, and leaves to each of its adepts full latitude to form an idea of it conformable to his faith or philosophy" *(L'Idéal initiatique).*

Moreover:

"Let us guard ourselves, therefore, from yielding to that idleness of mind which confounds the Grand Architect of initiates with the God of believers" *(Le Livre du maître).*

To take another, the Very Powerful Sovereign Grand Commander Brother Jean Marie Raymond: "We have desired to crystallise immortality in the symbol of the Grand Architect of the Universe, a kind of emblem of Cosmic Unity, supreme universal intelligence, which is nothing more than *Life* itself." Therefore like the Cabala, which is one of its bases, Masonry is pantheistic and its aim is to illuminate or deify man by means of astral or cosmic intoxication.

Mrs. Besant's "God" was pantheistic, this lifeforce in all nature, and her Christ was this astral force which illuminises; the same ideas are the bases of Theosophy, Rose-Croix, Masonry, and all Yoga. And what has been the attitude of the Grand Lodge of England to women in Masonry? (I) According to Albert Lantoine, the Anderson Constitution, 1723, says:

> "Slaves, women, immoral and dishonoured persons cannot be admitted, but only men of good reputation."

(2) On 3 September, 1919, the Grand Lodge Board of General Purposes issued the following: "... All such bodies which admit women to membership are clandestine and irregular; it is necessary to caution brothers against being inadvertently led to violate their Obligation by becoming members of them or attending their meetings..." (3) United Grand Lodge of England codified, 4 September, 1929, eight conditions for recognition of Masonic obediences throughout the world, one being: that the members of the Grand Lodge, as well as those of individual lodges, must be exclusively men, and that the obedience holds no relations of any kind whatsoever with mixed lodges, where the bodies admit women among their members *(An. Maç. Uni.,* 1930). (4) *The Morning Post,* 7 June, 1934, wrote:

> "The business before the meeting of the United Grand Lodge, in London, yesterday, included a motion for the exclusion of a brother who, it was reported, had attended meetings of an "irregular" body known as Co-Masons, which admitted women... having refused to take notice of a warning as to the probable result of his action, his expulsion had to be recommended, and Grand Lodge unanimously, and without discussion, accepted the motion. The Duke of Connaught, Grand Master, presided at the meeting, and his presence was greatly appreciated by the 1,800 brethren who were present."

Finally, as Oswald Wirth writes:

> "To become as Divinity, such was the aim of the Ancient Mysteries... To-day the programme of Initiation has not changed."

CHAPTER IX

RUDOLF STEINER AND ANTHROPOSOPHY

IN a leading article, 14 September, 1922, the *Patriot* warns its readers against 'The Subterranean War' and writes:

"For those who desire to learn we publish to-day the first of a series of articles by "G.G." (or 'Dargon'), a writer who has made a study of secret societies. The purpose of 'The Anatomy of Revolution' is not to take the reader deeply into any part of the subject, but to give a general and historical view of that complex of subversive organisation which is working for the destruction of Christianity, of Civilisation, and of the British Empire. The writer, who is a true Briton and a good patriot, has one purpose only — to warn the British public of the unsuspected danger which, as he believes and we believe also, imminently threatens it."

To quote G.G.:

"Here we must note that there has always been among the Arcane societies a dual movement — on the one hand mystical, on the other political. Such esoteric bodies as the Fraternity of the Rosy-Cross, the Martinists, the Swedenborgians, and Theosophists have consisted no doubt largely of harmless enthusiasts to whom mysticism or magic appealed. But they have also been used, as the cover for political intrigue, and as a net wherein to catch, test, and select persons who could be used for subversive ends. For it is one of the methods of the revolutionary directorate to use, wherever possible, harmless bodies as their cloak, and innocent people as their unconscious agents...

"I may refer briefly to the existence of an offshoot of the Theosophical Society, known as the Anthroposophical Society. This was formed as the result of a schism in the ranks of the Theosophists, by a man of Jewish birth who was connected with one of the modern branches of the Carbonari. Not only so, but in association with another Theosophist he is engaged in organising certain singular commercial undertakings not unconnected with Communist propaganda; almost precisely in the manner in which 'Count St. Germain' organised his dyeworks and other commercial ventures with a like purpose. And this queer business group has its connections with the Irish Republican movement... and also with another mysterious group which was founded by Jewish "Intellectuals" in France about four years ago (about 1918), and which includes in its membership many well-known politicians, scientists, university professors, and literary men in France, Germany, America, and England. It is a secret society ... although nominally a "Right Wing" society, it is in direct touch with members of the Soviet Government Russia..."

We have from time to time written of Dr. Rudolf Steiner's gnostic teachings and political activities. We now give a short summary of Edouard Schure's introduction to his translation of Steiner's book *Mystère Chrétien et les Mystères Antiques, 1908*. Schuré considered Steiner's teaching most luminous — it was so called Christian Illuminism — but much later left him because of his political activities, of which he did not approve. Later again, he returned to the fold. Our interest in this sketch of Steiner's life is that it shows how, from early years, he was watched, astrally prepared, and directed by some mysterious Master and initiator whose name and mission are not revealed.

According to Schuré, who was a Jew, Steiner was born in Upper Austria in 1861, and his youth was spent on the confines of Styria, the Carpathians, and Hungary. At the age of fifteen he made the acquaintance of a learned botanist who "had the gift of seeing the vital principle of the plants, their etheric bodies, and what occultists call the elementals of the vegetable world." His calm, coldly scientific conversation only further excited the curiosity of the young man." Steiner knew later that this strange man was an envoy from the Master, whom he did not yet know, but who was to become his real initiator, and who already supervised him from afar." From his talks with the botanist he was soon convinced that the basis of the "Great Universal" was the double current which constitutes the movement of the world the flux and reflux of the universal life-force, this occult and astral current which is the great propeller of life, with its hierarchy of powers. From the age of eighteen Steiner felt the double current: "He had from that time the irrefutable sensation of occult powers who acted behind and through him to direct him. He listened to this force and followed its warnings, because he felt himself profoundly in accord with it."

When nineteen he met his Master, for so long sensed, who was one of those powerful men who live unknown to the world in order to accomplish a mission; ostensibly they do not act upon human events. Incognito is the condition of their strength, making their action only more efficacious, "For they arouse, prepare, and direct those who act in the public eye." And Steiner's mission, according to himself, was: "To link together Science and Religion. Bring God into Science, and Nature into Religion, and so fecundate anew Art and Life." His Master was eminently a spiritual male as opposed to Steiner's more feminine sensibilities; he was a formidable dominator, for whom individuals scarcely existed. He spared neither himself nor others, his will was like a bullet from a gun which went straight to its aim, and swept all from its path.

Such was the powerful mind which dominated and used Steiner as a mere automaton, pulling the strings as his terrible ambitions required. For Steiner 1881 to 1891 was a period of study and preparation at Vienna; from 1891 to 1901 a time of struggle and combat at Weimar; from 1901 to 1907 a time of action and organisation at Berlin. About 1890 Steiner said: "The occult powers who were directing me obliged me imperceptibly to penetrate into the then current ideas of spiritualists." He came in touch with Nietzsche and Haeckel, who oriented him intellectually. As Schuré said: "He had the presentiment that in the incontestable discoveries of the naturalist he would find the surest basis of evolutionary spiritualism and rational Theosophy." Steiner, therefore, entered into contemporary materialism, and armed himself for his mission; in 1902 he found his battle-ground and support in the Theosophical Society, and became Secretary-General of the German section. In 1913 he left Mrs. Besant because of the Alcyone case, and founded the Anthroposophical Society.

As Schuré wrote:

"By his first Master and by the Fraternity to which he was associated, Steiner belonged to another school of occultism, that is, to Western esoteric Christianity and more especially Rosicrucian initiation… The tradition of esoteric Christianity, properly speaking, is directly and uninterruptedly attached to the famous and mysterious Manes, founder of Manicheism, who lived in Persia in the fourth century."

Brought up by Magi, Manes became Christian (Gnostic); his doctrine was: (I) the Master Jesus, prophet of Nazareth, was only the organ and interpreter of the Christ, who was the "arcanum of the planetary Word" — Solar manifestation; (2) he taught reincarnation and the numerous ascending (planetary) existences of the human soul; (3) what was called "evil" was only a necessary ingredient in the general economy of the world, a stimulant, a ferment of universal evolution!

Manes's disciples spread to Palestine, Greece, Italy, Gaul, Scythia, the Danube, and Africa. His doctrine was for centuries propagated by oral tradition, often under different names, Schuré writes, such as the Cathari, Albigenses, the Templars, and the Brothers of Saint John of Jerusalem. In the fifteenth century esoteric Christianity, inspired by the same tradition, became more laic and scientific under the influence of the Cabala and Alchemy, and it was about then that Christian Rosenkreutz founded the Order of the Rose-Croix. Rudolf Steiner as a Rose-Croix practised and taught Western occultism as opposed to Eastern. He did not believe in the annihilation of the body by asceticism — it must be trained and become as a magnet attracting and making use of the required forces.

Such is the account of Steiner, his Master and work as given by Edouard Schuré. The result of Yoga, meditation and processes for awakening the kundalini, whether Western or Eastern, is the same in all groups working under unknown Masters; it means that gradually the Master takes possession of the adept's mind and impresses his own will upon it, so that an advanced initiate, such as Steiner, would work under the impetus of the hidden Master and for his ends alone. As the so called Tibetan Master of Mrs. Alice Bailey, theosophist and occultist, New York, explains, contact with the Master is recognised by peculiar vibrations: (I) at the top of the spine; (2) in the forehead (pineal gland, where the adept's kundalini unites with the Master's forces from without, it is the seat of controlled knowledge); (3) at the top of the head (pituitary body). He continues: "In time the student comes to recognise the vibration and to associate it with some particular "Great One," for each Master has his own vibration which impresses itself upon his pupils in a specific manner." The forces are "these magnetic currents of the universe, that vital fluid, those electric rays, the latent heat in all bodies." Cold and calculating, "a Master is only interested in a man from the point of view of his usefulness in the group-soul and his capacity to help." The individual is as nothing to him; he is only a part in his world revolutionary machine, to be thrown aside when no longer an asset in their game!

Dr. Rudolf Steiner died at Dornach, Switzerland, 30 March, 1925, slowly but surely burnt out by the terrific forces working through him, and at his funeral Albert Steffen, poet and president of the Executive Committee of the Anthroposophical Society, delivered an address. Speaking of Steiner's "Spiritual Science" or Christian Illuminism, he said: "Rudolf Steiner opened out to us the prospect of a religious life beyond all sects." Fifty theologians went to him seeking a way to unite their work once more with the "eternal life of the Spirit," and Steffen continued: "Steiner was able to transmit to them the holy ceremony which the priests of the *Christengemeinschaft* are now enacting for himself." We understand this *Christengemeinschaft* is being revived, run by Heidenreyd with about 400 members in this country. What is this "Spiritual Science"? According to Steiner, "Anthroposophy is a path of knowledge to guide the Spiritual in the human being to the Spiritual in the Universe." Wholly cosmic and astral!

In his book translated by Schuré, *Le Mystère Chrétien et les Mystères Antiques,* Steiner writes:

> "In the early days of Christianity there sprang up in the old Pagan world, systems of the universe which seemed to be a prolongation of the philosophy of Plato, but which could be understood also as a spiritualisation of the wisdom of the Mysteries. *All these systems had their starting-point in Philo, the Jewish philosopher of Alexandria,* who said: 'It is necessary for the soul to come out of the ordinary "I." Then it enters into a state of spiritual ecstasy, of

illumination, when it ceases to know, to think, and to recognise in the ordinary sense of the words. For it has identified itself with the divine, they have become one…"

He is deified and has lost his own personality! And as Steiner says:

"God (the Creative Principle) is bewitched in the world, and it is his own force that is needed to find Him. This force (sexforce) must be awakened within you. Such were the teachings which the Myste received before initiation. And now began the great drama of the world, of which he made a living integral part. The aim of the drama was nothing less than the freeing of the hidden God; where is that God? God is not but Nature is. It is in Nature that he must be found. For he is enshrouded in her as in an enchanted tomb."

Here we have the pantheistic God Pan, who is merely the creative principle in all nature, including man — the life force. As Clemens of Alexandria said in speaking of the Greater Mysteries: 'Here ends all teachings, one sees Nature and things.'

Further, Steiner explains: 'The Cross of Golgotha is the whole cult of the Ancient Mysteries gathered into one fact… Christianity as a mystical fact is a degree of evolution in the Wisdom of the Mysteries.' This again is Manichaeism, which looks upon the Crucifixion, Resurrection, and Ascension of Christ as mystical experiences. A lecture given by Steiner at Oxford in 1922, 'The Mystery of Golgotha,' throws further light upon his Spiritual Science. Now, Steiner was also a Rosicrucian, and in explaining this 'Mystery of Golgotha' he based his ideas upon certain words said to have been written in the Book T., which, according to the Rosicrucian mystical legend, was found on the breast of Christian Rosenkreutz at the opening of his tomb in the fifteenth century.

These words were: *Ex Deo nascimur; In Christo* (or Jehesuah) *morimur; Per Spiritum Sanctum reviviscimus* — From God are we born; in Christ or Jesus do we die; through the Holy Spirit we rise again. That is through the Gnostic Trinity-Father, creator; Son or Solar Christ, the Logos or serpent, the vivifying force; the Holy Spirit, the Great Mother which reproduces all things. The whole is the eternal creation, destruction, and regeneration, as applied to Illuminism.

In the R.R. et A.C., which, under the late Dr. Felkin, was closely allied to Steiner and practised some of his processes and Eurhythmy for awakening the kundalini, the 5 = 6 ritual dramatically depicts the meaning of these words: the aspirant is led to the tomb wherein lay the Chief Adept in full regalia, representing Christian Rosenkreutz; the tomb is opened and the aspirant demands: "Out of the Darkness let the Light arise!" From within the tomb a voice is heard: "Buried with that Light in a mystical death, rising again in a mystical resurrection, cleansed and purified through Him our Master, O brother of the Rose and Cross!... Seek thou the Stone of the Wise!..." The Stone is the Quintessence or Pentagram — Illuminism.

As illustrated on the lid of the tomb, these mystical experiences represent the adept as a Christ crucified on the Cross of Light or Illuminism; the Great Dragon Leviathan — the kundalini — rises up to *Daath,* and from above descends the Lightning-Flash attracted by and uniting with the serpent within, linking the adept with the universal life-force without. He becomes the Jehesuah-Yod, He Shin, Vau, He — the Pentagram or deified man, losing his Selfhood. It is the Rosicrucian Chymical Wedding. It is thus described by the Jewish writer Kadmi Cohen in *Nomades:*

> "Abyss and pinnacle. The dizzy height of the one set off by the unfathomable depth of the other. Who will ever know the unspeakable sufferings of the ascension, the mortal terrors of the fall? But also the ineffable joy, superhuman, divine, to be upon the peak which overhangs the universe, beyond good and evil, above pure practical reason, to be Man, to be Self, who equals himself to God, who wrestles with Him, who absorbs Him. It is Israel, it is Ishmael who supplies these men to the world!"

His God is the God Pan, he is intoxicated by the astral Light!

Schuré explains that Christian Rosenkreutz left 'three spiritual truths' to his disciples, and that these truths were only scientifically proved four centuries later, namely: (I) the material unity of the universe — by spectrum analysis; (2) organic evolution — by transformation of species according to Darwin and Haeckel; (3) states of human consciousness different from the ordinary state — by hypnotism and suggestion. As the power used by Rosicrucians was said to be the "magnetic fluid" in man and in the universe, set in motion by concentrated thought and will-power, one can easily believe that such initiations, under unknown Masters, might mean hypnotism and suggestion. The spectrum is the resolution of light through the prism, and as the Rosicrucian ritual says: "Colours are forces and the signature of forces and Child of the children of the forces art thou." The Rosicrucians work with colours and geometrical figures, representing the forces of the planets, the signs of the Zodiac, the elements, etc., and the colours of the planets are the spectrum of the Rosicrucian 'Divine White Light,' that magnetic fluid which slays and makes alive. Steiner talks much of planetary hierarchies, Archangels, Angels, etc., but there is reason to believe that they can one and all be reduced to nature's universal forces, for the O=O ritual of the *Stella Matutina* says: 'For by names and images are all powers awakened and reawakened.

Therefore, is not Steiner's "Spiritual Science" merely the Hermetic fixation of the astral light in a material body-Illuminism-linking the adept, as a tool, to some "White Occultists" supposedly working for the weal, or is it not rather the woe of Humanity?

As expressing Steiner's Communistic, political dreams and schemes, we have his "Threefold State." As a symbolic basis for this "Threefold State" Steiner takes the human organism: (I) the system of the nerves and senses — the head system. (2) the system of breathing and the circulation of the blood — the rhythmic system. (3) the organs and functions of matter changes — the metabolic process. According to Steiner, these systems, comparatively speaking, function separately: "There is no such thing as absolute centralisation in the human organism." "In order to thrive, the social organism, like the natural one, requires to be threefold."

(1) Economic life — relatively as independent as the nervous and sensory system within the human body. "Its concern is with everything in the nature of production, circulation, and consumption of commodities."

(2) Public rights, political life — the State; "applied to a community possessing common rights."

(3) Mental and spiritual life; "everything that rests on the natural endowment of each single human being… spiritual and physical." All are apparently separate yet interdependent. "Alongside the political sphere and the economic sphere in a healthy society there must be the spiritual sphere, functioning independently on its own footing" — that is, religion, teaching, art, and intellectual life, and even technical and organising capacities as applied to the State or industrial economy.

> "It is the threefold line of evolution towards which modern humanity is striving… At the end of the eighteenth century, under different circumstances from which we are living to-day, there went up a cry from the hidden depths of human nature for a re-formation of human social relations (stirred up by the Illuminati and Grand Orient Lodges). Through all the scheme of the new order ran like a motto the three words: "Fraternity, Equality, Liberty.""

Admitting that equality and liberty are contradictory, Steiner is in sympathy with all three, and applies them to his threefold State. Economic life in the form of Associations is combined under brotherhood, the State under equality, and the spiritual field under liberty or freedom, and he says:

> "No social State, constructed on an abstract centralised scheme, can carry freedom, equality, and brotherhood pell mell into practice. But each of the three branches of the body social can derive its strength from one of these (contradictory) ideal impulses; and then all three branches will work fruitfully in conjunction."

Such is Steiner's, as it has been called, "headless" Threefold State, and this he would further extend, in the same headless way, to a Threefold World State.

> "Such a close interweaving of interests will grow up, as will make territorial frontiers seem negligible in the life of mankind.
>
> … The forces to which nationalities owe their growth require for their development free mutual interaction untrammelled by any ties that grow up between respective bodies of State and the Economic Associations. And the way of achieving this is for the various national communities to develop the threefold order within their own social structures; and then their three branches can each expand its own relation with the corresponding branches of the other communities. In this way, peoples, States, economic bodies, become grouped together in formations that are very various in shape and

character; and every part of mankind becomes so linked with the other parts that each is conscious of the life of the other pulsing through its own daily interests. A league of nations is the outcome arising out of root impulses that correspond to actual realities. There will be no need to 'institute' one built up solely on legal theories of right."

Finally, he says:

"There must be but one human race working at one common task, willing to read the signs of the times and to act in accordance with them."

The whole is just another form of Mazzini's "Associate, associate!" or Mrs. Alice Bailey's "World State" by means of "unification" under the control of some mysterious "Supermen."

This dream of a World State is far from being new. We know that Weishaupt's initiates had to take an oath swearing to help to their utmost the foundation of a Universal Republic; and at the end of the eighteenth century the Illuminatus Anacharsis Clootz's plan was: "All peoples forming only one nation, all the trades forming only one trade, all interests forming only one interest." Steiner was an Illuminatus said to have been linked to those who, towards the end of the nineteenth century, revived Weishaupt's Illuminism. He was, therefore, apparently, carrying on the tradition in his Threefold World State.

Moreover, with regard to intellectual interconnections, necessary for this World State, we might quote the report 1928-29, of the "Society for Cultural Relations Between the Peoples of the British Commonwealth and the Union of Socialist Soviet Republics," in which it was noted that the Anthroposophical Society (Steiner's) was one of the organisations in contact with it. A British Government Blue Book thus describes this S.C.R.: "The Communist International favours it as a fertile ground for Communist propaganda of the intellectual variety." And there is little doubt that to-day every nation is conscious of the Soviet life "pulsing through its own daily interests," largely detrimental and disintegrating economically, politically, and spiritually.

To take another phase of Anthroposophical teaching and practical application of its beliefs. In December 1932, Frau Lilly Kolisko, a leading member of the Anthroposophical Society in Stuttgart, came to London to lecture to an agricultural group of the Society which proposed to revive ancient astronomical or perhaps astrological customs, common among primitive people, adding to them, apparently, the science of Anthroposophy! Her theories were that plants and vegetables sown at the correct moon-phase grow much faster and more luxuriantly than when the moon-phases are ignored. That the earth breathes rhythmically, and that sowing, fertilising, and harvesting of crops can be worked into this rhythm. Further, that plants requiring much moisture grow a great deal better when planted two days before full moon, and those requiring little moisture during a waning moon.

Pearce, in his *Text-book of Astrology*, tells us that more rain usually falls during the *increase* than during the *decrease* of the moon, as was proved by many experiments throughout the years 1868 to 1881. Again, the ancients have said that oaks cut down in springtime, when the sap is rising, soon rot. All timber trees should be felled during the winter solstice, and the last days of the moon, then the timber would last in perpetuity. Practically this is affirmed by R. Reynell Bellamy, in his book *The Real South Seas*. He says of the Kanakas of New Caledonia that they maintain that the flow of the sap is upwards with the waxing moon and downwards when it wanes. They plant maize, beans, etc., before the full moon, and root crops after. Timber for building purposes they fell during the last phase of lunation, when the sap is at its lowest.

As for the rhythmic breathing of the earth, they no doubt refer to the Great Breath or *Swara* of the Universe, the *life-force* — *Pingala*, the positive or sun breath; *Ida*, the negative or moon breath; and the *Sushumna*, the central or uniting fire. There are also the five *Tatwas* of refined matter — ether, air (gaseous), fire (igneous), water (liquid), earth (solid). The whole process of creation on all planes of life is said to be performed by these Tatwas in their aspects of positive and negative. All these phases follow and merge into each other in regular and continuous procession. They are the basis of all magic, black or white. They are Nature's finer forces, but not spiritual or divine, except as instruments, the creative principle in all nature.

Again, to repeat what we have previously said, speaking of astrology among the Chaldeans, Dollinger wrote:

"These men found a support in the Stoic philosophy, which, starting with the principle of the substantial identity of God and Nature, had come to look upon the stars as eminently divine, and placed divine government of the world in the immovable course of the celestial globes."

In the time of Alexander the astrologers of the Chaldean and Alexandra-Egyptian schools were spread over Asia, Greece, and Italy, and taught that a secret influence from the planets descended uninterruptedly upon the earth and man, and that by magical cults and astrological prayers these planets could be acted upon and their forces directed as required. In Illuminised orders, such as the R.R. et A.C., these planetary influences are invoked, or attracted, by the Jewish symbol of power, the six-rayed star; and the higher grades are given at the various phases of the moon.

In *Od and Magnetism,* 1852, Reichenbach wrote:

"The element of odic force is thus radiated towards us so abundantly by sunlight and moonlight that we can lay hold of it at our ease, and make use of it in simple experiments. How unbounded its influence is on the whole of humanity, and even on the whole animal and vegetable kingdoms, will be proved shortly. Od is accordingly a cosmic force that radiates from star to star, and has the whole universe for its field, just like light and heat."

This Od or, as the Rosicrucians say, magnetic fluid, is the universal life-force, generated by the sun, and reproduced by the moon, which can be used for good or perverted for evil.

In support of what we have written above we find the following in the Programme of the Anthroposophical Summer School, held at Tetbury, August 1934:

"Dr. C. A. Mirbt will hold classes dealing with the anthroposophical conception of Agriculture. The subjects will be as follows: the soil as the work of Cosmos and Earth; the soil as a manifestation of the evolution of the Earth; Etheric formative forces in plant and soil; the true nature of manuring; the animal kingdom as manifestation of the astral world..."

Here we have the Cosmic forces of the stars and the magnetic forces of the earth. It is the basis of all the old pagan cults; it is the ancient Chaldean astrological lore and that of the old Rosicrucian medicinal herb-growers. Added to it all is the modern science of manuring! Further Steiner, like the learned botanist of his youthful days, claimed to be able to see the vital or life-forces in the plant, to arrest these forces, and use them as required in his healing. Hence his "New Therapy" and the British Weleda Co., Ltd., for dispensing the results of the "Anthroposophical Medical Research," incorporated in 1925.

By some it is maintained that this "Anthroposophical Agriculture" is based, not on Astrology, but Astronomy. Yet Steiner's astronomy in "Spiritual Science" appears to be a reversion to ancient and Eastern beliefs when Nature's forces and phenomena were everywhere looked upon as active and ruling gods, sometimes good and sometimes evil. In *Anthroposophy*-Michaelmas, 1928, E. Vreede writes of this astronomy, and explains that behind the veil of the past and Nature the stars reveal themselves as "Colonies of Spiritual Beings," nine stages of hierarchies towering above man. Together they have formed and governed the world and man, under a World Spirit.

In order that man should develop, these beings were seemingly withdrawn, and man was abandoned to mechanical laws;

> "yet in this mechanism, as in all natural phenomena, spiritual beings are working. The fact that in Spring the plants come forth from the soil, that blossom and fruit appear, and that the plants wither away in Autumn; the fact that when here we have Autumn, Spring begins to burst on the other side of the Earthall this is brought about by the Nature-Spirits, the gnomes, undines, sylphs together with the salamanders…"

Thus in the *Stella Matutina* four of its ceremonies end with the prayers of these nature spirits of water, air, earth, and fire, very beautiful as a piece of art, taking one back to childhood's wonderful fairy tales. Later, for the intellectual development of man, Ahrimanic beings (matter) were sent to consolidate the earth and veil spiritual reality.

Yet again it is said that man and Nature were, from the beginning, fashioned according to the laws of Rhythm and Periodicity, and the law of gravity held sway over the earth. Finally, as Steiner said: "When we observe the life of the world of stars, we are beholding the bodies of the Gods and ultimately of Divinity itself." This once more seems to reveal the pantheistic nature of Steiner's whole teaching, "the bewitched God" enshrouded in all nature. The Jehovah of the cabalistic Jew — the Creative Principle.

According to Steiner the Gods of the Sun, Moon, and Saturn — this Creative Principle... manifested in the body of Jesus of Nazareth as a Christ-impulse — the Serpent Power of the Yogis, the Logos or serpent of the Gnostics. "And the fact that it was possible for the Christ-impulse to enter humanity was brought about by the ancient Initiation principle becoming *historical fact.*" In *From Sphinx to Christ,* by Edouard Schuré, the French and Jewish exponent of Steiner's Neo-Gnostic Illuminism, we are given an account of this ancient pantheistic creed as applied to the Christ of the Christian Church, de-Christianising and Judaising Christian beliefs; making Christ merely a super "Deified Man." The Sphinx represents the prepared body, offered in sacrifice, into which the Christ-impulse was to descend. The whole means the rise and perversion of the sexforce or serpent within man, attracting and uniting with the Lightning-Flash or Solar Christ-impulse from without, controlled by unknown directors — it is called initiation.

According to Schuré:

> "It was still necessary that, from birth up to the age of thirty, when the Christ would take possession of His human habitation, the body of Jesus should be refined and harmonised by an initiate of the highest rank (one who had passed through many incarnations!), so that a man almost divine should offer himself up as a sacrifice, a consecrated vessel, to receive the Godmade man."

Therefore, it is said that Jesus was a reincarnation of the high initiate Zoroaster! Later the "Master Jesus" was placed under the instructions of the Essenes, a fraternity of initiates who lived along the shores of the Dead Sea, where finally the "voice within" told him: "Thou hast laid thy body upon the altar of Adonai (the Lord of the Universe) like a lyre of ivory and gold. Now thy God claims thee that He may manifest Himself to men.

He seeks thee and thou canst not escape Him! Offer thyself as sacrifice. Embrace the Cross!"

Then followed the initiation, the baptism in the Jordan by John the Baptist, of which Schuré writes:

> "It is forbidden to help the one who was being baptised to leave the water; the belief was that a breath of the Divine Spirit entered into him through the hand of the prophet and the waters of the river. The majority emerged from the test revivified; some died; others became insane as though possessed. These were called demoniacs."

As to the "Master Jesus":

> "He is aware of a sensation of drowning followed by a terrible convulsion... and for some seconds he sees a chaotic picture of his whole past life ... then the darkness of unconsciousness. The transcendent Self, the immortal Soul of the Master Jesus has left his physical body for ever, and he is received back into the aura of the Sun. At the same moment, by an inverse movement, the Solar Genius, the sublime Being, whom we call Christ, entered the abandoned body and took possession of it, animating with new fire this human lyre that had been prepared through hundreds of generations."

Lightning flashed from the sky, and as He emerged from the water, His whole body bathed in light, a luminous dove appeared above His head, "the mystery of the Eternal Feminine, the spirit of Divine Love, transformer and vivifier of souls, to be called later by Christians the 'Holy Spirit.'" Then came a voice from above: "This is My beloved Son; to-day have I begotten Him." (This version of the words is, Schuré says, to be found in the early Hebrew gospel; it works in better with his idea of this Cosmic Christ!) "The object of His mission is the spiritualisation of the world and of man," through love and the opening of the Mysteries to all who may aspire to them. That is illuminising as through the innumerable Mystery sects of to-day!

Now this whole account might well be the history of the preparation and initiation of the many illuminised tools now being used in the widespread Universal Movement of to-day. As in this baptism, so in these initiations, some died, some were illuminised, losing their personalities, becoming controlled by some unknown Master, as for example Krishnamurti of the

Theosophical Society, "Octavia" of the Panacea Society, and many others. The Illuminising Power was the Gnostic Trinity — the Father, the generating force; the Holy Spirit, the Great Mother, the reproducer; the Son, the Cosmic Christ, the manifestation of the Creative Principle, the illuminising force, of all Gnostic and Cabalistic sects.

Schuré further holds, thus in opposition to Mrs. Besant, that this Christ will not again occupy a material body, but will appear to such adepts who have astral vision. Just as in the 'House of Wisdom, Cairo,' the adepts were taught that Mohammed their prophet 'could be contacted spiritually through meditation on the mystical doctrines!' Also in the R.R. et A.C., which was closely allied to Steiner's group, their mysterious Master latterly appeared astrally to many members, masquerading as a Christ, demanding from the adepts complete sacrifice in service to the Great World Movement. And Schure says: "According to Rosicrucian tradition, the spirit which spoke to the world in the name of Christ and through the lips of the Master Jesus is closely related to the ruling star of our system, the Sun." This Christ-impulse is therefore a compelling power manipulated by these invisible directors, and the initiate penetrated by this force becomes merely the negative reproducer of the ideas and actions set in motion through this impulse. Under the mask of initiation he becomes diabolically possessed.

As M. Henri de Guillebert says:

> "The Jew looks upon himself as the Sun of humanity, the male, opposed to which the other peoples are but female, manifesting and assuring the coming of the Messianic era. In order to realise this sociological manifestation, the Jew organically extends his influence by means of secret societies created by him in order to spread everywhere his initiating force... [hoping to realise] the 'Universal Republic,' controlled by the God of Humanity, the Jew of the Cabala."

MAX HEINDEL

Max Heindel, who seceded from Steiner and founded "The Rosicrucian Fellowship" of California, published in 1911 his version of Steiner's teachings in *Rosicrucian Cosmo-Conception*. In this his teaching about the Christ, like that of Steiner, shows the Manichaean influences. To him the Christ is the Sun-Spirit, the King of Love, manifested magnetic life-force, the forces of attraction and cohesion; this Christ-Fire descended, he said, into the body of Jesus of Nazareth at the age of thirty, during his baptism in the Jordan, and he then became the initiate Christ Jesus. His mission was to unite separate races and nations in one Universal Brotherhood, of which he was to be the Eldest Brother. Ninety-nine did not require salvation, but were to reach perfection by way of rebirth and consequences, that is, Reincarnation and Karma. Christ was only to redeem the stragglers and open the way of initiation to all!

To illustrate their methods of shaping and hewing their dupes, Max Heindel explains:

> "Physiologists note that certain areas of the brain are devoted to particular thought activities... Now it is known that thought breaks down and destroys nerve tissues... [which] are replaced by the blood... When through the development of the heart into a voluntary muscle, the circulation of the blood finally passes under the absolute control of the unifying life-spirit — the Spirit of Love (so-called Christ-Force) it will then be within the power of that Spirit to withhold the blood from those areas of the mind devoted to selfish purposes. As a result these particular thought centres will gradually atrophy. On the other hand, it will be possible for the spirit to increase the blood supply, when the mental activities are altruistic, and thus build up the areas devoted to altruism."

Here we appear to have a more or less diabolical hypnotic method, gradually muting all strong and sane faculties, creating single-eyed fanatics, false idealists, soft peace-mongers, yet willing to revolutionise nations and break up Empires. As Max Heindel puts it: "Working toward Universal Brotherhood in accordance with the designs of our invisible Leaders, who are none the less potent in shaping events because they are not officially seated in the councils of the nations." Again: "The national, tribal, and family unity must first be broken up before Universal Brotherhood can become a fact." Everywhere we see these unities being acted upon for this apparent purpose! All methods are employed to ensnare the unwary but desired prey.

PANACEA SOCIETY

In his *Essai sur la secte des Illuminés,* the Marquis de Luchet, a Mason, wrote in 1789:

> "There exists a crowd of small anti-philosophical groups, composed of learned women, theological Abbés, and some so-called Sages. Each group has its beliefs, its prodigies, hierophants, missionaries, adepts, and its detractors... Each professes to explain the Bible in favour of its system, to found its religion, fill its temple, and multiply its catechumens. Here Jesus Christ plays a great role; there it is the Devil; elsewhere it is Nature, and again Faith. Everywhere reason is null, science is useless, experience is a chimera."

Speaking of Rosicrucianism, Paul Vulliaud says: "As it progresses, this movement augments the number of its Masters by linking to itself all isolated Theosophists: Boehme, Jane Lead, etc., forming a kind of patristic chain." Enlarging on the precursors of Freemasonry, Gustave Bord, 1908, tells us that Boehme, a more or less uneducated shoemaker, was born near Garlitz in 1575. Known as the Teutonic Philosopher, he was a mystic, theosophist, and visionary; influenced by the philosophies of Paracelsus and Cornelius Agrippa, he was led to mysticism, and

> "was convinced that he held, by special grace from God, the universal and absolute science, which he communicated to his readers without order, without proofs, in a language borrowed from the Apocalypse and alchemy... We find in Boehme a vast system of metaphysics, the foundation of which is an unbridled pantheism."

After reading Boehme's *Six Theosophic Points,* and other works, we are forced to come to a similar conclusion.

Coming to the present day, most of the many sects we have written about can be referred to as belonging to one form or another of Theosophical mysticism or Rosicrucian illuminism-gnostic and pantheistic, the cult of Nature and Naturalism. One of the most insistent and ambitious of these is the Panacea Society, about which we have written much in the past. Briefly, its history is as follows: A mystic sect, under the name of "Philadelphians," was founded in 1652 by Jane Lead, an enthusiastic admirer of Boehme, for the purpose of explaining his writings. She herself was said to have received mystical revelations, which were published as "Sixty Propositions to the Philadelphian Society, whithersoever dispersed as the Israel of God." Like the writings of Boehme, these revelations were Gnostic and Rosicrucian Illuminism. From Jane Lead and their seven successive prophets, forming a patristic chain, was evolved the present Panacea Society, with "Octavia" as mystic leader and Rachel Fox as president. Their Trinity is similar to that of the Universal Gnostic Church, which invokes thus: "Glory be to Father and to Mother, to Son and to Daughter, and to the Holy Spirit without and within." The Panacea Society recognises: The Father of Light, the generative fire; the Holy Ghost, the Great Mother; the Son, Christ, or active manifestation of the Father, the Bridegroom; the Daughter, the negative manifestation of the Mother, Shiloh, the Bride, who, they said, descended into "Octavia," the latter thus becoming the passive instrument, receiving and transmitting the power from above — that of her Master!

They, too, received revelations, published as *The Writings of the Holy Ghost — A Series of papers for My beloved.* Their means of enlightenment were limited to these writings, the Bible, the Apocrypha, and the writings of their prophets. They had two fixed ideas: the opening of Joanna Southcott's mysterious box in the presence of twenty-four bishops, six Jews of repute and others, and which they claimed contained the means of saving England in the coming storm, and bringing deliverance to Judah; the other was magnetic-healing by charged sections of linen and water, "a sure deliverance and protection, so that death may become non-existent." Further, 144,000 "Israel or the Immortals" were to be sealed and set apart for service, and recently we heard that twelve square miles of land had been bought, where on these 144,000, when chosen, were to be settled.

As showing their attitude towards the Jews, the two following advertisements, taken from Jewish papers, are interesting:

(1) *"Not anti-Semitism, but anti-Hamitism* — The Panacea Society is anxious to help the Jews (descendants of Shem) to deliver themselves from the abominable charges which bring about anti-Semitic persecution. The first thing to learn is that it is the

descendants of Ham, who say they are Jews, and are not, who are, and always have been, the enemies of God and man."

(2) *"Good News for the Jews* — the Prophet's promises and the Pharisaic ideals of a kingdom ruled by God upon earth are on the edge of becoming FACT, for the week of 6,000 years of 6 days of 1,000 years each is rapidly closing, and the Sabbath of Rest for Israel and for Judah during the reign of the Messiah on earth is about to commence. Enquire, Panacea Society, Bedford."

This, they say,

"will be the end of the Adamic age, which followed the Atlantean, Lemurian, and other ages, the history of which is shrouded in Mystery... God's Sabbath of Rest is the seventh thousand from Adam ... [when] men will live on earth delivered from sin, sickness, and death by reason that Satan will be cast off the earth into the place prepared for him..."

Again, in a leaflet headed 'To Our Brethren of the tribe of Judah,' they say that it is for the union of Judah and Israel the world is waiting, and these isles are their place of gathering; that King George V is descended from Zedekiah, King of Judah; therefore the Hebrews have a king, a country, and because the Union Jack means, they say, the union of Jacob, they have also a national flag! But both Judaism and Christianity have, they say, sinned, in that the former rejects the Son and the latter rejects the Daughter! Needless to say, the Panacea Society has accepted both, and therefore, alone of all religions or cults it possesses the whole truth! Again they say they have forsaken "all contrivances of man in philosophies, philanthropies, governments, churches, cults, such as Higher Thought, Christian Science, Theosophy, Occultism, etc.," and are seeking "alone for a New Life." Nevertheless, their cult is built up of mystic Illuminism, Rosicrucianism, and Gnosticism, and one of their admired predecessors was Jacob Boehme, the Teutonic Philosopher and Theosophist!

Finally, we have another leaflet, headed "The Last Religion for the Last Times — the "whosoever" Religion," based on the text, "Whosoever shall call on the name of the Lord shall be delivered." They continue:

"We do not for a moment discount the religions which have served our and other nations during the 6,000 years of comparative peace, when it was right to follow the religious teachings of childhood. But this 'whosoever' religion is for a time of war the final war between God and the devils — and when such things as earthquakes … wars and rumours of wars, and distress of nations with perplexity are about, as they certainly are to-day, it is most reasonable to suppose that a very simple form of religion, such as a straightforward command to call upon God for deliverance (for "myself and my family") … would be provided."

Curiously enough, we have heard much in recent months of a somewhat similar but anonymous "Whosoever" religion, publicly calling upon the people of the nation to pray for "deliverance and protection for myself and my family, etc." It would be satisfactory to those who have in good faith responded to this anonymous call, which is still persisting, September 1935, and signed the petition, if this mystery of similarity could be solved.

We hear the Panacea Society is once more stirring, making last desperate attempts to get the notorious Joanna Southcott box opened. In order to hasten matters they have made a small concession, in that they will allow twenty-four clergy nominated by the Bishops to open the box, and if the contents do not prove to be the panacea for world ills as expected by the Society, the box and all it contains may be burned. Is it that the cold winds of doubt are entering into some of their souls!

Joanna Southcott, 1792–1814, was the second link of the patristic chain of seven visitations based on Jane Lead's writings, on which the Panacea Society builds its mission to England. In a short statement of "The Doctrines of the Dispensation of the Holy Ghost (during which death will cease)," published by the Society in 1922, the following points refer to the box and its mission: (4) You have probably heard that Joanna Southcott left a box, corded and nailed, of sealed MSS. The box is the Ark of the Testament, alluded to in Rev. xi. 19, called so because it contains God's Will and Testament for this country (!). (5) You may also have heard that this box can only be delivered up and opened by twenty-four Bishops of the Church of England, who are the twenty-four elders mentioned in Rev. xi. 16, and are the executors of the Will.

(6) The box was originally left in the care of the Rev. Thomas Foley, Vicar of Old Swinford, Worcester, and upon his death it was given into the care of his son Richard, Vicar of North Cadbury. The present custodian (1922), also a Churchman, is under an oath not to deliver up the box except to twenty-four bishops who will comply with certain conditions laid down by the Lord (!). (7) The box will be applied for in a time of grave national danger. The ark or box will prove publicly the truth of what has so long been developing privately, and also will prove the integrity of the Church, by placing before her the proof of a New Divine Revelation, before which she must bow or cease to exist.

Is this in reality a New Revelation? Is it not rather old as the cults of the remotest past which went to build up the Jewish Magical Cabala-Sabeists and workers in "fluidic magic"? Here are a few points of their revelations at that time, which seem to show relationship to these ancient beliefs:

> "What do the Bishops know of (1) Spirit, soul, and body, and their relation to the glories of the sun, moon, and stars [astral influences]? (2) Of the coming immortal state of man and woman upon Earth, and how it will be brought about [Illuminism!]? (3) Of the Eternal and Enduring Motherhood of the Holy Ghost [Jerusalem above], who is the Third person in the Blessed Trinity?"

We have seen that their Trinity is cabalistic and gnostic, in which its aim is illumination or illuminism, the Son being the vivifying force which, as the gnostics say, creates "Christs," or deifies man. It is union with the universal life-force which would appear to be eternal, and by this union, they believe, man would become immortal in his body — would never die!

"Octavia" writes in *Healing for All:*

> "To sum up, Joanna plays on the same strings as Jane Lead [under the influence of Jacob Boehme], the coming restitution of all things at the end of 6,000 years, and all to be brought in by Woman [passive mediumistic instruments!] ... the last hour of the 6,000 years is running out..."

Again, she writes to the Rural Deans:

"The Diocesan Bishops have been adjured to inform the clergy of sacred and secret revelations made in this country upon the coming cataclysm and upon the protective measures which the Lord has prepared, whereby a remnant will be saved out of the overthrow, but they have with one consent rejected every overture... Meanwhile, there is time to approach the Bishops and to demand that the records be searched, particularly that the Ark containing the word of the Lord through the Prophetess Joanna Southcott be opened, for the "time of grave national danger," which is to mark its opening, is here" (May 1923).

Thousands of pounds, they say, have been spent, and for twenty years or so statements have been sent to the Bishops; they even, in May 1924, sent a petition signed by 11,208 persons in England requesting the Archbishop of Canterbury and other Bishops to open the box. In this instance the statement was sent to forty-two Bishops, the Chaplain-General of the Forces, and the Dean of Westminster. The Archbishop replied that he had done his part "to meet the wishes of those, whoever they may be, who have control of the box or boxes, for my correspondents tell me there are rival boxes." As we know, in 1927 a box was opened by the National Laboratory of Psychical Research, but the result was more a farce than a fiasco!

Moreover, an organisation known as the "Fishers of Men," whose notepaper, according to the *Evening Standard,* was headed by a drawing of a serpent being stabbed by a dagger, though believing in the Divine Mission of Joanna Southcott, they dissociated themselves from the Panacea Society's decision to allow the box to be opened by twenty-four nominated clergy instead of twenty-four Bishops. As they said, such a concession "can only result in disaster and not the hoped-for blessings."

This symbol of the "Fishers of Men" appears to place the Society among modern cabalistic Illuminati, for according to Eliphas Levi, in his *History of Magic,* "The secret of the Great Work, which is the fixation of the Astral Light by a sovereign act of will, is represented by the adepts as *a serpent pierced with an arrow,* thus forming the Hebrew letter Aleph." The Trinity in Unity of the Cabalists! The Patristic mission of the Panacea Society and its affiliations is apparently to illuminise England by means of controlled Illuminati, and their overmasters are no doubt the ever-ubiquitous Brothers of the Great White Lodges, who are cabalists!

STEINER'S COMMUNITY CHURCH

To return for a moment to Rudolf Steiner, we would note that Rom Landau, in his book, *God is My Adventure, 1935*, writes about the Anthroposophical Community Church as told to him by one of its young ministers. No doubt it is the same movement spoken of by Albert Steffen in 1926 as the *Christengemeinschaft*, whose priests were present at Steiner's funeral.

Steiner, it would seem, was the adviser and "spiritual inspirer" of this Community Church, which was initiated in June 1921, by a group of young ministers and laymen at Stuttgart, where Steiner gave a "Lecture Course to Theologians." The group collected again at Dornach, and once more Steiner lectured to them on his teachings about Christ. Their traditional beliefs were deeply shaken: they decided to form a new Church based on Steiner's revelations, and they evolved a constitution which was approved of by Steiner. In September 1922 he ordained Rittelmeyer by laying on of hands, and Rittelmeyer in turn ordained a number of young ministers.

According to Steiner: "Anthroposophy addresses itself to man's need of knowledge and brings knowledge; the Christian Community Church addresses itself to man's need for resurrection and brings Christ." That is awakening the "God within" or kundalini, bringing about illuminism! Now we know Steiner's teaching on Christ is that of the Manichaeans and the Jews of the Alexandrian School. His God is the Universal Creative Principle, and his Christ-Impulse is merely the vivifying and illuminising force of that same Principle; and the Resurrection, Crucifixion, and Ascension are no more than mystical teachings as taught by the Manichaeans.

Therefore one wonders if this Christian Community Church is not an attempt to revive the old heresy of the Albigenses! Rom Landau tells us that these Churches exist in Germany, several other Continental countries, and in England.

CHAPTER X

FRATERNITY OF INNER LIGHT AND YOGA

L ET us now turn to another, perhaps less known, of our modern *Illuminés*, the "Fraternity of the Inner Light," whose head is Dion Fortune. Its teaching is largely based on the Jewish Cabala. She writes that it

"is one of these Mystery Schools; it is contacted on to the Western Esoteric Tradition, and it works the Christian, the Hermetic, and the Keltic aspects of that Tradition (hence its pilgrimage centre at Glastonbury)... The Fraternity is an independent and self-contained organisation, and is not affiliated to any other organisation on the physical plane, but holds its contacts direct from the Great White. Lodge ... the Great White Brotherhood, the Masters, or Elder Brethren. It is with these that the initiate of the Mysteries comes in touch when his higher consciousness is sufficiently developed."

Dion Fortune explains her real attitude towards Christianity in her book, *The Esoteric Orders*, when, speaking of Hermetic traditions, she writes:

"Its highest development was in the Egyptian and Cabalistic systems, and it was blended with Christian thought in the schools of the Neo-Platonists and the Gnostics; but the persecuting energy of the Church, long since exotericised, stamped it out as an organised system. Its studies were only kept alive during the Dark Ages among the Jews, who were the chief exponents of its Cabalistic aspect. Its Egyptian aspect was reintroduced into Europe by the Templars after the Crusades had put them in touch with the Holy Centres in the Near East. [As we have shown, the secret doctrine of the Templars was Manichaean and Johannite, and they were allied to the Assassins!] Stamped out again by the fear and jealousy of the Church, it reappeared once more in the long line of Alchemists who flourished after the power of Rome was broken by the Reformation;

and it is still alive to-day. [For] During the last half-century innumerable attempts have been made to induce the soul of the Mysteries to reincarnate, and these attempts have met with varying success. Out of many abortive efforts a tradition is gradually being reformed; the smouldering fire of occult knowledge has been fanned to a blaze, and *the gods have again drawn near to man.* "

Further to Dion Fortune, Christ is "Lord of the Purple Ray," classed with Krishna and Osiris. He is the Cosmic Christ, a regenerative and reconciling world force which can be contacted by meditation and used for Cosmic purposes; he was never a personality nor of our humanity, but Cosmic Fire, having the Sun as his symbol. And, she says, "by inspiration we can open our consciousness to it, and align ourselves with its lines of power until consciousness is suffused by it and illumination occurs." And showing its pantheistic nature she continues: "Union with the divine aspect of the self, the God within, must precede awareness of the God of the Whole of which it is but a part. The spiritual level of man's nature is but a circumscribed portion of the One Spirit, the All, the Noumenal aspect of manifestation."

We must therefore conclude that the first aim of the Fraternity, like all illuminised groups, is to unite the Creative Principle within to the Creative Principle without, attracting and drawing down the Cosmic Christ or Fire — the illuminising force — thus forming the magnetic link with the dominating minds of their Masters, for as she again explains: "By thinking of the Masters we attract their attention, and it is unbelievably easy to establish a magnetic link with those who are always more ready to give than we are to receive." As the Masters said to the present writer, "We have need of thee and all thy gifts!" Their plan is to rule over a Universal World State, and for this purpose they have need of passive yet gifted instruments. As Dion Fortune, herself, writes:

> "The Masters receive souls as pupils, not for the benefit of the soul, but for the benefit of the Great Work; a man is not trained for the sake of curiosity or enthusiasm, but only in so far as he is of value as a servant."

Having duly become illuminised servants, the adepts must train and initiate other dupes for a similar service in one direction or another as required by these Masters. Therefore:

"An officer who rightly understood his function would dwell upon the force which should act through his office till his personality became so saturated with it that he radiated its influence upon the candidate he was helping to initiate. The united action of all the officers builds a group-mind which is capable of transmitting and focussing potencies of a much more massive or cosmic type than could be transmitted through the channel of a single consciousness"

Colour and sound play an important part in transmitting these forces. As Max Heindel said and Dion Fortune repeats:

"These invisible sound vibrations have great power over concrete matter. They can build and destroy. If a small quantity of very fine powder is placed upon a brass or glass plate, and a violin bow drawn across the edge, the vibrations will cause the powder to assume beautiful geometrical figures. The human voice is also capable of producing these figures; always the same figure for the same tone. If one note or chord after another be sounded upon… preferably a violin… a tone will be finally reached which will cause the hearer to feel a distinct vibration in the back of the lower part of the head. Each time that note is struck, the vibration will be felt. That note is the 'key-note' of the person whom it so affects. If struck slowly and soothingly, it will build and rest the body, tone the nerves, and restore health. If, on the other hand, it be sounded in a dominant way, loud and long enough, it will kill as surely as a bullet from a pistol."

And Dion Fortune sums up:

"All these influences are employed to construct a great thought-form in the group-mind of the Lodge, and into this thought-form are poured the potencies evoked by the Names of Power used in the initiatory work, and these influences are focussed upon the candidate while he is in a state of exalted consciousness, This is the rationale of initiation."

This takes us back to the Order of the Élus Coens of Martinez de Paschalis and the Jewish Magical Cabala with its "fluidic magic" and the power generated by pronouncing the so-called divine names, so much used in all magical orders, Eastern as well as Western. As the ancient Chaldean Oracles said: "Change not barbarous names in evocation, for they are names Divine, having in the sacred rites a power ineffable." And colours, we know, are the signatures of forces, therefore their vibrations are similar to their corresponding forces.

As an excuse, the usual excuse of all such Fraternities and Orders, for the oath of secrecy, Dion Fortune explains:

> "The knowledge is reserved in order that humanity may be protected from its abuse in the hands of the unscrupulous... The mind has certain little-known powers, which are so potent and so subtle that, used for crime, they could overturn the social system of a nation. The courts recognise that undue influence can be exercised by one person over another, but they have little realisation of the kind of influence a trained mind can exert over an untrained one."

It is, therefore, reasonable to ask: Has Dion Fortune any real proof that these so-called Masters and Brethren of the so-called Great White Lodge are not unscrupulous and ambitious occultists and magicians, using and abusing these subtle powers of the minds of men in order to bring about their own mad and fanatical world ambitions, overturning the social, religious, and political systems, not of one nation but of all? If not, is she willing to take the enormous responsibility and risk for herself and more especially her confiding candidates and dupes? She teaches that the Manus, by means of suggestion or thought-transference, planted ideas in human consciousness! Who are these supposed Manus? — a name borrowed from the East for what end!

Again:

> "It is for this reason [Illuminism] that the Masters found and support such organisations as the Theosophical Society, the Anthroposophical Society, the Rosicrucian Fellowship, and many others, less known but not less useful..."

Curiously enough, we find among their books, for sale to the members, Crowley's *Magick,* containing "a reprint of the famous "777."" This latter book was largely built up from correspondences given in the cabalistic "Knowledge Lectures" of the Golden Dawn, of which Order Crowley was a member in London from 1898 to 1900, when he was expelled! ·

Finally, like many other *Illuminés,* the "Fraternity of Inner Light" professes to abstain from political activities as an organisation, but any member, having been oriented by teaching from these Masters on the Inner planes, "it is his duty as a citizen to keep himself informed concerning matters of national and local policy and administration, and to bring his influence to bear upon these in the cause of justice and righteousness."

His influence would naturally be that of his Master and control!

Who, then, are these Masters? And what is their Great Work? Have things changed since de Luchet wrote in 1789:

> "here was formed in the heart of thickest darkness a society of new beings, who knew each other without being seen, who understood each other without explanation, who served one another without friendship. Their society aims at governing the world, appropriating the authority of sovereigns, usurping their thrones by leaving them the mere barren honour of wearing the Crown. It adopts the Jesuitic régime, blind obedience, and the regicide principles of the seventeenth century; from Freemasonry the tests and exterior ceremonies; from the Templars the subterranean evocations and incredible audacity. It uses the discoveries of physics in order to impose upon the ignorant multitude."

The invisible manipulators of Illuminism may be few, but their methods have the secret subtlety of the serpent, and their dupes are many. It is by binding together half qualities in men and women into groups of three, five, seven, twelve, etc., that the power of magic lies; it is, as it were, the seven colours of the prism, united to form the "Divine White Light" of the Rosicrucians, each individual representing the characteristics of a colour, therefore, of a force. This applies to material, mental, and emotional magic. There are also many other correspondences attached to each force, as shown by Crowley in "777," which when combined together add to the potency of that particular force. As Dion Fortune expresses it:

> "A system of Correspondences consists of a set of symbols which the concrete mind can apprehend and a knowledge of the association chains which connect them with each other; this knowledge is absolutely essential for occult development."

Or for magic, black or white!

KUNDALINI-YOGA

The Kundalini-Yoga in one form or another is found in all these sects; it is the basis of their attraction and power. Without it they could not exist, there would be no mysterious Overmasters pouring out suggestive and intriguing teachings, giving directions and seemingly wise advice; there would be no seeing of visions and hearing of voices, there would be no going out into the profane world orienting minds by means of these insidious teachings, drawing into the nets the unwary and sometimes genuine seeker after truth, but more often the craver after excitement, looking for something to enhance or give interest to an otherwise colourless life, enticed by the promise of awakening hitherto unsuspected and mysterious powers — but always under control and ostensibly for the betterment of collective Humanity. Binding the members together with an oath of secrecy and blind obedience — the secrecy of their contact with these Masters or Elder Brethren who, through these pseudo-mysteries and their dupes, would govern the world and usurp authority.

In his book *Serpent Power*, 1919, Arthur Avalon (Sir John Woodroffe) writes:

> "The Tantras say that it is in the power of man to accomplish all he wishes if he centres his will thereon ... for man, they say, is in his essence one with the Supreme Lord [Universal Creative Principle.], and the more he manifests spirit [astral light] the greater he is endowed with its powers... The object of the Tantric rituals is to raise these various forms of power to their fullest expression."

The centre and root of these powers in man lies in the Kundalini. Therefore we can understand why the God of all these modern mysteries is the Universal Creative Principle, and the Kundalini within man is called the "God within" or hidden god, and finally why man, when filled to intoxication with this astral light, looks upon himself as God, a deified and illuminated man.

Briefly, the Kundalini is the sex-force lying in three and a half coils at the base of the spinal column. It is that part of the Great Breath or *Swara* which is "the mightiest manifestation of creative power in the human body." It is formed of three energies: *Ida,* on the left side of the spinal column, the Moon or feminine channel (or Nadi); *Pinggala,* on the right-side, the masculine or Sun channel; *Sushumna,* the channel of the uniting and dissolving Fire, within the column itself. It is the "Serpent Power," the creator, preserver, and destroyer, the I.A.O. of all Hermetic, Cabalistic, and Gnostic sects.

> "She, the subtlest of the subtle, holds within herself the Mystery of creation, and by her radiance, it is said, the universe is illumined, eternal knowledge awakened [subconscious] and liberation attained... She maintains all beings of the world by means of inspiration and expiration."

The Kundalini must first be roused by powerful mind and will, along with suitable physical actions; certain modes of training and worship are prescribed, the use of images, emblems, symbols, pictures, mantras, and processes, etc. Thus rendered active, it is drawn to the cerebral centre, "as in the case of ordinary positive and negative electric charges which are themselves but other manifestations of the universal polarity which affects the manifested world."

Pinggala when roused goes upward from right to left, encircling the lotuses or chakras, these centres of physical and psychic force, reaching the pineal gland, at the root of the nose, between the eyebrows; *Ida* goes from left to right, also encircling the chakras, rising to the same centre between the eyebrows. These two, together with the *Sushumna*, form a plaited knot at this same pineal gland. To be led up the "Middle Path" the vital force must be withdrawn from both the *Pinggala* and the *Ida*, devitalising the rest of the body for the time being, and made to enter the *Sushumna*, piercing the chakras on its upward path, absorbing into itself the tattvas of each chakra, also the sub-tattvas with which each in turn is intercharged. Thus we have the *earth* tattva of the chakra at the base of the spine; *water*, the spleen; *fire*, the navel or solar plexus; *air*, the heart; *ether, the throat*. Passing from the gross to the subtle the earth is dissolved in water, water absorbed by fire; fire is sublimed by air and air by ether, and in absorbing these tattvas the Kundalini is, as it were, rendered subtle and freed from the gross. This by some is called transmutation of the sex-force, leading to spiritual things, but in reality it is only astral. Having united with the universal in the cerebral centre, it then descends, at the same time projecting back the tattvic forces into the various chakras, again taking up its latent potential position at the base of the spinal column, and the body resumes its vitality. The longer it can be retained in the cerebral centre, the seat of the "Supreme Lord," the greater, it is said, will be the power and knowledge acquired by the Yogi.

Such is the "God within" of all these various sects. It is represented by the Caduceus of Hermes, with its twin serpents, negative and positive, twining round the central rod, the spinal column, surmounted at the pineal gland by the wings of what is called liberation; the ball at the top of the rod being the pituitary body, the seat of supreme power. Or as the Emerald Tablet of Hermes expresses it:

> "What is below is like that which is above, and what is above is similar to that which is below to accomplish the wonders of one thing [manifestation]. Its father is the Sun; its mother is the Moon. It is the cause of all perfection throughout the whole earth [equilibrium].. The power is perfect *if it is changed into earth* [fixation of the astral light in a material basis]. Separate the earth·from the fire, the subtle from the gross, acting prudently and with judgment. Ascend with the greatest sagacity from earth to heaven, and then descend again to earth and unite together the things inferior and superior; thus you will possess the light of the whole world, and all obscurity will fly away from you [the ascent of the Kundalini or Serpent Power and the descent of the Lightning Flash. It is the serpent pierced with an arrow, fixation of the astral light in a material body, producing illumination or Illuminism]. This thing has more fortitude than fortitude itself, because it will overcome every subtle thing and penetrate every solid thing. By it the world was formed."

It is the Universal Creative Principle, electro-magnetic forces of life. It is force which can slay or make alive! Further, Max Heindel, in his book *Rosicrucian Cosmo-Conception,* gives the diagram of the three paths taken by the Kundalini or unused sex-forces. He calls them, right of the spinal column, mystic; left, occultist; and central, adept. They all lead to illumination, that is, clairvoyance, clairaudience, and impressional teaching. These, in the form of mental suggestive processes, were received by Dr. Felkin from Dr. Steiner, and given, along with certain of Steiner's meditations and breathing exercises, to the members of the *Stella Matutina,* who were merely told that these processes would awaken their inner senses. To each of these three processes was attached one of the three following names: Jakin, Boaz, or Macbenac, representing the Kundalini forces, the three Pillars found in all Masonry, the cabalistic Pillars of Mercy, Severity, and Mildness of the Tree of Life. According to Dr. Wynn Westcott, the cabalistic Tree of Life is simply the Rabbinic form of the union of the creative principle within man, with the Universal Creative Principle without. And as Max Heindel explains:

> "It will give first-hand knowledge of the superphysical realms."

The great danger of this Yoga as practised among Western and modern *Illuminés* would, therefore, appear to be not only an intoxication of astral light, producing illusions and deception, even mania, but also the serious risk of a stronger mind, working on the astral plane, taking possession of a weaker and less-informed mind, using it for its own ends as in the case of these Masters and Elder Brothers, who seem to be taken on trust by the leaders of these cults. As Dion Fortune writes:

> "By thinking of the Masters we attract their attention, and it is unbelievably easy to establish a magnetic link with those who are always more ready to give than we are to receive; and if anyone, after thinking about the Masters and formulating a wish to be accepted as a pupil, finds that the circumstances of his life are beginning to blow up a storm, he will know that his application has been accepted and that the preliminary tests have begun."

The Masters never take the pupils on trust, they test them, they shape and hew them, until they are humbly and blindly obedient, ready to do their appointed work in the Great Plan of these "Supermen." And thus we see the Western world permeated with leaders in Yoga cults, only a little less ignorant than the men and women they would instruct, all preparing the way for the "Masters," whoever they may be.

OUSPENSKY

First we will take P. D. Ouspensky, a Russian, as depicted in his book *A New Model of the Universe.* As regards Occultism, there is nothing really new in this book, for it is based largely on the work of other writers, with the idea of showing that most religions, cults, and occultism are merely "pseudo." As the author says: "When we find that religion is centuries… behind science and philosophy, the main inference is that it is… pseudo-religion." The only real thing in his opinion is "esotericism," which apparently means sensations and teachings obtained by mysticism, induced by some form of Yoga. All this is interwoven with his own vague experiments, theories, and feelings.

He believes the world is controlled by an "inner circle." "True civilisation," he says, "exists only in esotericism… It is the inner circle which is, in fact, the truly civilised portion of humanity." Here is his theory of the growth of the inner circle: Adam and Eve were issued from Nature's Great Laboratory and appeared upon earth; for a time they were helped by the powers who created them. Men at first were incapable of making mistakes, and so advanced rapidly, but as time went on they, believed they knew good from evil, and were able to guide themselves. They then made mistake after mistake, until they gradually fell to the level from which they rose "plus the acquired sin"! A certain number made no mistakes, and were able to preserve all knowledge that was really valuable for culture; these then became the "inner circle" (we presume the Elder Brothers of the Great White Lodge!). This inner circle took the place of the powers who created men. Their religion is esotericism; all others, therefore, are "pseudo." Such are the uninspired and uninspiring theories of Ouspensky; which appear to us to be not even original!

His chapters on the Tarot cards and the various forms of Yoga are taken from books already well known. He thus explains the powers gained by means of first *Raja-Yoga:*

> "As a result man attains a state of extraordinary freedom and power. He not only controls himself, but is *able to control others.* He can read the thoughts of other people whether they are near him or at a distance; *he can suggest to them his own thoughts and desires and subordinate them to himself.* He can acquire clairvoyance, he can know the past and future."

Karma-Yoga, which means *non-attachment,* "teaches man … that in reality it is not he who acts, but only a power passing through him." He rarely acts "independently, but in most cases only as part of one or another great whole" — no doubt governed by forces and laws often set in motion by the "inner circle" for their own ends! *Hatha-Yoga* is attainment by control over the body and physical nature of man. "By learning to govern their own bodies Yogis at the same time learn *to govern the whole of the material universe,*" that is, the development of will and thought power. *Jnana-Yoga* uses the methods of *Raja-Yoga,* and is said to educate the mind and reveal the fundamental laws of the universe. *Bhakti-Yoga* teaches how to believe, pray, and attain certain salvation; in it differences of religion do not exist.

Ouspensky insists that Yoga must be practised only under a teacher, yet apparently he carries out, on his own, mystical experiments which, if controlled by some unknown group, might lead to anything from outside suggestion to obsession. He writes:

> "During the first experiments... I felt that I was disappearing, vanishing, turning into nothing ... in one case it was All that swallowed me up, in the other it was Nothing ... in subsequent experiments the same sensation of the disappearance of "I" began to produce in me a feeling of extraordinary calmness and confidence... When I felt that I did not exist, everything else became very simple and easy."

Then he began to get teaching! This is common to all occult schools, and more generally means control by some outside influence. Also, as we know, the so-called transmutation or rather perversion of sex-force is the basis of all such experiments in Yoga. As he explains, sex-force is used for "the development of man in the direction of the acquisition by him of higher consciousness and the opening-up of his latent forces and faculties. The explanation of this latter possibility in connection with the using of sex-energy for this purpose, forms the content and meaning of all esoteric teachings."

He speaks of Yogi Ramakrishna, who was a Bhakti-Yogi, and lived in the "eighties" of last century, in the monastery Dakshineswar, near Calcutta. "He recognised as equal all religions with all their dogmas, sacraments, and rituals." For twelve years he (the Yogi) experimented, in the way of asceticism, with all religions, and according to himself, he attained the same results of ecstasy, in each one, and therefore concluded that all great religions were one. But his divine Mother was the Great Mother Nature! and his ecstasy meant union with the Universal Creative Force!

It is interesting and enlightening to know that Swami Vivekananda, who went to America in 1893 to take part in the "Parliament of Religions," was one of Ramakrishna's disciples! In his book, *Mysticism in the Court of Russia,* J. Bricaud says: "Certain writings of Dostoiewsky, Tolstoi, and Merejkovsky have revealed to Western people the secret nature of the Russian soul, tormented and eager for the marvellous." Is Ouspensky not just one more of these Russian souls, eager for the marvellous,. as shown in his experiments, and his vague self-induced pseudo-mystic sensations described as felt by him at the Pyramids, Taj Mahal, etc.? Is it not this pseudo-mysticism in their tools that is required by those who would secretly control and dominate mankind?

Ouspensky was for a time a disciple of Gurdjieff, that strange man who, for a time, held extraordinary sway over many and varied followers at Fontainebleau, and who is now apparently in New York. It is small wonder that we see America, to-day, rotten with the canker of these cults so that even those who would save their country are dominated by "Elder Brothers" of one kind or another or steeped in a dangerous and mistaken mysticism, and spiritism.

VIVEKANANDA

In *The Confusion of Tongues, 1*929, Charles W. Ferguson tells of the great Swami and Yogi invasion of America during the last forty years. Of Swami Vivekananda he says: "He was the first and greatest zealot of the East to offer up the Hindu mysteries in palatable form for American consumption." In 1893 this Swami went to America, chosen by his followers to represent them at the Parliament of Religions which, in September of that year, was held in Chicago. Arriving there in July, he settled in one of its richest hotels. Soon his money ran out, and, being without credentials, he was told he would not be received at the Parliament of Religions when it opened. Sad and sorrowful, he set out for Boston, and on the train a kindly lady took charge of him and made her home his headquarters. In Boston he was taken up by the Harvard professors, and when the time came he was dispatched to Chicago armed with the required credentials, and finally found his way to the Parliament of Religions. There, among the varied sects and cults, he was an immense success, and gave great impetus to all movements which preached the "divinity of man"; he was lionised, and lectured far and wide. In New York he established a Vedanta Society, which spread and was well supported. It was his avowed purpose to unify and synthesise the East and West, but what he chiefly did was to prepare the way for a horde of lesser figures, who, no doubt, carried his mission far beyond his own ultimate aim. He made America India conscious and made Hindu philosophy popular.

In his philosophy and teachings as given in *The Life of Swami Vivekananda,* by his Eastern and Western disciples, 1912-15, his lectures on Raja-Yoga, or the conquering of interior nature, teach that the goal of life "is to manifest this divinity within by controlling nature, internal and external," and that all Indian philosophies have one object, 'that is, the liberation of the soul [the 'god within'!] through perfection.' Further:

> "When the Yogi becomes perfect, there will be nothing in nature not under his control. If he orders the gods to come, they will come at his bidding. All the forces of Nature will obey him as slaves, and when the ignorant see these powers of the Yogi they will call them miracles. Nature is ready to give up her secrets... through concentration. There is no limit to the power of the human mind. The more concentrated it is, the more power is brought to bear on one point, and that is the secret."

As Mr. Ferguson remarks:

> "Raja-Yoga, disclaiming and discounting the religious motive, proposes none the less to make man the king of high heaven and the engineer of the cosmos... If we may judge from testimonials, what those who follow the Swamis and Yogis want in the way of modern religion is a quick relief from neurasthenia and frustration ... and a temporary surcease from the fascinating but at times maddening world in which we live."

He then briefly gives the eight steps of Raja-Yoga which lead to full initiation, and which must be practised under an inspired teacher: *Yama,* in which the pupil masters himself, becomes trustful and self-reliant, and surrenders himself to what he conceives to be God; *Asana* a series of exercises and postures designed to put the body completely at the mercy of the mind. *Pratyahara,* a method of making the mind relentlessly introspective; *Dharana,* a process through which concentration is achieved; *Shyana,* or holy meditation upon lofty ideas; and *Samadhi,* in which the individual at last rises to complete·super-consciousness and lives in a realm where ailments and limitations of the body exercise no influence over him. Again: 'If one stays doggedly at the ritual of breathing, the sacred fluid of kundalini [sexforce], having its residence at the seat of the spinal column, will be aroused ... then the book of knowledge will be opened.' This is obtained by controlling the *Prana,* the dual forces of the universe, which manifests itself as motion, gravitation, and magnetism in the cosmos, and as nerve-currents and thought-force in the body.

YOGANANDA

Among the horde of Swamis and Yogis who have exploited these powers by Americanising and commercialising Yoga, Swami Yogananda is, or was, apparently one of the most successful. He arrived in America, 1920, to attend the International Congress of Religions at Boston, and his first centre was organised there, but later headquarters were at the Mount Washington Centre of Yogoda and Sat-Sanga, in California. Yogoda means a system which "teaches one to harmonise all the faculties and forces that operate for the perfection of mind, body, and soul." Sat-Sanga means "Fellowship with Truth." In 1929 he claimed 20,000 students of his system, with centres in eight leading cities, and also a bi-monthly magazine *East-West Magazine.* He wishes to establish "How to live schools" throughout the world.

Roughly, the science of Yogoda lies apparently in magnetising the spinal column and using this electricity stored in the body and lodged in the brain as the chief power-house, and ultimately bliss is said to settle over the physique and the pleasures of the flesh are forgotten. Finally, advertised as a system of bodily perfection for the "busy aspiring Western peoples," it "uses the will to re-charge the body-battery from the cosmic life-current, and thus produce a fatigueless state." Further:

> "It also includes the highest technique of meditation and concentration by the psycho-physiological methods taught by the great saints and sages of India. How to see the vital force and hear the cosmic vibrations... Yogoda quickens man's evolution through an intelligent co-operation with cosmic law. It restores his eternal heritage, and gives him realisation of himself as the *immortal life energy.*"

In England we are not without our quota of exploiting and proselytising Swamis and Yogis, and what we would emphasise is, that such a crude form of Eastern Yoga, when applied to Western mentality, whether in the form of Indian or Tibetan systems or the Magical Cabala of the Jews, merely results in a hypnotic passivity or unbalance, through an over-charge of astral light, and is destructive to Western virility and mental power, which will end in submerging Western and Christian traditions, leaving the nations an easy prey to domination by their ever-watchful and secret enemies. Also we must never forget that these cosmic and vital forces can both slay and make alive, bodily and mentally, and in the hands of ambitious and unscrupulous men, "Supermen," "Elder Brothers," or the whole gamut of those who astrally control these sects and cults which have eaten into the life of the Western World to-day, this Yoga teaching can be a deadly weapon of power for evil domination or vengeance, under the masquerade of soul-development or religious attainment.

MEHER BABA

Another less powerful but more theatrical figure is Shri Meher Baba, known as "The New Messiah." *John Bull, 7* May, 1932, published, "after having completed a thorough investigation into his operations of recent years," some interesting details as to who he is and how he arose out of obscurity into publicity, using theatrical methods which gave him a certain notoriety. His agent for Europe and America was a man not unknown among circles of Illuminati in England, and it was at his farm in the south of

England, where a colony of devotees numbering about twenty, men and women, young and old, white and coloured, settled down for some little time to attain "the Greater Realisation," through Meher Baba's teaching. Paul Brunton, in *A Search in Secret India,* tells us that "his personal name is Meher, but he calls himself Sadguru Meher Baba. Sadguru means 'perfect master,' while Baba is simply a term of affection in common use among some of the Indian peoples." His father is a Persian and Zoroastrian, and Meher Baba was born at Poona in 1894 and led a normal life until he was about twenty, when he came in contact with "a well-known Muhammadan woman faqueer, Hazrat BabaJan," who in some way unbalanced his mind. Some believe he has never completely recovered.

John Bull informs us that up to his somewhat recent "call" to Messiahship his means of livelihood was selling native liquor in the byways of Nasik, where, in 1932, he had apparently only a few thousand followers. Although his fame in India is but limited, many of his followers are wealthy, and he was able to raise large sums, which he used to finance various schemes for publicity purposes. One was a cinema to be built in Nasik, but because of calls from creditors and lack of funds it was never completed. Another was a school at Ahmadnagar for boys of various castes, creeds, and races, who were to be spiritually trained to act as his "ambassadors" or minor Messiahs in all parts of the world. He even attempted, by means of an emissary, to draw European boys out to this school; final arrangements were concluded by his agent, but the authorities intervened, and the boys remained at home.

As to Meher Baba's cult, it is so-called yoga, a speeding-up method of working on the Kundalini and awakening the latent senses or, as they say, becoming "acquainted with those forces which, when liberated, will enable the student to realise greater possibilities in accordance with the inner laws of Nature and Life." To further this process there was sun-bathing, violent physical exercises in the open air, the study of all psychological problems, and a general leading of the simple life under Meher Baba's instructions. One may ridicule such mushroom-growths, gurus who cover their comparative ignorance and incapacity as teachers by spectacular stunts such as the "silence," which for quite a number of years Meher Baba has imposed upon himself as a preparation for his future mighty calling, his lack of speech being supplied by an alphabet board, which he works like a typewriter while a disciple interprets his meaning and teachings. He believes there will be a great war, and when that comes his tongue will be loosened and he will teach and lead all peoples and bring in peace; until then silence!

Paul Brunton adds as a note to his account of "The New Messiah":

> "Meher Baba has since appeared in the West, and a Western cult has started to gather around him. He still promises wonderful things, which will happen when he breaks his silence. He has several times visited England, has acquired a following in France, Spain, and Turkey, and has been twice to Persia. He made a theatrical journey across the continent of America with a mixed retinue of men and women. When he arrived in Hollywood, he was given a royal reception;, Mary Pickford entertained him in her home, Tallulah Bankhead became interested in him, while a thousand leading people were presented to him at Hollywood's largest hotel. A large tract of land was acquired in the United States to establish his Western headquarters. Meanwhile, dumbness still lies on his lips, the while he flits impulsively from country to country on brief visits. At last he has been brought into the glare of notoriety."

Summarising Meher Baba and his experience with the old fakir woman, he says:

> "I believe that the youthful Meher became quite unbalanced as a result of this unexpected experience. This was obvious enough when he fell into a condition of semi-idiocy and behaved like a human robot, but it is not so obvious now that he has recovered sanity. I do not believe that he has returned to normality as a human being. To some people, a sudden overdose of religion, Yogic trance, or mystic ecstasy, is as unbalancing as a sudden overdose of certain drugs…"

As we know, however, this pseudo-liberation, as practised in all these modern groups, carries with it no uncertain dangers — mental, moral, and physical — but fanatical and perhaps somewhat hypnotised enthusiasts are always ready to take risks in their search for the excitement of what they call spiritual-uplift, which so often ends in mediumship exploited by some unknown powers for political and subversive ends. We have only to look among our so-called intellectuals to realise this. America, where Meher Baba goes to spread this Yogacraze, is perhaps more susceptible than England to the virus of this poison, which acts as a dope, playing up to the restless craving of some of its citizens for psychical experiences, so often in that country quite frankly applied to mere material business and commercial ends, or it may even be, to further subversive political schemes.

Moreover, the modern craze for Illuminism is not less disintegrating and demoralising. Felix Guyot, apparently a Martinist, in a book on *Yoga for the West,* reveals some dangerous methods which, he claims, lead to illumination and contact with the Masters, methods which he has been practising for over thirty years, and which are curiously akin to those taught in the Stella Matutina and R.R. et A.C., the Anthroposophical Society, etc., which are Martinist and Rosicrucian. He says that "humanity is moving backwards, we are under the rule of the Beast." But is it not rather the rule of the cabalistic Jew, using the serpent or sex-force in his system of Illuminism?

To act upon the Kundalini or sex-force and bring about union with these Masters, monoideism or concentration, with gymnastic, breathing, and psychic exercises, some of them exceedingly and admittedly dangerous, leading to possible death or obsession, are expounded by M. Guyot. He says:

> "[Sexual desire] is a rich source of energy which, if properly employed, can be of very great assistance in the sphere of occultism... If you check and control the reserve of force of which the sexual organs are the source, you will be able to direct it towards the goal you have in view, and *use it for your own ends...* and when the time comes, on another plane."

To forward this Illuminism students "must not only wipe out their own special hatreds but really *suppress the capacity of hatred...* in favour of love." This is perhaps the underlying cause of so much unnatural and unbalanced pacifism, especially seen among members of these sects.

Further:

"Students will have to adopt a religion to sustain and help them during their psychic training [to give them the uplift!] ... for the moment it is not a matter of believing but of acting as though you did believe... The mythical entities of the religion chosen will play a considerable practical part in the various psychic exercises... We think the best religions are the Jewish religion, as set forth in the Cabala, the Roman Catholic religion in its esoteric aspect, Buddhism, and especially Hinduism. Finally, Freemasonry can very adequately take the place of a religion, but it must be based on Martinism, which is its source."

This means Illuminised Masonry as in France in 1789 and since, and this Jew-dominated Masonry has always been, and still is, the well-spring of all modern revolutions.

Abstract diagrams and mantrams along with breathing exercises are, he says, the key to supernormal cognition. He thus explains this dangerous magical practice:

"If the experiment is successful ... you will experience a feeling of cold at the extremities, especially in your hands, and you will tremble slightly. At the same time you will feel a sensation, which cannot be explained to those who have not experienced it, *as though an extraneous entity entered into you.*

... You will then find that a series of images, and afterwards of intuitions, come into your mind very quickly, but characterised by the fact that it seems to you that it is not you who are thinking, and that things are being revealed to you by another through the medium of a sort of internal illumination."

The author notes: "This is the inspiration of the pythonesses of antiquity. It is the first degree of ecstasy. By various processes the Rosicrucians and Martinists tried to bring about this ecstasy, and that is why the Martinists called themselves the *Illuminated.*"

The author puts this on the Mental Plane and says: "By means of thought transmission you will be able to communicate with the Masters, which will be of great assistance in completing your initiation (or illumination)." He claims that "the experimenter is not possessed." Nevertheless, he is for the time possessed and controlled on the astral plane, and is being shaped and hewn, receiving the Master's: forces and instructions which eventually orient his whole outlook on life; or if the experimenter be a leader of a group, the result is devastating to the mentality of many. Again, M. Guyot says: "By becoming more proficient in certain exercises we can succeed in bringing other people under the same influence, that is, we can convert our own particular hallucination into a collective hallucination. That is true both of positive and negative hallucinations." Here we have a terrible and dangerous power, mass suggestion often creating a powerful body of hypnotised and fanaticised adepts and others working out the World Plan of an unknown and invisible group of ambitious mystics and occultists, themselves fanatics.

Of the Pythonesses of the ancient Mysteries we read in *Dieu et les Dieux*, by des Mousseaux:

> "It seems that the immodesty of the phallic cult crept even into the Delphic sanctuary of Apollo-Bacchus, even into the method of putting the priestess [or as she was called, pythoness] into communication with her God [creative principle], uniting the two in order to make Divinity speak through a mortal mouth... In this temple the prophetess is seated on a tripod. Soon her hair bristles, her eyes roll with blood and flame, her muscles are convulsed, the breath of the God animates her, and the vapours from the sacred cave penetrate into her through the tripod... She is exalted to fury... and often the last of her prophetic movements is death... To predict, is for her a terror..."

There is an American group which is a striking political example of this Illuminism, communications psychically received by its leader from some unknown "Elder Brother," whose watchword is apparently "Peace." Here and there in the publications of this association, of which we will speak later, we find this same occultism — the use of the sex-force, speculations on reincarnation and karma, and messages and instructions received from their Master, for some would-be great political regeneration.

The following is another, a religious example, of these same methods of invisible control. There was given in the *Morning Post*, 2 February, 1931, a short account of a trance sermon delivered at the Fortune Theatre, through Mrs. Meurig Morris by her control, who called himself "Power." To those who have any knowledge of illuminised sects, there is absolutely nothing new in what he said. He thus explains himself: "Remember that I, like others who have changed, am still an intelligent being." That is, though "regenerated" or illuminated, he is still a man of flesh and blood, like all masters of Illuminism, invisible or otherwise.

For example, in the Golden Dawn the "Hidden Chiefs" were "Great Adepts of this Planet still in the body of the flesh." And the Mithraic Sun Masters of the same Order said: "The Masters of Wisdom are mortal men ... in thy higher self *[Kether* of the Cabalistic Tree of Life] thou shalt hear my voice; when thou art willing to obey that voice of silence... I am guiding thee." Thus this "voice within" is not that of a spirit nor yet is it divine, but merely that of a controlling "mortal man," influencing the medium from outside, and it may be from a distance — an unknown illuminatus!

"Power" further explains: I use her in this way:

> "At the top of her head there is a large cone-like shape [pituitary body!]. It is down this cone, like a passage [or funnel] that the power is poured. I am able to play and work on the brain, and use the whole body as I will, while the control is taking place."

This is hypnotic control or possession, and appears to be somewhat similar to the method taught and attempted by the R.R. et A.C. masters when seeking to gain permanent control over the Chief and the Order. According to them the transmission of the forces, set in motion by thought and willpower, from the mental plane above to the material plane below, is in the form of a double cone or hour-glass; the power from above transmits the force through the upper cone, and by means of the lower translates it to the passive and prepared medium below, along the etheric thread of communication (see *Light Bearers of Darkness,* pp. 124 and 134). This method has also been compared by other occultists to the action of a waterspout or whirlwind, creating a vortex down which the forces rush.

Again "Power" says: "Why, it may be asked, do I arrive the minute the hymn begins?" Now it is known that in illuminised sects and Yoga *mantras* and *rhythmic movements,* such as the vibration of so-called divine names and formulas, the Eurhythmy of Steiner, and in other groups specially intoned hymns are used to awaken the necessary vibrations, setting in motion the whirling forces which attract and bring down the Master's forces from above, creating the etheric link, concentrating the forces on the prepared focal-point-in this case Mrs. Meurig Morris. As we have seen this method is applied to religious, political, and educational groups, all for the purpose of subversion.

"Power" is therefore one of these hidden Masters, men who have investigated and experimented with laws of nature unknown to most people, and have become adepts in manipulating these finer secret forces, creative forces of the universe, using their knowledge to gain power over their fellow-creatures, and through them aspiring to World Domination. No doubt he is an "Elder Brother" seeking through Mrs. Meurig Morris to create a magnetic chain of religious ideas necessary for the Great Plan.

The following curious piece of intriguing information is given by René Guénon in his *Théosophisme:* Eliphas Levi, the occultist and Martinist, who died in 1875, had announced that in 1879 a new "Universal Kingdom," political and religious, would be established, and that this kingdom would belong "to him who would have the keys of the East," that is, the Keys of Solomon, and that these keys would be possessed "by the nation whose life and activity was most intelligent." This prediction was contained in a manuscript which was in the possession of an occultist of Marseilles, pupil of Eliphas Levi, the Baron Spedalieri, who gave it to Edward Maitland, who in turn passed it on to Dr. Wynn Westcott, Supreme Magus of the *Societas Rosicruciana in Anglia,* member of the *Theosophical Society,* and one of the founders of the *Golden Dawn.* Finally, the latter published it in 1896, under the title of "The Magical Ritual of the *Sanctum Regnum."* It is said that Spedalieri was a member of the "Grand Lodge of the Solitary Brethren of the Mountain," an illuminised Brother of the Ancient Restored Order of the Manicheans, "a high member of the Grand Orient," and also a "High Illuminate of the Martinists." The drearri of the Grand Orient is, as is well known, Universal Masonry.

Now, Eliphas Levi, in his book *Transcendental, Magic,* describes this *Sanctum Regnum* as magical omnipotence, the knowledge and power of the Magi for which is required an intelligence enlightened by study, indomitable courage, and a will which cannot be broken, and finally prudence, which nothing can corrupt or intoxicate. "To know, to dare, to will, to keep silence." It is the invisible "Holy Empire" over all peoples and over all nations. The Pentagram is its guiding star, the symbolism of Illuminism, the star of revolution. Its symbol of power is the Interlaced Triangles, the Seal of Solomon, the seven powers representing complete magical power through the knowledge, in all its combinations, of the magnetic currents of attraction and repulsion in all nature. He who has this power and can wield it has "the Keys of the East."

The Great Work which is to prepare the way for the establishment of the "Universal Kingdom" is the formation of the magnetic-chain. To form this is, according to Eliphas Levi,

> "to originate a current of ideas which produces faith and draws a large number of wills in a given circle of active manifestation. A well-formed chain is like a whirlpool which sucks down and absorbs all... To be able to apply these currents and direct them is to be Master of the World. Armed with such a force you may make yourself adored, the crowd will believe you are God."

For many years we have seen the insidious cankerous growth of this magnetic-chain of these ideas, not only in England, but throughout the entire world, largely set in motion by the Invisible Power which works through these many secret revolutionary movements, even those apparently innocent and harmless, perverting, debasing, and disintegrating religion, ethics, art, literature, politics, sociology, and economics, making way for the "Universal Kingdom," political and religious, which is to be ruled by the Signet of Solomon, the Hebrew Talisman!

As M. Flavien Brenier remarks in his book *Les Juifs et le Talmud*[3]:

> "One cannot fail to be struck by the similarity which exists between the doctrines of the Pharisees twenty-five centuries old [borrowed from the Chaldeans of Babylon] and those professed in our days by

---

[3] *Les Juifs et le Talmud: Morale et Principes sociaux des Juifs*, published by Omnia Veritas Ltd, www.omnia-veritas.com.

the disciples of Allan Kardec or of Mme Blavatsky. The most important difference is that the final blessing is reserved by the Talmud for Jews alone, whilst Spiritists and Theosophists affirm that all beings will attain it."

As the Talmud says:

> "The Messiah will give the Royal Sceptre to the Jew, all peoples will serve him, and all kingdoms will be subject to him."

Rabbi Benamozegh, in *Israël et l'humanité,* wrote of the coming power of the Jewish Magical Cabala:

> "Is it surprising that Judaism has been accused of forming a branch of Freemasonry? What is certain is, that Masonic theology is, at the bottom, merely Theosophy, and corresponds to that of the Cabala. On the other hand a profound study of Rabbinic monuments of the first centuries of the Christian era furnishes numerous proofs that the *aggada* was the popular form of a reserved science, offering, by methods of initiation, the most striking resemblances to the Freemasonic institution. Those who will take the trouble to examine with care the connection between Judaism and philosophic Freemasonry, Theosophy, and the Mysteries in general, will lose, we are convinced, a little of their superb disdain for the Cabala. They will cease to smile in pity at the idea that cabalistic theology may have a role to play in the religious transformations of the future... We do not hesitate to repeat that this doctrine, *which draws together to the heart of Judaism the Semite and Aryan elements,* contains also the key to the modern religious problem."

CHAPTER XI

ALEISTER CROWLEY AND
THE GOLDEN DAWN

AGAIN, to quote the *Anatomy of Revolution,* we find G.G. writing:

> "And just as we found that the group of German, Irish, Indian, Turkish, and Egyptian societies was linked together by an interlocking membership, so we find that these Arcane orders are also in like manner connected. This is not the place to go into the ramifications of the strange mystical revolutionary societies of Europe, America, and the East. I shall refer only to the "Ordre Renove des Illuminati Germaniae" and the "Rose-Croix Esotérique." both founded by men with names that are either German or Jewish. [Leopold Engel and Franz Hartmann.] The latter society appears to be the inner ring of the Order of the Templars of the Orient, founded about a generation ago by another man with a German name. [Dr. Karl Kellner, 1895, and from 1905, Theodor Reuss.) And with this Ordo Templarum Orientis, we find associated the notorious Aleister Crowley, whose relations with Germans and Irish revolutionaries during the war earned for him the attention of the police of the United States of America.

At the end of his book, *Les Illuminés de Bavière,* 1915, R. le Forestier speaks of the revival of the Order of the Illuminati by Leopold Engel. He is rather indefinite as to date, but says it had its centre in Berlin, and had, as required, been reported to the police. He quotes Engel as saying:

> "They gradually came to believe that it would be possible to give something definite to the adepts in order to reach an ideal goal by means of Weishaupt's theories."

We need not repeat what we have already written about Aleister Crowley in *Light Bearers of Darkness*[4], except to give a few necessary facts for the understanding of what follows. He is a man of many aliases, such as: Count Svareff, Count Skellatt, Count Skerrett, Edward Aleister, Lord Boleskine, Baron Rosenkreutz, Count Macgregor, Count Mac Gregor, Eerskine, Perdurabo Baphomet, The Beast, Therion, and Thor Kimalehto.

He was born at Leamington, 12 October, 1875, and was undergraduate at Cambridge from 1895 to 1898. In November 1898 he became a member of the "Order of the Golden Dawn," where he was known as Perdurabo; however, on account of his well-known reputation, he was refused admission to the London Inner Order, the R.R. et A.C. In 1900 he acted as emissary for Macgregor Mathers, the Chief of the Golden Dawn, who was at that time in Paris and who had sent Crowley to London to put down the rebellion which had arisen there owing to Mather's arrogance. Crowley, however, failed in his mission, and found himself eventually and finally expelled from the London Temple of the Golden Dawn. He nevertheless retained possession of all the rituals and certain MSS., and from 1909 to 1913, by direct orders, he said, of the Secret Chiefs, he published these documents in his *Equinox*, "The Review of Scientific Illuminism," under the title of "The Temple of Solomon the King." This review, with these rituals as teaching basis, was also the organ of his Order of the A.A., the "Atlantean Adepts" or the Great White Brotherhood, and closely allied to that were his "Ordo Templi Orientis" and his "Mysteria Mystica Maxima." His doctrine was: "Do what thou wilt, shall be the whole of the Law; Love is the Law; Love under Will."

To go through the ten numbers of Vol. 1 of his *Equinox*, is to realise the reason why he has been called "A Master of Corruption." These, along with many of his other writings, are a strange medley of sexualism, mysticism, indecencies and blasphemies. And underlying all this pseudo-mysticism are to be

---

[4] Inquire Within, *Light Bearers of Darkness*, Published by Omnia Veritas Ltd, www.omnia-veritas.com.

found subversive political activities. In the 19 *Patriot*, October 1922, a credited authority writes:

> "We have before us, for example, a manifesto issued by the National Grand Lodge and Mystic Temple Verita Mystica of the Ordo Templi Orientis, or Hermetic Brotherhood of Light, dated 22 January, 1917, at Ascona, Switzerland, and signed by J. Adderley, Secretary. The manifesto announces that the headquarters of the Brotherhood has been transferred to Switzerland 'since the commencement of the World War.' The ostensible object of the manifesto is to end the war and to establish a new order of Society, 'based on the principle of co-operation of all, on the common possession of the soil and the means of production by all.' To this end it proposes a National Congress, to be held at Ascona from the 15th to the 25th August following, and announces that one of the attractions is to be a representation of Aleister Crowley's mystic poem 'The Ship.' The document also states that another centre of the 'O.T.O.' is New York, and we may reasonably suppose that Aleister Crowley was organising this centre during his war-visit to the U.S.A. It is at least certain that he was busy in America from 1914 onwards."

We have in our possession a copy of Crowley's book *Magick*, by the Master Therion, 1929. We can only give a few extracts and notes, showing the nature of its contents and teachings.

The book opens with a Hymn to Pan! Io Pan! Io Pan!, which seems to express the essence of his creed, for, throughout, his book is tainted with gnostic and sexual imagery. He writes: "There is a single main definition of the object of all magical Ritual. It is the uniting of the Microcosm with the Macrocosm. The Supreme and Complete Ritual is therefore the Invocation of the Holy Guardian Angel; or, in the language of Mysticism, Union with God." That is, rousing the kundalini, and uniting it with the universal magical agent! And of this God he explains:

> "The testing of the spirits is the most important branch of the whole tree of Magick. Without it, one is lost in the jungle of delusion. Every spirit, up to God Himself, is ready to deceive you if possible, to make himself out more important than he is.
>
> ... Remember that after all the highest of all the Gods is only the Magus... For the Gods are the enemies of Man; it is Nature that Man must overcome ere he enter into his kingdom.

The true God is man. In man are all things hidden. Of these the Gods, Nature, Time, all the powers of the universe are rebellious slaves. It is these that men must fight and conquer in the power, and in the name of the Beast that hath availed them, the Titan, the Magus, the Man, whose number is six hundred and threescore and six."

The power of the Beast is universal generation, the universal magnetic agent. Speaking of the Eucharist of Scientific Illuminism he says:

"Take a substance symbolic of the whole course of nature, make it God, and consume it." [It must be, he says, consumed daily.] "The magician becomes filled with God, fed upon God, intoxicated with God. Little by little his body will become purified by the internal lustration of God; day by day his mortal frame, shedding its earthly elements, will become in very truth the Temple of the Holy Ghost. Day by Day matter is replaced by Spirit, the human by the divine; ultimately the change will be complete; God manifest in flesh will be his name."

But his God is merely Nature's creative principle, again universal generative powers. Pan, lo Pan!

Requiring concentrated energy for his magical operations, he explains:

"*The blood is the life.* This simple statement is explained by the Hindus by saying that the blood is the principal vehicle of vital Prana... It was the theory of the ancient Magicians, that any living being is a storehouse of energy varying in quantity according to the size and health of the animal, and in quality according to its mental and moral character. At the death of the animal this energy is liberated suddenly. [For magical purposes.] The animal should therefore be killed within the Circle, or the Triangle, as the case may be, so that its energy cannot escape. An animal should be selected whose nature accords with that of the ceremony... For the highest spiritual working one must accordingly choose that victim which contains the greatest and purest force. A male child of perfect innocence and high intelligence is the most satisfactory and suitable victim... Those magicians who object to the use of blood have endeavoured to replace it with incense... But the bloody sacrifice, though more dangerous, is more efficacious; and for nearly all purposes human sacrifice is the best. The truly great Magician will be able to use his own blood, or possibly that of a disciple, and that without sacrificing the physical life irrevocably."

He apparently would have us believe that the Great War was the necessary bloody sacrifice for the Initiation of a "New Aeon"! He concludes: "The animal should be stabbed to the heart, or its throat severed, in either case by the knife." He refers us to Frazer's "Golden Bough" for practical details! Into such details we need not enter here.

In Chapter XI of his book *Magick*, headed "Of our Lady Babalon and of the Beast whereon she rideth," Crowley writes:

"The contents of this section, inasmuch as they concern Our Lady, are too important and too sacred to be printed. They are only communicated by Master Therion to chosen pupils in private instructions."

Towards the end of the book, page 345, Liber XV, he gives the ritual of the O.T.O. (Ordo Templi Orientis), The Catholic or Universal Gnostic Church. The Creed is:

"I believe in one secret and ineffable Lord; and in one Star in the company of Stars of whose fire we are created, and to which we shall return; and in one Father of Life, Mystery of Mystery, in His name Chaos, the sole viceregent of the Sun on Earth; and in one Air the nourisher of all that breathes. And I believe in one Earth, the Mother of us all, and in one womb wherein all men are begotten, and wherein they shall rest, Mystery of Mystery, in her name Babalon. [Babylon, the Great Mother of the idolatrous and abominable religions of the earth.] And I believe in the Serpent and the Lion, Mystery of Mystery, in his name Baphomet. [According to Eliphas Levi the Lion is the celestial (astral) fire, while the serpents are the electric and magnetic currents of the earth, the spirit of the seed.] And I believe in one Gnostic and Catholic Church of Light, Love and Liberty, the Word of whose Law is Thelima. And I believe in the communion of Saints. And, forasmuch as meat and drink are transmuted in us daily into spiritual substance, [life-force] I believe in the miracle of the Mass. And I confess one Baptism of Wisdom whereby we accomplish the Miracle of Incarnation. [Generation. And I confess my life one, individual, and eternal that was, and is and is to come. [The universal magnetic life-force.]"

The Priestess enters with a positive child on the right and a negative child on the left and having placed the paten before the

"Graal" on the altar — that is the material basis for the operation and the astral light or vital force with which it is to be united — she, followed by the children, "moves in a serpentine manner involving three and a half circles of the Temple ... and so to the Tomb in the West." It represents the rousing of the kundalini serpent with its three and a half coils at the base of the spinal column.

The Priestess is enthroned upon the altar in the East by the Priest, who consecrates her with water and fire. There are three steps to the altar. On the first step the Priest invokes:

> "O circle of Stars ... not unto Thee may we attain, unless Thine image be Love. Therefore by seed, root and stem and bud and leaf and flower and fruit we do invoke Thee:..."

The Priestess completely unrobed, answers:

> "But to love me is better than all things... Put on the wings, and arouse the coiled splendour within you (kundalini); come unto me! Sing the rapturous love song unto me!..."

The Priest invokes, on the third step:

> "Thou that art One, our Lord in the Universe, the Sun, our Lord in ourselves whose name is Mystery of Mystery... Make open the path of creation and of intelligence between us and our minds... Let thy light crystallise itself in our blood, fulfilling us of Resurrection."

The whole ceremony is a sensuous adoration of the Great Mother Babalon in the person of the Priestess, embodying their doctrine, "Do what thou wilt shall be the whole law. Love is the law; love under will." It ends with the Mystic Repast, the consecration and consummation of the elements, the Mystic Marriage! It is, to say the least of it, a symbolic representation of universal generation.

With regard to the "Communion of the Saints," according to this ritual they are those who have from generation to generation adored this Lord of Life and Joy and manifested His glory to men. They include among many others: Lao-tze, Dionysus, Hermes, Pan, Priapus, Osiris, Melchizedeck, Amoun, Simon Magus, Manes, Pythagoras, Merlin, Roger Bacon, Christian Rosenkreutz, Paracelsus, Andrea, Robertus de Fluctibus, Adam Weishaupt, Goethe, Carl Kellner, Dr. Gerard Encausse (Papus),

Theodor Reuss, and *Sir Aleister Crowley!* "Oh, Sons of the Lion and the Snake!... May their Essence be here present, potent, puissant, and paternal to perfect this feast!" So much for his Eucharist!

Of his Order of the A.A. — Atlantean Adepts — or Great White Brotherhood, he divides it into three orders:

(1) The S.S., being the grades 8 = 3 to I0 = I; (2) The R.C. (Rosicrucian), being the grades from 5 = 6 to 7 = 4; (3) The G.D. (Golden Dawn), being the grades from 0 = 0 to 4 = 7 with a connecting link (Portal?). As has already been stated, his book *777* is largely compiled from correspondences culled from the early Golden Dawn cabalistic "Knowledge Lectures," applied to the Tree of Life. He has also apparently adapted the early rituals of the Golden Dawn and the 5 = 6 ritual of the R.R. et A.C. to suit his own idiosyncrasies. As he expresses his rules:

> "All members must of necessity work in accordance with the facts of Nature... They must accept the Book of the Law as the Word and the Letter of Truth, and the sole Rule of Life. They must acknowledge the authority of the Beast 666 and of the Scarlet Woman as in the book it is defined, and accept Their Will as concentrating the Will of our whole Order. They must accept the Crowned and Conquering Child as the Lord of the Aeon, and exert themselves to establish His reign upon Earth. They must acknowledge that "The Word of the Law is *Thelima*," and that 'Love is the Law, Love under Will'." [That is the Universal Gnostic Church as already described.]

His Order "Mysteria Mystica Maxima" is, it would seem, for the study and practice of his own adaptation of Raja-Yoga, etc.

It is curious to find, in *The Inner Light* book service, May 1933, organ of Dion Fortune's 'Fraternity of Inner Light,' the following statement:

> "The remaining stock of Crowley's *Magick* is growing steadily less. The type has been dispersed, and reprinting is therefore impossible. This book will go to a very high price in a few years' time. We may mention that it contains a reprint of the famous 777, which consists of the Tables of Correspondences." [Correspondences for magical conjurations and such operations!]

Some of Dion Fortune's followers are seeking for something truly spiritual; is this what she feeds them on!

What is Magic? Papus, Dr. Gerard Encausse, occultist and Martinist, from documentary and experimental evidence shows "how all magical operations are scientific experiments carried out with forces still little known but analogous in their laws to the most active physical forces such as magnetism and electricity." He adds, "The works of magic are dangerous." Three principles are required in such works: the human will and intelligence, the directing principle; the material basis on which it acts, the passive principle; the intermediary, through which the mind and will act upon the material basis, that dynamic vital force carried by the blood to all organs, acting upon the nervous system, it is the motor or life-principle. It is the OD of the Jews, the astral light of the Martinists, the magnetic fluid of the Rosicrucians. As Eliphas Levi in his *History of Magic* explains: There is a natural composite agent, a fluid, a force, receptacle of vibrations and images, by the mediation of which every nervous apparatus is in secret communication together. The existence of this universal magnetic life-force and the possible use of it is the great secret of practical magic; it is the wand of theurgy and the key to black magic.

It is, he says, a blind force which warms, illuminates, magnetises, attracts, repels, vivifies, destroys, coagulates, separates, breaks, and conjoins everything under the impetus of powerful wills, some for the great good and others for the great evil. It is the fire which Prometheus stole from heaven, a consuming danger to those who make it subserve their passions. As Eliphas Levi explains: "Black Magic may be defined as the art of inducing artificial mania in ourselves and others"; and by acting upon the nervous system, through a series of almost impossible exercises, "it becomes a kind of living galvanic pile capable of condensing and projecting powerfully that light which intoxicates or destroys." It is the force "which slays and makes alive," used in all illuminised sects, whose God is the Creative Principle, this magnetic life-force in all nature, the vivifying force being their Christ; these forces are, therefore, said to be divine and spiritual, although being merely Mother Nature's forces of creation, preservation and destruction, universal generation. As has been said, all so-called divine or barbarous names used in their evocations simply set up vibrations, awakening and reawakening these hidden forces in man and in the universe as required for the end in view, hence Crowley's *777*. Most of these sects and orders are in fact merely nurseries, training unwitting men and women to become the passive material instrument in the hands of so-called "White Brothers" or more truly black magicians.

As Paracelsus writes: "The Chaldeans and Egyptians used to make images according to the constellations of the stars, and these images moved and talked, but they did not know the powers that acted in them. Such things are done by faith … but a devilish faith supported by the desire for evil." As a modern example of this necromancy we read, in *Letter on Occult Meditation*, 1930, by Alice A. Bailey, of New York, theosophist and occultist:

"As you know, the Master makes a small image of the probationer, which image is stored in certain subterranean centres in the Himalayas. The image is magnetically linked with the probationer, and shows all the fluctuations of his nature. Being composed of emotional and mental matter, it pulsates with every vibration of those bodies. It shows their predominating hues, and by studying it the Master can rapidly gauge the progress made and judge when the probationer may be admitted into closer relationship. The Master views the image at stated intervals, rarely at first, as the progress made at the beginning stages is not so rapid, but with ever-increasing frequency as the student of meditation comprehends more readily and more consciously cooperates. The Master, when inspecting the images works with them, and through their means effects certain results … at certain times the Master applies certain contacts to the images and via them stimulates the bodies of the pupil. A time comes when the Master sees, from his inspection of the image, that the needed rate of vibration can be held, that the required eliminations have been made, and a certain depth of colour attained… He becomes then an accepted disciple."

Such is the teaching given to Mrs. Bailey by her Master of the Great White Lodge; it reads extremely like black magic and devilish! Adepts trained in these magic schools lose their "I" and become mere robots, even as these images, and are thrown aside as empty husks when no longer useful to their evil taskmasters.

Study of the history and workings of all these secret sects proves the truth of this, and always it has ended in perversion for the purpose of domination, individual or universal.

In *La Messe Noire*, 1924, J. Bricaud writes:

> "To-day, when our society is invaded by the eroticism of the Middle Ages sorcery, the words Black Mass have last their primitive meaning... The mystic element weakening, sadism and sensualism alone remained, degenerating these last years into a vulgar orgy, so-called revival of pagan ceremonies, accompanied by lewd scenes, excited by the rhythm of libidinous poetry and the intoxication of oriental perfumes."

It is mysticism inverted, it is a denial of Christ, and as they say, homage to "Him to whom wrong has been done, the ancient outlaw unjustly driven out of Heaven." Lucifer! As Eliphas Levi exclaims:

> "Lucifer — Light Bearer — how strange a name attributed to the Spirit of Darkness! It is he who carries the light and yet blinds feeble souls."

Gilles de Rais, Marechal of France, Sire de Laval, Baron de Bretagne, was one of the most terrible examples of the magical use of Black Mass in the desire for riches, etc. Bricaud writes of him:

> "In these terrifying scenes the mind of Gilles appeared to darken; veritable fits of madness seized him. Desirous, at all price, of obtaining from Satan the secret of the philosophic Stone (in order to obtain gold), on the advice of his magicians he immolated children, consecrated them to the Devil, extracted their blood and brains in order to form powerful philtres destined to produce the expected prodigies... The deed of accusation at the opening of his trial reproached him with having sacrificed 140 children in his diabolical conjurations... The secular Court pronounced the penalty of death and confiscation of his goods."

In London and elsewhere, we are told, Black Mass is still performed, no doubt in a less terrifying form, but nevertheless erotic and vicious, pandering to neurotic and depraved minds, who in turn contaminate others, insidiously infecting the sanity of the nation, sowing seeds of chaos and putrefaction, moral, physical, and mental. In the *Morning Post*, 16 January, 1931, there was an interview with Mr. Harry Price, founder and director of the National Laboratory for Psychical Research, beaded "Devil Worship in London." It says:

> "Mr. Price spoke from close personal experience of the practices which he described, and among a number of other striking allegations he asserted that black magic, sorcery, and witchcraft are practised in the London of to-day on a scale and with a freedom undreamed of in the Middle Ages. Professors and leaders of the cults, for the most part foreigners, make use of the same formulas and incantations as the medieval necromancers. The cults are increasing and attracting interest at such a pace that they will soon assume such dimensions as to become a genuine menace to the morals and sanity of the nation... Celebrants of the Black Mass and Devil Worship practised entirely without risk of consequence, because there is no existing law under which proceedings can be taken... "Interest in the occult," continued Mr. Price, 'is spreading by leaps and bounds, and I can safely say that there are more devotees of the Black Arts in London to-day than ever there were in the Middle Ages. They try by forms of black magic to order events and to make things come to pass — they try to raise the dead or injure people who are at a distance; they even make use of wax dummies and the instruments of the mediaeval wizard.' [Or the magnetised photograph used "to help people" in the R.R. et A.C.!]

Mr. Price talked of attempts to transmute metals Mr. Price's allegations have been supported by incontrovertible evidence of those who have been present, and an account of a Bloomsbury Black Mass and its inevitable and abominable conclusion was given in the *Morning Post,* 19 January, 1931. The writer also stated that Oxford and Cambridge and certain districts of London are infested by these Black Art scoundrels, who thus play·on the senses of their victims by a form of mass hypnotism.

It has been said that, after the seizure of documents and the exposure of Weishaupt's Illuminati in 1786, a law was passed by the English Parliament in 1799 prohibiting all secret societies with the exception of Freemasonry, and that this law has never been annulled!

Concluding his book on Black Mass, 1924, J. Bricaud says:

> "It is certain, as we have shown, that the sacrilegious ceremonies, the scenes of profanation have not disappeared. But they have lost

their primitive meaning and their psychological aspect is no longer the same. To-day the followers of Satan put all their ardour into the accomplishment of what they believe to be the highest expression of sacrilege; they give themselves up to sensual pleasures before a derisive Christ, the better to defy Him. Under Louis XIV, it was still the rule to sacrifice a little child on the altar. To-day it is no longer watered with blood, it is soiled with filth. Modern Black Mass is no longer true Satanism. It is no longer the monstrous revolt of the creature against the Creator, the criminal revolt of man lost in hatred against the Divine Power. His disgusting saturnalias and his orgies against Nature are merely sadism."

In a small pamphlet arranged by Dr. Wynn Westcott, Supreme Magus, of *Societas Rosicruciana in Anglia,* and published by John M. Watkins, Cecil Court, London, 1916, we are given what is called "Data of the History of the Rosicrucians." What chiefly interests us are the notes on the founding of the S.R.I.A. and later the Golden Dawn as follows:

"In 1865 the *Societas Rosicruciana in Anglia* was designed by Robert Wentworth Little (who rescued some rituals from the store-room of Freemasons' Hall), and Kenneth R. H. Mackenzie, who had received Rosicrucian initiation in Austria, while living with Count Apponyi as an English tutor, and also Authority to form an English Masonic Rosicrucian Society. In 1866 the Metropolitan College was founded; R. W. Little was chosen Supreme Magus...

"Frater R. W. Little died in 1878, and Dr. William Robert Woodman became Supreme Magus... In 1880 the Soc. Rosic. in U.S.A. was founded and recognised.

"In 1887, by permission of S.D.A. ('Sapiens Dominabitur Astris'), a Continental Rosicrucian Adept, the Isis-Urania Temple of Hermetic Students of the G.D. (Golden Dawn) was formed to give instruction in the medieval Occult Sciences. Fratres M. E. V. (Magna est Veritas et Praevalebit — Dr. Woodman), Supreme Magus of S.R.I.A., with S.A. (Sapere Aude — Dr. Wynn Westcott) and S.R.M.D. (S. Rioghail Mo Dhream Macgregor Mathers), became the Chiefs, and the latter wrote the rituals in modern English from old Rosicrucian MSS. (the property of Frater S.A.), supplemented by his own literary researches. Frater D. D. C. F. (Deo Duce Comito Ferro—Mathers's Inner motto), in 1892, supplied the ritual of an Adept Grade from materials obtained from a Frater, L. E. T. (Dr. Thiesen of Liège, 'Lux e Tenebres,' according to Dr. Wynn Westcott), a Continental Adept. Several other Temples sprang from the Isis-Urania, viz. the Osiris, at Weston-super-Mare; the Horns, at Bradford; the Amen Ra, at Edinburgh, and the Ahathoor, in Paris, in 1884 (1894), which was consecrated by F.E.R. (Fortiter). Frater S. A. (Dr. Wynn Westcott) resigned from the Association in 1897, and the English Temples soon after fell into abeyance (1900, when the Temple in London revolted against Mathers)…

"The revived Rosicrucian Lodges on the Continent of Europe are carried on with great privacy, and their members do not openly confess to their admission and membership. Several centres are in active work under conditions derived from previous centuries of usefulness. While studying and teaching theories of life and its duties, and admitting members by ceremonial and ritual, many groups of the Continental Rosicrucians are, as formerly, of both sexes, and so are not necessarily Freemasons. As in the earliest times the Rosicrucians not only studied, but went about doing good and healing the sick and diseased, so now the Fratres to-day are concerned in the study and administration of medicines [such as., Steiner!], and in their manufacture upon old lines; they also teach and practise the curative [also magical] effects of coloured light, and cultivate mental processes which are believed to induce spiritual enlightenment [Steiner's processes for rousing the kundalini!] and extended powers of the human senses, especially in the directions of clairvoyance and clairaudience. Their teaching does not necessarily include any Indian or Egyptian symbolism."

"Dr. Woodman in 1891 died during Xmas week… and early in 1892 Dr. Wynn Westcott … was installed as Supreme Magus…"

In 1900 the London Temple of the Golden Dawn broke with Mathers, who was then recognised Chief. For two years it was ruled by an appointed Committee, but in 1902 it returned to the rule of three Chiefs, the following being elected: Dr. Felkin, Mr. Brodie Innis, and Mr. Bullock. In 1903 this group took the name of the Stella Matutina under the same chiefs. In 1913, Dr. and Mrs. Felkin received certain higher grades on the Continent and linked up with Dr. Steiner.

Neither Dr. Wynn Westcott nor Aleister Crowley ever had any connection with the Stella Matutina, official or otherwise The present writer was initiated into the Stella Matutina in 1908, and was appointed one of the Ruling Chiefs of the S.M. and R.R. et

A.C. in 1916, and at no time ever had anything to do with the Golden Dawn or Aleister Crowley.

CHAPTER XII

AMERICAN GROUPS

WE find much about this mysterious "Inner Government of the World," which apparently ruled Mrs. Besant and through her the Theosophical Society, of which she was head, in a book, *Initiation Human and Solar, 1933*, by Mrs. Alice A. Bailey, occultist and theosophist, New York. It is published by the Lucis Publishing Co., New York, and is dedicated "To the Master K. H. (Koot Humi)." This is the same "Koot Hoomi" of Mme Blavatsky and Mrs. Besant! Of these Masters Mrs. Besant wrote in a pamphlet, *The Masters, 1912*:

> "A Master is a term applied by Theosophists to denote certain human beings, who have completed their human evolution, have attained human perfection ... have reached what the Christians call 'Salvation' and the Hindus and Buddhists "Liberation.".... Those who are named M. (Morya) and K. H. (Koot Hoomi) in *The Occult World* by Mr. Sinnett were the two Masters who founded the Theosophical Society, using Colonel Olcott and H. P. Blavatsky, both disciples of M., to lay its foundations; and who gave Mr. Sinnett the materials from which he wrote his famous books, the one named above and *Esoteric Buddhism* which brought the light of Theosophy to thousands in the West. H. P. Blavatsky has told how she met the Master M. on the bank of the Serpentine, when she visited London in 1851."

We would add, to show how in reality all these groups, whether Theosophical or Rosicrucian, are linked up under one sinister group of esoteric men, fanatically imbued with the idea of World Domination: Dr. Felkin, late head of the R.R. et A.C., possessed a fine photograph, said to be "Maitreya," which hung over his desk, and his daughter had one of "Koot Hoomi" in her room; both were looked upon, by their owners, as "Holy"!

In her book Mrs. Bailey writes that this Inner Government is a Hierarchy of Light, Elder Brothers. First, there is the King *Sanat Kumara,* who is said to live in Shamballa, a somewhat mythical or perhaps mystical centre in the Gobi desert; he is the Lord of the World and initiator (representing the Creative Principle) — and around him is the Triad of manifestation. Below him, manifesting the light or energy to the world, is this Triad of Departmental heads: (1) *Manu:* racial government, founding, directing, and dissolving racial types, producing those required for their plans. He visualises that which has to be done, and by sound transmits the required creative and destructive energy to his assistants. He is said to live at Shigatse in the Himalayas. (2) *Lord Maitreya:* Religion, World Teacher or Christ, initiator of the mysteries and liberator. He is said to live in the Himalayas. (3) *Manachohan:* he manipulates the forces of Nature, and brings about civilisation as required.

Under these, she says, work the Masters of the (Great White) Lodge, representing the seven rays or planetary aspects of the Light. These as regents hold in their hands the reins of government for continents and nations, guiding their destinies; they impress and inspire statesmen and rulers; they pour forth mental energy on governing groups, bringing about desired results wherever co-operation and receptive intuition can be found. They are: *Master Jupiter:* lives in the Nilgherry Hills. Holds the reins of government of India and a large part of the Northern Frontier, and he must eventually guide India out of her present chaos and unrest and form her diverse people into a synthesis. *Master Morya:* lives in Shigatse, but is a Rajput Prince. He works in connection with many organisations of an esoteric or occult kind as well as through the politicians and statesmen of the world, influencing more especially those with international ideals. *Koot Humi:* lives at Shigatse, but is a Kashmiri. Is in the line for World Teacher to the sixth root race. Was educated at a British university, widely read in current literature. Concerns himself with vitalising certain great philosophies, and interested in philanthropic agencies. His work is largely Love — awakening the brotherhood idea. *Master Jesus:* he lives in a Syrian body somewhere in the Holy Land. He works with the masses rather than individuals; he is preparing the way in Europe and America for the eventual coming of the World Teacher. "Certain great prelates of the Anglican and Catholic Churches are wise agents of his." *Master Djwal Khul:* lives in Shigatse, is a Tibetan, and is called "The Messenger of the Masters." Has profound knowledge of the rays and planetary and solar influences, and works with healers, welfare and philanthropic world movements, such as the Red Cross.

Master Rakoczi: is a Hungarian, and lives in the Carpathian Mountains. Was known as Comte de St. Germain, Roger Bacon, and later Francis Bacon. Works with the occult side of affairs in Europe, largely through esoteric ritual and ceremonial, being vitally interested in the effects of the ceremonial of the Freemasons, of various fraternities, and of the Churches. Acts practically in America and Europe as general manager for carrying out the plans of the executive council of the Lodge, which is an inner group of Masters round the Three Lords. *Master Hilarion:* is a Cretan, but lives chiefly in Egypt. He works with those who are developing intuition, and his energy is behind Psychical Research, and he initiated the Spiritualistic Movement, and has all higher psychics under observation. There are two English Masters; one lives in Great Britain, and guides the Anglo-Saxon race and is behind the Labour movement throughout the world and guides rising democracy. The key for the future is to be co-operation, not competition; distribution, not centralisation. *Master Serapis:* called the Egyptian, energises music, painting, and drama. *Master P.:* Irish, works under Rakoczi in North America; works esoterically with Christian Science and New Thought; is training disciples for the Coming of the Christ towards the middle or close of the present century. Some of the Masters are expected to come out among men towards the close of the century.

Moreover, she says, prior to the Coming, adjustments will be made, *so that at the head of all great organisations will be found either a master or an initiate,* as also at the head of certain great occult groups of the Freemasons of the World and of the various great divisions of the Church, also residing among many of the Great Nations. Everywhere they are gathering in those who in any way show a tendency to respond to high vibrations seeking *to force* their vibrations and fit them to be of use at the time of the Coming. "The work may proceed through one medium or another (disciple or movement), but always the life-force persists, shattering the form where it is inadequate and utilising it when it suffices for immediate need." At will these monstrous masters would use their power to shape and hew, slay and make alive!

With regard to her statement that "at the head of all great organisations will be found either a master or initiate," did not the Jewish writer, Dr. Angelo Rappaport, say in his book, *The Pioneers of the Russian Revolution:*

> "There was not a political organisation in the vast Empire which was not influenced by the Jews or directed by them; the Social-Democrats, the Revolutionary Socialist Parties, the Polish Socialist Party, all counted Jews among their directors; Plehve was perhaps right when he said that the combat for political emancipation in Russia and the Jewish question were practically identical."

As to the expected consummation towards the close of the present century, in *Cheiro's World Predictions*, we find some significant statements, whether inspired or not it is not possible to say:

> "From 1980 ... will, in my opinion, see the restoration of the Twelve Tribes of Israel as the dominant power in the world.
>
> ... Another law giver, like Moses, will arise ... and so in the end through this 'despised race' universal peace will be established."

In all illuminised sects the means of communication with their unknown directors is to begin with invariably pseudo-yoga in one form or another and later by formulae. In another of her books, *Letters on Occult Meditation,* she throws some interesting light on the methods and nature of these Masters' world schemes. This book is dedicated "To the Tibetan Teacher who wrote these letters and authorized their publication," 1922. Much is camouflage, meant to deceive; and to cover themselves and the possibility, always great, of harmful results from their diabolical experimentations with men, women, and nations, they talk much of the dangers to be encountered from "Dark Brothers," evil entities, and elementals! It is more likely that they are "Dark Brothers" themselves!

By means of this pseudo-yoga, the pupil's personality is in turn withdrawn from the physical, etheric, astral, and mental bodies, until "the man recognises himself as a part of the Master's consciousness... The Master is only interested in a man from the point of view of his usefulness in the group soul and his capacity to help." The forces used and set in motion are "those magnetic currents of the universe, that vital fluid, these electric rays ... the latent heat stored in all forms." We are told there are two special methods of setting these forces in motion, so as to bring about unity with the Masters. *Mantrams—rhythmic* sounds, words, and phrases, a compelling force.

> "A mantram, when rightly sounded forth, creates a vacuum in matter, resembling a funnel. The funnel is formed betwixt the one who sounds it forth and the one who is reached by the sound. There is then formed a direct channel of communication... [and when] a similarity of vibration is somewhat achieved ... the pupil [becomes] custodian of a mantram whereby he may call his Master... It is purely scientific and based on vibration and the knowledge of dynamics."

It is destructive, removing obstacles; and constructive, building up the Masters' kingdom of power.

Rhythmic Movements, which, according to the rhythm, brings "those who use it into line with certain of Nature's forces ... permitting of the rhythmic flow of force in certain specified directions for certain specified ends." It stimulates the sex-organs and brings about illumination. Its effect is tremendous, and can be worldwide in its radius. Further, we are told this may be applied on special occasions as follows:

Politically. — It is said the time is coming when those who are manipulating nations, sitting in the assemblies of the people, administering law and justice, 'will begin all their work with great rhythmic ceremonies [ritual dancing!],' putting themselves in touch with *Manu,* so as to carry out his plans and intentions. The funnel made, they will proceed to business, having placed two men in their midst as the focal point for receiving the Master's instructions. What about the League of Nations?

Religious. — The priest will be the focal point, and after due ceremony and rhythm the united congregation will be the transmitter of forces and information from *Maitreya* even as in the Liberal Catholic Church!

Educational. — All universities and schools will start the sessions with this rhythmic ceremony, the teacher being the focal point, thus stimulating the students mentally and intuitionally, inspired through the funnel by *Mahachohan.*

Here apparently we have an explanation of the Steinerite Eurhythmy and the "Goetheanum Speech Chorus," from Dornach; by rhythmic movement and sound the kundalini is stimulated, the centres vivified, and the vacuum created through which the required forces and influences are directed by their Master, affecting not only the performers, but the whole audience, merging and orienting them for occult purposes. Magnetising the hall and preparing the people for illumination!

> "In all these three branches of service you will notice that the faculty of working with groups is one of paramount importance... It may be either a band of Church workers among the orthodox; it may be in social work, such as the labour movements, or in the political arena; or it may be in the more definitely pioneer movements of the world, such as the Theosophical Society, etc... I would add to this one branch of endeavour that may surprise you. *I mean, the movement of the Soviet in Russia and all the aggressive radical bodies that sincerely serve under their leaders for the betterment [sic] of the masses.* "

These, then, are some of the tools and their rhythmic methods of black magic, inspired by these mysterious directors, with their camouflaged teachings, and camouflaged names, seeking for World Domination, not through the betterment, but the enslavement and spiritual death of mankind.

As de Luchet said with truth:

> "If several men mix together half qualities, they temper and strengthen each other ... the weak yield to the stronger, the most skilful draw from each what he can supply. Some watch while others act, and this formidable ensemble arrives at its goal, whatever it may be... It was according to this principle that the sect of the Illuminati was formed."

The Illuminati are still with us, ruled from behind by the same mysterious and invisible power!

Maurice Joly, in his revolutionary pamphlet, *Dialogues aux Enfers*, 1864, makes Machiavelli say: "Before thinking of actually directing the public opinion of all peoples one must stun it … dazzle it by all sorts of movements; mislead it insensibly in its ways." From Mrs. A. Bailey's books we have shown the basis of the secret World Government, its work and method of rhythmic control. We will now consider, from the same source, the establishment of a world-wide chain of occult school, whereby it proposes to impose its will upon all peoples.

Of these movements her Tibetan teacher says:

> "Experiments are being made now, unknown oft to the subjects themselves… people in many civilised countries are under supervision and a method of stimulation and intensification is being applied which will bring to the knowledge of the Great Ones Themselves a mass of information that may serve as guide to their future efforts for the race. Especially are people in America, Australia, India, Russia, Scotland, and Greece being dealt with. A few in Belgium, Sweden, and Austria are likewise under observation… Schools have been already started … when they are firmly grounded, when they are working smoothly and with public recognition, and when the world of men is being somewhat coloured by them and their *subjective* (astral) emphasis, when they are precluding scholars, workers, politicians, scientists, and educational leaders who make their impress on their environment, then mayhap will come… the true occult school.

> … This subjective reality being universally admitted, will therefore permit of the founding of a chain of inner schools … that will be publicly recognised (there will always be a secret section)… H.P.B. [Mme Blavatsky] laid the foundation stone of the first school … the keystone… If all that is possible is done, when the Great Lord comes with His Masters the work will receive a still further impetus… and become a power in the world." ·

And the whole idea of this tentative plan is to control the bodies of man through the so-called 'God within,' linking him by means of the Masters to this central control in Shamballa. 'The Himalayan Brotherhood [of Light] is the main channel of effort, power, and light … and is the only school, without exception, that should control the work and output of true occult students in the West. It brooks no rival.' The occult schools will be situated where some old Mystery magnetism lingers.

The National subdivisions will be: *Egypt:* in Greece and Syria the preparatory schools, and in Egypt, much later, the advanced school profoundly occult. *United States:* the preparatory school in the South Middle-West and an extensive advanced occult college in California. *Latin countries:* South France the preparatory school and in Italy an advanced school. *Great Britain:* the preparatory in one of the magnetised spots in Scotland or Wales, and later, after Ireland has adjusted her internal problems, the advanced school will be in one of her magnetised spots, and will be under *Maitreya.* In *Sweden:* a preparatory school for Northern and German races. *Russia* may later be the headquarters of a more advanced school. *New Zealand:* preparatory school, and later an advanced school in Australia. *Japan:* a preparatory school and a most esoteric branch in West China under *Manu.* None at present in South Africa nor in South America. Preparatory schools are in process of being founded, the more advanced will precede the Coming of the Great Lord (1980). A beginning will be made with members of the different occult schools, such as the esoteric section of the Theosophical Society, etc.; the work in Britain, America, and Australia is already started. 'This much of the plan has been permitted publication as an incentive to all of you to study and to work with more strenuous application.' For what? slavery under these masters!

Preparatory schools should be close to a big centre or city, preferably near sea or expanse of water — water is a conductor of force. Contact with many and varied people is required as also outside mental training. The advanced schools should be far from men in isolated strongholds in mountainous regions; there they must contact the Masters and the centre at Shamballa. The preparatory staff consists of the Head, an accepted disciple, the focal point through which the Master's forces flow. Six instructors, one at least clairvoyant, will be complementary to each other, a miniature replica of the Hierarchy of Light. To these will be added three women, intuitive and good teachers. Under these will be others, dealing with the emotional, physical, and mental equipment of the pupils. The staff of the advanced school will consist of an Initiate Head who, under the Master, will be sole judge and autocrat. Under him two other teachers, accepted disciples. Their work will be supervisory, as all occultists are "esoterically self-taught" that is, directed by a Master. Much emphasis is laid on so-called purification, physical, emotional, and mental, for unless the body is purified and the brain stilled, the shattering forces transmitted by the Masters, in their experimentations, would, they well know, cause grave physical and mental disease, even such as ever follows in the train of these occult schools. This purification is attained by dieting, and the use by the Masters of coloured lights and sound, shattering, stilling, stimulating, and attracting, until initiation or hypnotic control by the Central Power is accomplished for "the great Law of attraction draws you to Him, and nought can withstand the Law" — the compelling force! The control is so complete that the tool "cares not if he loses friends, relations, children, popularity, etc. ; he cares not if he seems to work in the dark, and is conscious of little result from his labours." His "personal self" is sacrificed!

When these so-called mysteries are restored, their custodians will be "the *Church and the Masons*"! That was written first in 1922.

In 1934 Mrs. Balley wrote a booklet, *The Next Three Years*, purporting to be the World Plan, for the uplift of Humanity by the realisation of man's divinity through the guidance of some so-called "Elder Brothers or Supermen." According to Mrs. Bailey: "Out of the medley of ideas, theories, speculations, religions, churches, cults, sects, and organisations, two main lines of thought are demonstrating." These are, she says, the "reactionary dogmatists," who bow to a prophet, a bible, or a church, and are doomed eventually to die out. The other, the "subjective group of intellectual mystics," regarding themselves as members of the Universal Church, destined to grow and strengthen until they form the new subjective religion. Apparently the latter are not free as they bow to the authority of this unknown Hierarchy of Elder Brothers, who seek to order and dominate the world by the "unification of effort in all departments of human enterprise, religious, scientific, and economic."

Thus to-day, she writes, we have

> "a breaking away from old-established tradition, a revolt from authority, a tendency towards self-determination and an overthrowing of the old standards, of old barriers, of thought, and of the divisions hitherto existing between races and faiths. Hence we find ourselves passing through an intermediate stage of chaos and of questioning, of rebellion, and of consequent licence."

Or as Lady Emily Lutyens, one of Mrs. Besant's followers, wrote in the *Herald of the Star,* March 1927:

> "We are witnessing the birth of a new world consciousness, of a world civilisation... Old traditions are being broken down, old customs destroyed, old landmarks swept away... There must be anarchy before there can be creation."

Thus they pave the way for the New Age, new civilisation, new science, and the new religion of so-called Illuminism and intuition.

Mrs. Bailey explains:

> "The Plan as at present sensed and for which the World Knowers (under the Elder Brothers) are working might be defined as follows: It is the production of a subjective synthesis in humanity and of a telepathic interplay which will eventually annihilate time ... it will make men omnipresent ... and omniscient."

It is Illuminism! The time, she says, in which these Elder Brothers must complete their Plan is limited by the Law of Cycles, "when forces, influences, and energies are temporarily at work, and of these the World Knowers seek to make use." It is what they call the Aquarian Age! "which will last astronomically 2,500 years, and which can, if duly utilised, bring about the unification, consciously and intelligently, of mankind and so produce the manifestation of what may be called "scientific brotherhood."" Therefore their aim is to break up family, national, and racial pride.

Since the fifteenth century, she continues, in order to build a more synthetic unity, seven groups have been formed — cultural, political, religious, scientific, and later philosophical, psychological, and financial. These were to bring about certain preparatory conditions as part of the Hierarchical programme. The philosophers, including ancient Asiatic philosophers, powerfully mould thought, psychologists talk about man's urges and characteristics, and the purpose of his being. Financiers control and order means whereby man exists, "constituting a dictatorship over all modes of intercourse, commerce, and exchange... Their work is most definitely planned and guided. They are bringing about effects upon earth which are most far-reaching." All these groups, she says, are co-operating with the Hierarchy and build for posterity. These world workers

> "are necessarily cultured and widely read ... they do not regard their country and their political affiliations as of paramount importance. They are equipped to organise, slowly and steadily, that public opinion which will eventually divorce man from religious sectarianism, national exclusiveness, and racial bias."

1934 to 1936 are to be test years. In politics, the development of. an international consciousness, economic synthesis among nations.

> "Material stress and strain, the wrecking of old political parties, the overthrowing of trade relations ... demonstrating the necessity of establishing a spirit of international dependence and interrelation, that the nations would be politically forced to realise that isolation, separateness, and the cultivation of national egoism must go."

Thus bringing about the Brotherhood of Nations — a *World Federation State!* She further classes together the following dictatorships: The Soviet *dictatorship of the proletariat,* "... behind all the mistakes and the cruelty, behind the rank materialism there lie great ideals [Jewish!]"; the *dictatorship of racial superiority* in Germany; the *dictatorship of organised business* in America; the *dictatorship of empire* in Britain; Italy, Turkey, etc., and all such national movements, according to Mrs. Bailey, are in reality under the impelling impulse of the ideas thrown into men's minds by the secret Hierarchy, but because of ignorance, they are "distorted, selfishly applied, and separately utilised."

Further, from 1945 the World Faith will take shape, and she explains: *"The three words, electricity, light, and life, express divinity and their synthesis is God."* This is merely the life-force, and is sheer pantheism and Illuminism. Again she says, the scientists set themselves the goal of expanding man's consciousness, the unfolding of his latent senses, and so widening his horizon that a synthesis of the tangible and the intangible will take place in education, science, and psychology. Finally, for the next three years we are asked to drop antagonisms, antipathies, hatreds, and racial differences, and to think in terms of one family, one life, me humanity. The end and aim being unification and mental control by the so-called 'Hierarchy of Supermen.' Who are they? What of the dreams and activities of *L' Alliance-israélite-universelle*! Such a monstrous robot is even now showing signs of materialising, but the dream is too fantastic and too fanatical to succeed among Western peoples.

Theosophists are not alone in being dominated by these mysterious "Elder Brothers" of the Great White Lodge. A message was received in the New Zealand Temple vault, 10 July, 1919, by the late High Chief, Dr. Felkin, purporting to come from 'Christian Rosenkreutz,' that mythical Head of the Rosicrucians, in reply to grave doubts expressed about these mysterious Brethren, by one of the Ruling Chiefs of the London R.R. et A.C. The message ran:

> "The Brethren are indeed the Elder Brethren and the messengers of the Lord [of Light], but they are neither infallible nor do they belong to the company of the gods. They are but men highly advanced indeed, and waiting for the torch [of Illuminism] to be kindled in their midst, yet are they not of those of whom ye know as Masters, and it is not in their power either to kindle the torch nor yet to say at what day or hour the flame of Pentecost [Illuminism] shall descend."

We have already sketched the secret world plan of these 'Elder Brothers' as given by Mrs. Bailey, one of their most faithful dupes and disciples. Some time ago we received a book published in Canada, 1930, said to be 'Unsigned Letters from an Elder Brother,' written from January, to December, 1929, to a group working under him. In the foreword he says:

"The whole Earth is upon the very verge of that which threatens it. This present year, 1930, and those immediately following, shall see the dissolution of almost all these things upon which men and nations do rely. First the overthrow — then the Silence — then the *Restoration.* Think ye on these things."

In this book a certain light is thrown on these Brothers, their plans and methods of drawing unwary and confiding men and women into their sinister and deadening net of Illuminism.

"Every Elder Brother is a ranking member of one or other of the Twelve Hierarchies [the Great White Lodge and the twelve signs of the Zodiac]... He has no life apart from them." He can 'neither admit nor refuse admittance to the status of discipleship.'

He trains students to receive the new knowledge by direct contact, forming instruments to orient humanity.

This knowledge, the Elder Brothers say, is confined to the *Illuminati* and initiates, who are few in number. The existing order is to be overturned and destroyed, they are preparing the way, *by changing the thought currents of the world,* for the restoration of the Mysteries and the knowledge which underlies them. 'The Knight Templars are gathering again,' they say, and 'through their efforts the ranks of Freemasonry and other similar orders will know a great Renaissance.' None may enter discipleship and at the same time maintain allegiance to any occult order or teacher, but existing membership in Freemasonry, co-Masonic movements, Oddfellows, or similar fraternal organisations is not debarred. 'Our prohibition applies only in those cases where religious or spiritual teaching is avowedly the chief end or work.'

The one modern authority on the 'Masters' whom 'we entirely endorse is H. P. Blavatsky.' Those who have been called

"are members of a select and powerful group... We have first to link, to draw together the scattered members of our Great Order... Later we will bind; through their efforts we will unify many movements, giving them new knowledge, purpose, and direction... Plainly we wait for the breaking of the storm which shall clear the ground for our own efforts... From the Centre there shall ultimately go forth Light, Knowledge, Leadership, and finally Rulership... Those who have the knowledge and are in possession of the Plan will take up the reins. In that day we will set up *the Standard of the Lion and the Sun.*"

As Dr. Ranking said: "During the Middle Ages the main support of the Gnostic bodies and the main repository of this knowledge was the Society of the Templars." And we already know what their record was.

The new knowledge is to be obtained by direct contact with the Brotherhood, the means used being Love-attraction and repulsion. Sex-force and passion, or love, is not only a means of creating life in this world, it creates forces on the psychic plane, it is 'a magnetic and cosmic phenomenon,' attracting and binding the negative instrument, the disciple, and the positive directing Brother using him. It means a fusion of dual consciousness, mental and emotional.

> "Most often the Brothers work on the etheric and mental levels of consciousness: they do not wear physical bodies, they work indirectly through one or other of their attuned disciples, giving him or her clearer ideas, intuitions, and a general fund of knowledge far in advance of what he or she possesses in themselves."

In this way many books are written. Not all channels are clear, and lucid, personal ideas creep in.

"If there is any obstinacy or personal pride or contumaciousness, then that disciple is discarded, the informing consciousness is withdrawn, and some other channel is used." Further, if the Brother is to work in a physical body, he selects the parentage and environments, and in case of failure two bodies born about the same time are prepared. "He takes such a body in order that the mind and will of the group as a whole may be expressed through that personality." If one body fails it is cast adrift like a rudderless ship! By such diabolical prostitution of Nature's forces do these fanatical Supermen seek to dominate and control humanity!

Early in 1935 Mrs. Bailey was in this country endeavouring to advertise the secret World Plan of these Supermen as stated in *The Next Three Years.* She distributed 25,000 copies, the object being to 'educate public opinion,' and an attempt to form a defined active group which 'can salvage a distressed world and bring light and understanding to humanity.' Their aim is to 'eventually divorce man from religious sectarianism, national exclusiveness, and racial bias,' in preparation for a World Federation State and World Illuminised Religion! To forward this idea the pamphlet has been translated into French, German, Italian, Spanish, and Roumanian, but funds were lacking for printing this attempt to inoculate Europe with this American virus of pernicious Illuminism, as if Europe past and present had not suffered enough from this terrible scourge which so often ends in some mad, political, social, and pseudo religious obsession!

SILVER SHIRTS

In 'The Silver Shirts' of America we have an example of the political plans of these 'Elder Brothers,' being inaugurated and built up. According to their magazine, *Liberation,* from which we have drawn our information, the Silver Shirts of America claim to be a Protestant, Christian organisation with a constructive plan for 'turning the United States into a true democracy, sensitive to the dictates of a sovereign people.' A mass movement of units, 'A Christ Democracy, under which the entire nation has been turned into a Great Corporation with its voting citizens, the common stockholders.'

To materialise this project a "League of Liberation" was formed by William Dudley Pelley at Ashville, N.C., the whole based on prophecy and inspiration received by him clairaudiently via the "psychic radio" from so called 'Great Souls' on the higher realms of life who state that the Soviet rule is but "a cog in their Plan," as also Hitlerism, and they speak of 'the temporary upset of Jewry.' The leader is an unseen 'Prince of Peace'! Under the auspices of this League he founded the Galahad College, Ashville, where the following subjects were taught to a maximum of 250 students a year: *Ethical History* — studying from the Creation through the civilisations and culture of Lemuria, Maya, Atlantis, Egypt to the Jewish Dispersion and the Holy Roman Empire as a background for modern times. *Public Stewardship*— "a gripping, battle of Light Forces against Dark Cohorts." *Spiritual Eugenics* — expounding William Pelley's psychic scripts and training students how to receive similar communications. *Social Metapsychics* — training the student to recognise the light and dark factors in the "Great Obsessions" of history, recognising and dealing with similar factors in present day subversive movements. *Christian Philosophy* — new economics, banks, and issue of money a governmental function, public utilities owned by the public. *Educational Therapy* — applied suggestive therapy, doing away with paupers and criminals. *Cosmic Mathematics* — understanding the laws of vibrations, individual and group. Here we have apparently a super-Americanised College for training psychics!

William Pelley advocates development of the psychic senses — super-seeing, clairvoyance; super-hearing, clairaudience. He first realised these powers in himself May 1928, and says: "I have left my mortal body in broad daylight and travelled and been seen 3,000 miles away..." He further states that night after night he has listened for and heard the "voice of unseen but living teachers" whose teaching, as heard, he repeated to a stenographer; their Life-Plan offers a complete change of thinking about God and After-life, they believe in passing through, it might be, 200 bodies, say, in 50,000 years! From the higher realms of life, in plain, uncompromising words, were given the following methods necessary to awaken these latent senses:

> "In the process called intimacy there is a moment when the third eye of the spirit (pineal gland) is awakened or opened and a tremendous rush of self-force is literally projected into the other's aura. That moment is precious in occult phenomena and can be attained constantly by men and women attuning themselves to the enticements of love without the devitalising effects of passion."

That is, arousing and perverting the unused sex-forces in order to bring about the required psychic conditions.

And as the teacher continues:

> "To persons of rightful attainments, sincerely desirous of perfecting themselves in the Hidden Higher Truths, there comes a time when the practice of certain rites awakens slumbering senses, and such see beyond the known, and into the unknown.
>
> ... One of the capabilities ... *should be the going in and out of the physical mechanism at will,* in order to be the perfect instrument."

Although nominally protected, this might well end in possession of the vacated body by some obsessing teacher or mentor, so-called! As an inducement they are told that with awakened senses "they could command men and women by the power of thought to do anything at their bidding. They could heal even to raising the dead..." Vastly dangerous powers in the hands of evil men, master or disciple!

As to their Protestant-Christianity, it might be classed with the early Gnostics or even the Cabalistic Jews as expressed to-day in many illuminised sects. As William Pelley's Mentor says:

> "We [as Christians] invent so to speak the Christos-idea, we recognise in the Christ the Creative Principle set apart in a peculiar order of Avatar Spirit... rendering a certain mission to Itself and to the Man-Race, which likewise is "part" of Itself... Christ Jesus the *man*, and Christos-Lord, the Holy Angelic avatar Spirit come to earth to epitomise good [light] are as distinct and separate"

as adult and schoolchild. They go on to explain that the ancient 'you,' in each man, is the God-spirit, the God-stuff, the Christos Magic Man, the individualised Logos, the individual word made flesh. This is simply the creative principle in each, positive and negative, the Gnostic Good and Evil, light and matter.

Again we get the echo of the Manichaean "phantom" Christ: "The Jews as a people did not crucify Christ." He was crucified by certain "deterrent and malign psyches" that incarnated in Jewish bodies "to strike back at the Logos of Light which they recognised as having burst into flame in Jesus, the man... It was Jesus the Avatar *psyche* [illuminising force] that they evilly schemed to get out of the way."

William Pelley adopts the Great Pyramid teaching of Dr. Davidson, declaring it contains a divine revelation and is the key to all daily events, and asks:

> "How did it happen at the time of the American revolution, when next to nothing was known of the mathematical interpretation of the great monument, that its symbolism was used in concrete exactness on the Great Seal of the United States, indicating that it was the part of America to reinstate the rule of Christ on earth?"

Now Charles Sotheran, New York, Mason of many degrees, initiate of the Rosy Cross and other secret societies, wrote to Mme Blavatsky, 11 January, 1877: "In the last century the United States was freed from the tyranny of the Mother country by the action of secret societies more than is commonly imagined." Was the United States Seal not the inspiration of these secret societies?

It is curious to find the same Seal with the Statue of Liberty used as symbols of the "New Order of the Ages," Rosicrucian and Illuminism, whose head is Dr. Swinburne Clymer, apparently under the direction of the mysterious International Secret Council of Nine, said to be Rosicrucian, with its centre in France. Dr. Randolph, original founder of the Group, 1864, takes the Rosicrucians, a vast Secret Brotherhood, back to the Sabeans and calls them founders of the "Semitic civilisation." William Pelley is hot-footed up against, above all, the Jew of International Finance, but does not his mentor's psychic teaching of the Christos-Logos of Light point to the Sabean primitive cult of the stars and the serpent, out of which the "Semitic civilisation" arose? He knows nothing of his psychic mentors but what they have chosen to impart to him; might not their aim be de-Christianisation of the United States and establishment of this "Semitic civilisation," a Gnostic so-called "Christ Democracy" ruled and directed by "voices unseen but living teachers"? As the *Jewish Encyclopaedia* has pointed out, Gnosticism "was Jewish in character long before it became Christian."

A pamphlet was issued giving a general idea of the doctrine of this proposed "Christ Democracy," from which we give a few extracts:

"Do you know that there are men and women in this nation who are able to look into the immediate future with transcendent vision and discern accurately a complete metamorphosis of our present institutions along more wholesome lines? This means in plain language that they can see what improvements in our political and economic order are going to arise from this present period of distress and turmoil.

"They see these improvements crystallising between 31 January, 1933, and 4 March, 1945, both dates written large in Great Pyramid

Prophecy. They see a real democracy established in the United States, under the conditions of which the following innovations are to be effected without altering our governmental structure in the slightest:

"A *Christ Democracy* under which the entire nation has been turned into a Great Corporation with its voting citizens the Common Stockholders.

"A *Christ Democracy* in which these Common Stockholders as one of the principles of citizenship, automatically and irrevocably receive a monthly dividend of 83,33 dollars from the Corporation to assure them a livelihood, and for ever keep them from starvation attendant on unemployment.

"A *Christ Democracy* in which large sums of the Great Corporation's dividend-paying Preferred Stock are issued to the citizens in varying amounts from the lowest to the highest, to furnish them with incentives towards initiative, industry, ambition, and thrift — such Stock paying dividends in addition to the Starvation Dividend of the Common citizenship stock, which cannot be bought, sold, or exchanged or otherwise manipulated by predatory groups or individuals.

"A *Christ Democracy* in which annual production is strictly regulated by the consuming capacities of the whole citizenry and not by their monetary buying power.

"A *Christ Democracy* in which money in form of currency is discarded as archaic, and all citizens do business by a form of Cheque through a Federal Bank, which cheque is only used once exactly like express money orders of the present.

"A *Christ Democracy* in which all rights to private and personal property are militantly conserved and protected by the Government.

"A *Christ Democracy* in which there are no more taxes on the citizen of any description, taxation being as archaic as currency. A *Christ Democracy* in which there are no rents for the occupancy of homestead property, rents being as archaic and predatory as currency taxes, and interest, but replaced by a system under which every occupant paying to live in a structure is engaged in buying that property, either in whole or part.

"A *Christ Democracy* in which foreclosures on property for any nature whatsoever are illegal.

"A *Christ Democracy* in which all citizens enter a Federal Civil Service that is reconstructed upon an efficiency basis and graduated as to compensation according to a worker's industry or talents.

"A *Christ Democracy* in which all legislation, no matter what its character, cannot become law until it has been passed upon a private vote of 51 per cent. of the citizenry to whom it applies.

"A *Christ Democracy* in which dishonest or incompetent officials can be instantly recalled by a 51 per cent. vote of the citizenry in any district wherein they function.

"A *Christ Democracy* in which all voting, either for or against office holders, is done through the postal service instead of the cumbersome and archaic polling place.

"A *Christ Democracy* in which all votes so cast, for or against a man or a measure, are preserved as public property and fully published, thus forestalling dishonest tally of returns.

"This neither Socialism nor Communism, but an entirely different principle in human government which endured for 300,000 years in Atlantis, over untold generations in Peru before the coming of Spaniards, and for 2,500 years in China before the overthrow of the Manchus — details concerning which are rigorously suppressed and censured by modern educational institutions supported by endowments from the present predatory element in the modern barbaric State."

Such is the Government Plan proposed by William Pelley's 'Elder Brother,' under a mysterious 'Prince of Peace.'

The following is a further example of the methods of these invisible wire pullers who would govern the world through trained and psychically developed men and women. In this the Psychical Research of America appears to be involved.

A friend in America sent us a little book, *Let us in,* which purports to be communications received in 1931 from Professor William James, who died in 1910. It is said, however, by one who for years lived near him, that this book does not represent James either living or dead! Judging from the contents, it can be concluded that behind that name is in reality one of these mysterious master minds. In this case a group of two men and a woman (the receiver) were used as mediums, one being Bligh Bond, then editor of *Psychic Research* for the American Society of Psychical Research, also well known to Spiritists and Illuminés in this country through his Glastonbury books, *The Gate of Remembrance* and *The Hill of Vision*. In a note to this book he writes: "Their unseen control (William James and his group) of the policies of *Psychic Research* has again and again been impressed upon me in the course of my daily work here." A few extracts from *Let us in* will give an idea of this secret communicator and his aims in using this group, giving teaching which, when published, would orient the psychically inclined public, drawing others into his net.

Their God is the God of Masonry, the Yahveh of the Jews: "The inner secret of evolution is that God, the *life principle*, is evolving from within his creation every part thereof..." Of the Manichaean dual forces, light and darkness, good and evil, it is said:

> "It is of the utmost importance that men on earth should fully realise the existence of these two camps and avail themselves of the help of the Light-Bearers [Luciferian] whose weapons are love and life... The forces of ignorance have also reincarnated, and it is that war between darkness and light that is now upon us... The substance which we call love is more enduring than steel ... there are laws connected with its use."

It is the magnetic fluid of the Rosicrucians! "It is the primary stuff of the universe. It is God himself, the Ultimate (life-force). It is manipulated by thought and will."

For mental healing:

> "By your faith in the existence of this great primary substance you are capable and at liberty to employ it. Your spoken word or clearly formulated thought is the wire, as it were, over which you conduct the power to the person in need... Then call us in!" This magnetic healing, therefore, means linking the patient to these Master-minds! And this is to be used to remove so-called "invading entities," but these communicators must themselves be included under that term, for they say: "In reality it is not a case of let us in; we are already in, and we want you to know it; already in for good or ill!"

Again for political purposes:

> "Sit right where you are and turn the power of your thought as directly on that far-away and perhaps powerful leader, calling upon

the help of your own special psychic forces (guide) to aid you in bringing the God-power upon that person or group of persons!..."

to co-operate with or controvert their schemes as suits these masters! Again opening up a focal point of attack for these hidden manipulators! In a similar way the members of the R.R. et A.C. were taught to concentrate on Russia in 1917-18!

Of Russia it is said:

> "The Russian problem is of the utmost importance. The whole universe is constructed on the principle of focal points... Russia is the place where, by common consent of forces outside your ordinary ken [!], an experiment is being launched which is intended to involve the whole human race. This has been foreseen for centuries. *The events which led up to it, the seed from which it sprang, were sown ages ago!"* — Illuminising Judaism!

What was said by the Mason de Luchet of Illuminism in 1789 is just as true to-day:

> "There are a certain number of people who have arrived at the highest degree of imposture. They have conceived the project of reigning over... opinions and of conquering the human mind."

The *Morning Post* New York correspondent on 13 May, 1935, reported:

> "An editorial defence of a report by Dr. Harold Cummins, published in London, on ectoplasmic finger-prints, has caused the American Society of Psychical Research to dismiss Mr. Frederick A. Bond, editor of its journal...

> "Following his dismissal, Mr. Bond made the charge that the policy of the trustees was fixed by a group "more or less pledged to support a particular interest, namely, the mediumship of Mrs. Crandon ["Margery"] and the advocacy of its supernormal character." This is the second time that American psychical circles have split over "Margery."

So much for the value of investigations carried out by the Psychical Research Society; they so often drift into nothing but Spiritualistic seances and playing around with mediumistic phenomena.

CHAPTER XIII

SECRET SOCIETIES IN AMERICA, TIBET, AND CHINA

THE *A.M.O.R.C.* — *The Ancient Mystic Order of the Rosy Cross* or *Antiquae Arcanae Ordinis Rosae Rubeae et Aureae Crucis* — whose Supreme Grand Lodge is now in San José, California, was founded by Dr. H. Spencer Lewis, formerly president for many years of the New York Institute for Psychical Research. He went to France, it is said, in 1909, and there the European Rosicrucian Supreme Council agreed to his plans and authorised the French Jurisdiction to sponsor them. He returned to America, and after much official activity their Supreme Council was organised in New York City, I April, 1915, and in 1916 a national convention was held at Pittsburgh, in·Pennsylvania; a constitution was adopted, and the·order founded, which is now said to be worked under a Charter received from the International Council in Europe.

They claim that "in the United States, etc., there are College, University, and Lodge branches as well as study groups in every important city and town;" also that its foreign jurisdiction includes Grand Lodges "in England, Denmark, Holland, France, Germany, Austria, Russia, China, Japan, East Indies, Australia, Switzerland, and India. The College of the Order in the Orient is located in India." They have also a centre in London and apparently headquarters in Bristol. Their magazine is called, *The Rosicrucian Digest.*

They say they are "not affiliated or connected in any way with any other society, or with any cult or movement," but it is curious to note the similarity of name with that of the Inner Order of the

Stella Matutina — Ordinis Rosae Rubeae et Aureae Crucis — which has also a centre in Bristol! Further, besides having, according to René Guénon, several theosophists as adherents, Mrs. Ella Wheeler Wilcox, they say, was one of their strong co-workers, and we know that her poems, for example "New Thought Pastels," are also variously quoted in support of the ideas both of the New Thought Movement and Max Heindel's Rosicrucian Cosmo-Conception. From information received from America, 1930, we learn that A.M.O.R.C. had its temple in Boylston Street, Boston, Mass.; the Imperator was Harve Spencer Lewis, Ph.D., F.R.C., who was also said to be Member of the Supreme Council R.C. of the World, Legate of the Order in France, Ordained Priest of the Ashrama in India, Honorary Consular of the "Corda Fratres" of Italy, Sri Sabhita, Great White Lodge, Tibet, Rex Universitatis Illuminati, and Fellow of the Rose-Cross College of the Rosicrucian Order. They finally claim to be the only Rosicrucian organisation in America invited to take part in all recent international conventions or Council sessions held in foreign lands.

They look upon Egypt as one of the early arcane schools of Light, hence their pamphlet, *The Light of Egypt,* by Sri Ramatherio, 1931, in which they tell us that their symbol is the cross with a single red rose in the centre: the use, they say, of more roses is not the ancient emblem. The Steinerites and Max Heindel use seven! The R.R. et A.C. has one in the centre of the cross, which is divided into twelve, seven and three petals — the zodiac, planets, and elements, a symbol of the universe — and in its heart is again the rose of ruby and the cross of light, the whole signifying man or the microcosm crucified on the cross of Illuminism, sacrificed to the ambitions of the Power behind the Order. In the registered emblem of the A.M.O.R.C., above the Red Cross of sacrifice, is the Hebrew Talisman of power, the Signet or Seal of Solomon, the interlaced Triangles — as above so below.

In the U.S.A. they advertise their Order by holding national conventions and by hundreds of newspaper and magazine articles showing forth the advantages offered.

In this country, by full-paged magazine advertisements, they promise personal power, success, health and prosperity to be attained by means of "atonement with the Cosmic creative forces and inspirational guidance." They claim to be non-sectarian, with no limitations of race or sex, and they believe in universal brotherhood, as do most other such cults. They further claim to be the One Rosicrucian movement throughout the world operating as a unit.

One of their methods for attaining this unity is a form of private correspondence-teaching, for study and experiments in development of the psychic centres and aura, and also methods for using the law of the Triangle, involving breathing exercises, vibrations, thought forms, rhythm, methods and experiments for receiving Cosmic Illumination, all to be used and tested in daily affairs! It is suggested that part of every Thursday evening should be set aside for these experiments and concentrations, "For this is the Rosicrucian Night throughout the world, and it means greater power through the multitudes who are thus attuned." And in this union universal and international, the A.M.O.R.C. offers its members association with the master-minds of the laws of nature — the Brethren of the Rosy Cross.

They talk of the urge of the Cosmic-Mind, the still small voice which they call intuition, but is it not rather the voice of the international master minds who, under cover of "saving civilisation," are seeking to pervert it and dominate the world through the united and oriented dupes of all these never-ending illuminised societies?

CONFEDERATION OF INITIATES

Another Rosicrucian group is the Secret School, Confederation of Initiates, using the Philosophical Publishing Company, Beverly Hall, Penn., U.S.A., and we are told the latter superseded the Humanitarian Society, founded in 1864, under the name of Rose-Cross Aid, by Dr. Paschal Beverly Randolph — friend of Lincoln — who also, it is said, started the American true Rose-Cross Order in 1852. The Illuminati Rose-Cross College was founded in the United States in 1774.

The present head of the Philosophical Publishing Company is R. Swinburne Clymer, M.D., descendant of George Clymer, who signed the Declaration of Independence; he practises in Philadelphia, lectures in various medical colleges, is now about fifty-nine years old, and a 32nd degree Mason. In 1932, he was Supreme Grand Master of the Order Sons of Isis and Osiris — 38 degrees, supports the College of the Holy Grail and the New Church of Illumination. All three movements are included in Man-Isis, the New Order of the Ages. Man-Isis teaches the development of the ancient fire, the spark of the Cosmic Christ, the dual creative forces in man, bringing about deification; they welcome the coming of the Grand Master John as forerunner to Apollonius of Tyana, and to them the Essenes represented the Great White Lodge (Jewish!). They profess to embrace the esoteric side of all religions.

Dr. Clymer has written many books on Rosicrucians and their teachings, and some, at least, have been fully endorsed by the mysterious International Secret Council of Nine, which apparently direct the Confederation of Initiates. We have the following message purporting to be issued by this Council with regard to the admission of aspirants, dated 5 February, 1932:

> "This is the New Dispensation, and the work of the Spiritual and Mystical Fraternities must be re-established throughout the world, so that all peoples may be taught the Law and thereby enabled to apply it towards universal improvement as the only means of saving mankind... We, the Council of Nine, have selected your organisation, as one of the oldest in America, to help do this work. This must be brought about in such a manner that there can be no question of personal self-interest. May we suggest that you select as your method that of the pre-Christian Essenian Order in which Jesus was trained [?] ... accepting in good faith all students who apply, on an absolutely freewill basis, instructing them in the ancient manner and permitting these students to compensate you on an exchange basis? ..."

> (signed) COMTE M. DE ST. VINCENT, Premier Plenipotentiary of the Council of Nine of the Confraternities of the world.

It is said that Dr. Randolph's writings "positively fix the Secret School in France." Further, he thus "authoritatively" explains Rosicrucians:

"Many, though by no means all, the alchemists and hermetic philosophers were acolytes of the vast Secret Brotherhood which has thrived from the earliest ages … the members of this mystic union were the Magi of old, who flourished in Chaldea ages before one of its number left his native plains and on foreign soil founded the Hebraic confederation. They were the original people of Saba, the Sabeans, who for long ages preceded the Sages of Chaldea. They were the men who founded the Semitic civilisation… Of this Great Brotherhood sprung Brahma, Buddha, Lotze, Zoroaster, the Gnostics, the Essenes, and there Jesus, who was himself an Essene, preached the sacred doctrine of the Fountain of Light… They were the men who first discovered the significance of fire… Whatever of transcendent light now illumines the world, comes from the torches which they lighted at the Fountain whence all light streamed upon that mystic mountain [of initiation]… There is nothing original in Thaumaturgy, Theology, Philosophy, Psychology, and Ontology, but they gave it to the world…"

Rosicrucians, therefore, are Illuminés of that Magical Cabala of the Jews, born by the Waters of Babylon!

As Dr. Clymer quotes in his *Philosophy of Fire:*

"There is in Nature one most potent force, by means of which a single person, who would possess himself of it, and know how to direct it, could revolutionise and change the whole face of the world. This force was known to the ancients and the secret is possessed by the Secret Schools of the present day. It is a universal agent, whose supreme law is equilibrium; and whereby, if science can but learn how to control it, it will be possible to send a thought in an instant around the world; to heal or slay at a distance; to give our words universal success, and to make them reverberate everywhere."

It is always the same explanation;

"There is a Life Principle, a universal agent, wherein ·are two natures and a double current of love and wrath. This ambient fluid pervades everywhere … the Serpent devouring its own tail.

… With this electro-magnetic ether, this vital and luminous caloric, developable in everyone, the ancients and alchemists were familiar… Quiescent, it is appreciable by no human sense; disturbed, or in movement, none can explain its mode of action except the Initiate, and to term it a 'fluid' and to speak of its 'currents' is but to veil a profound mystery under a cloud of words."

Like the Jews of Alexandria, Dr. Clymer teaches that the Sacred books of all religions, including those of the Jews and the Christians, are no more than parables and allegories of the Secret Doctrines of the inner Mystery, the "creation or evolution of worlds and of man. In the Secret Doctrine there was not one Christ for the whole world, but a Potential Christ in every man." That is an illuminised man, the Pentagram!

Speaking of the Greco-Judaic literary falsifications of the Jewish School of Alexandria, Silvestre de Sacy notes in Saint-Croix's book on the *Mysteries of Paganism*, 1817:

> "If some writers of to-day, notwithstanding their profound learning, appear to be dupes of these impostures, it must not be forgotten that often the indulgence in paganism increases proportionately as the respect for revealed religion diminishes, and that those who find in the mythology and beliefs of the Greeks, the fundamental dogmas of an enlightened and spiritual religion, or a system of subtle and transcendent philosophy, are oftenest, in fact, those who see in the Old and New Testaments only a mythology made for the childhood of society and adaptable only to simple and rude men.'"

JULIA SETON

Another of these de-Christianising groups of Illuminati is "The Modern Church," and its School of Illuminism, claimed to be founded in 1905 by Dr. Julia Seton for the purpose of preparing the way for the "New Civilisation." She calls herself an international lecturer for U.S.A., Europe, and Australia. She tells us that the

> ""New Church"… is redeemed out of all nations, all races, all peoples, all creeds, into the One Life that is in all [universal life-force] … shown forth in non-resistance, love, service, and worship… The Illuminati School is the modern school of higher psychology and mysticism, where ancient and occult wisdom is revealed. It teaches new methods of social, ethical, industrial, religious, international, and national liberty. The teaching is standardising the world and passing all thought into one great universal impulse."

Again she writes: "The New Age mind asks, "What is God?"" and the answer is:

"God is Cosmic Spirit, manifesting in all and through all as a ceaseless unerring intelligence; all nature is the body of God, and manifests as a perfect plan of creation… All things emerge new-born from Cosmic Spirit, all things return reborn to it. *Cosmic Spirit is waiting to be acted upon and man is the actor…* It cannot choose but bring forth after the kind of intelligence which commands it… Man is the highest expression of Cosmic Spirit in form on earth. He is not part of God, nor a creation by God; he is universal Intelligence or Cosmic Spirit itself…"

That this is no new religion any student of ancient pantheistic creeds will recognise. As M. Flavien Brenier, in *Les Juifs et la Talmud*, says:

"Now the dominating philosophic doctrine among learned Chaldeans… was absolute pantheism… identified as a kind of breath of Nature, uncreated and eternal; God emanated from the world, not the world from God … ideas which they [Hermetic Freemasonry] have inherited from the alchemists of the Middle Ages, who held them from the Cabalistic Jews."

Here we have the mindless-mind, the blind God of Dr. Julia Seton's "Modern Church," which is waiting to be acted upon by man! Thus do we see in the making the negative illuminised "New Civilisation" standardised into one great universal impulse set in motion by the Master minds of the "Great White Lodge," in the name of Higher Psychology and Mysticism. It is Luciferian perversion, an obsession.

ROERICH

Another destroyer of Western civilisation is Nicholas Roerich and his "New Era" creed.

In 1925 Serge Whitman wrote, in the *Foreword:*

"We who search the paths of international understanding and the structure of universal peace, must look upon Roerich as the apostle and forerunner of the new world of all nations."

Nicholas Roerich, a Russian living for a time in America, is a world-known painter, philosopher, and scientist. He was secretary of the Society for the Encouragement of Arts in Russia and director of its school, organising and co-ordinating the native and new impulse in painting, music, drama, and the dance, and his work was appreciated by such men as Andriev, Gorky, Mestrovic, Zuloaga, Tagore, and others who represented the *newness*. Later he was invited to exhibit his paintings in America, and remaining there, he continued his work, uniting arts so as to unite men. For that purpose he established the Corona Mundi, which in 1922 finally took the form of the International Art Centre of the Roerich Museum, New York.

In 1929 he presented the Roerich Museum, which contained 734 of his own paintings, to the American nation. The other affiliations to the Roerich Museum are: the Master Institute, 1921, for teaching his new ideals in all arts; the Roerich Museum Press, 1925, to spread the New Era ideals by publication of books; also Urusvati, Himalayan Research Institute, 1928, for scientific research in medicine, botany, biology, geology, astrophysics, archaeology, etc. Branches and groups of the Roerich Society have been organised in Europe, Asia, Africa, South·and Central America, and the United States.

From 1924 to 1928 he headed an expedition which passed through India, Tibet, Turkestan, and Siberia. His diary of these wanderings is given in his book *Altai Himalaya,* which is illustrated by many reproductions of his mystical paintings. In his other book, *Heart of Asia,* Part II, Shambhala — he gives an account of what he believes this New Era will mean. It is the key to his work and philosophy, and his resultant world influence. A few extracts will make this clear:

> "In the limitless desert of the Mongolian Gobi, the word Shambhala, or the mysterious Kalapa of the Hindus, sounds like the most realistic symbol of the great Future... In the Temple of Ghum monastery, not far from the Nepalese frontier, instead of the usual central figure of Buddha you see a huge image of the Buddha Maitreya, the coming Saviour and Ruler of Humanity [probable date 1936]... The teaching of Shambhala is a true teaching of Life. As in Hindu Yogas, this teaching indicates the use of the finest energies, which fill the macrocosm [universe], and which are as powerfully manifested in our microcosm [man] ... [it expresses] not a mere Messianic creed, but a New Era of mighty approaching energies and possibilities ... the epoch of Shambhala will be attended by a great evolutionary momentum... The teaching of Life

by the Mahatmas of the Himalayas speaks definitely of it... That which but recently was commonly known as the teaching of will power and concentration has now been evolved by Agni Yoga into a system of mastering the energies which surround us. Through an expansion of consciousness and a training of spirit and body, without isolating ourselves from the conditions of the present day, this synthetic Yoga builds a happy future for humanity...

"Agni Yoga teaches: 'Understand the great meaning of the psychic energy-human thought and consciousness — as the great creative factors... People have forgotten that any energy once set into motion creates a momentum. It is almost impossible to stop this momentum; therefore every manifestation of psychic energy continues its influence by momentum sometimes for a long time. One may already have changed his thought, but the effect of the previous transmission will nevertheless permeate space. In this lies the power of psychic energy... [in order to be receptive to this psychic energy man's nerve centres must be developed]. The centre of the third eye [pineal gland] acts in co-ordinance with the chalice [heart or feeling knowledge] and with kundalini [sex force]. This triad characterises in the best way the basis of activity of the approaching epoch. (That is perverting sex-force to bring about illumination and induce negative receptivity!]...

"During the development of the centres humanity will feel incomprehensible symptoms, which science, in ignorance, will attribute to the most unrelated ailments. Therefore the time has come to write the book of observations regarding the fires of Life... Physicians do not neglect!"

One might well wonder how many of present-day mental, moral, and bodily ills are due to the psychic practices of these innumerable esoteric and illuminised cults which actually obsess a large portion of modern humanity! It is the making of a monstrous robot set in motion by fiendish but unknown fanatics and madmen!

Although Roerich has written: "The evolution of the New Era rests on the corner-stone of Knowledge and Beauty," yet he says it is the Knowledge and Splendour of Shambhala! And the spirit of all Roerich's work has been described by Claude Bragdon in his introduction to *Altai Himalaya* as the search for "the hidden truth, the unrevealed beauty, the *Lost Word*, in fact." That is *I.N.R.I. — Igne Natura Renovatur integra* — All nature is renovated by fire. The fire of universal generation! The Serpent Power!

Thus the new world is to be unified by means of these cosmic and psychic energies, which would undoubtedly culminate in world domination and control by some very powerful and positive group superior over all others in development of will power and intense concentration, having profound knowledge of the laws of these energies, as well as of human nature and its weaknesses, using these energies to prepare and rule negatively developed men and women — a happy future indeed for enslaved humanity!

TIBETAN INITIATION

Writing in *Isis Unveiled,* Mme Blavatsky said:

> "The astral and sidereal light as explained by the alchemists and Eliphas Levi in his *Dogme et Rituel de la Haute Magie,* and under the name of 'Akasa' or life-principle, this all-pervading force was known to the gymnosophists, Hindu magicians, and adepts of all countries thousands of years ago; it is still known to them and used by the Tibetan Lamas, fakirs, thaumaturgists of all nationalities, and even by many of the Hindu "jugglers.""

Further, all Theosophists who derive their doctrines, in part or in whole, from Mme Blavatsky's writings believe their Masters to be either dwellers in Tibet or linked to some powerful hierarchy there.

In *Tibet's Great Yogi Milarepa,* edited, with an introduction, by W. Y. Evans Wentz, we are told that "throughout Tibet and extending into Nepal, Bhutan, Sikkim, Kashmir, and parts of Mongolia there are three chief schools of Buddhist philosophy." In Tibet the adherents of these schools are: (1) The Yellow Caps or Gelug-pas, the established Church of Northern Buddhism, wielding through its spiritual head, the Dalai Lama, both spiritual and temporal power. (2) The Kargyutpas or "followers of the Apostolic Succession." That is the transmission of the "Divine Grace" from the Buddhas through their Supreme Guru Dorje-Chang to the line of Celestial Gurus and thence to the Apostolic Guru on earth and from him to each subordinate Guru and by them through the Mystic Initiation to each of the neophytes. It is a veritable magnetic-chain. (3) The Red Caps or Adi-Yoga school, the Unreformed Church. The Yellow Caps acknowledge the superiority of the Red Caps in all questions connected more or less with magic and the occult sciences.

Then there are the Bons, known as Black Caps, surviving monastic orders of primitive pre-Buddhistic religion. Evans Wentz also compares the Kargyutpas with so-called Christian Gnostics, and says that, according to some Gnostic schools, "God the Father was mystically the Primordial Man, the *Anthropos* or I.A.O. (the life principle) comparable to the Adi-Buddha of the Kargyutpas and other sects of Northern Buddhism." In both faiths Deliverance depends on one's own efforts; there is a similarity in the initiation ceremony, and both use mantras; both personify the Female Principle in nature as "Wisdom," both believe in rebirth. To the Great Yogis there is one family, one nation-Humanity!

As for the Mystical Initiation, Mme A. David-Neel, in her *Initiations and Initiates in Tibet,* gives us many and enlightening details showing the close similarity of the methods and beliefs of the Lamaist sects to those of the many gnostic and cabalistic sects of to-day. In Tibet, the idea of a Supreme personal God, an eternal omnipotent Being, the Creator of the World, has never held sway; they consider nothing but the law of cause and effect, with its manifold combinations. Under the name of esoteric or mystical methods, Lamaists really include a positive psychic training and salvation [Liberation] is an arduous and scientific attainment. The Tibetan Initiation or "angkur" is above all the transmission of a power, a force, by a kind of psychic process, so as to communicate to the initiate the capacity to perform some particular act or to practise certain exercises which tend to develop various physical or intellectual faculties. There are three kinds of teachings, methods, and initiations: exoteric, esoteric, and mystic.

Exoterically there are powerful beings or "Yidams" who, they say, protect those who worship them. Esoterically these "Yidama" are depicted as occult forces, and mystics regard them as manifestations of the energy inherent in body and mind.

Mystic Initiations are therefore psychic in character. The theory is that the energy emanating from the Master or from some more occult sources may be transmitted to the disciple who is capable of "drawing it off" from the psychic waves into which he is plunged during the celebration of the angkur rites. The disciple is offered an opportunity "of endowing himself with power."

By meditation the Masters develop in their pupils certain psychic faculties by means of telepathy or symbolic gestures, a strong form of suggestion, awakening ideas. Before a mystic angkur the initiating Lama for a few days or several months, according to the degree to be conferred, remains in a state of profound concentration, or as Mme David-Neel expresses it: "The Lama stores himself with psychic energy just as an accumulator stores itself with electricity."

After the initiation the aspirant goes into retreat, and mentally and physically prepares himself to receive the force which will be transferred to him. He regulates his religious practices, food, and sleep as directed by his Master. "He also endeavours to empty his mind of all reasoning activity so that no mental or physical activity may take place, and thus form an obstacle to the stream of energy which is to be poured into him." A certain degree of skill in the exercise of Yoga, principally the mastery of the art of breathing, is necessary for success. The candidate of the "Short Path," when seeking admission as a disciple, is reminded of the risks he runs of incurring dangerous illness, madness, and certain occult happenings that may cause death. Considering the forces being used, this can be understood. The disciple must have faith in his initiating Master and in the efficacy of the angkur he confers.

One can, therefore, realise the dangers to which the adept is exposed in these high mystic and psychic initiations, common to all gnostic and cabalistic sects, more especially when one remembers that in all such modern sects the initiating adept and teacher is himself merely an intermediary, oriented and controlled, carrying out the commands of some unknown and ambitious Hierarchy of Supermen who, as related by Mrs. A. A. Bailey of New York, would dominate the nations through such tools, moulded to occupy their several appointed posts, light bearers of darkness leading the peoples to commit mental, religious, national, and racial suicide so as to make way for some monstrous New Era, new civilisation, new subjective religion.

SECRET SOCIETIES IN CHINA

In *Les Sociétés Secrètes en Chine*, 1933, Lieut. Colonel B. Favre shows the antiquity of these Chinese secret societies and how their methods and organisations are in many ways similar to those in Europe and elsewhere, and above all, how their influence was manifested during the revolts of the eighteenth and nineteenth centuries. He states that discoveries made during little more than twenty years in Turkestan, China, Mongolia, Persia, and Afghanistan reveal a closer connection between ancient peoples than has hitherto been believed. The secret of these societies, he says, veils their work, and a complicated ritual, magical and religious practices, and ceremonies of initiation create among members, bound by an oath, the necessary atmosphere to awaken great enthusiasm. "To lead the people is to place the passions at the service of an idea." In China these political secret societies rest chiefly on Taoism and Confucianism, and the family and clan idea is utilised to bind members together.

He tells us that the Han Dynasty was one of the most brilliant in Chinese history; immense conquests brought the Empire in contact with distant peoples, cultural interchanges of the greatest importance were established, and during this period, when passions of all sorts were displayed in the extreme, secret societies flourished. After the fall of the Han, Buddhism attained considerable development, and among the ten great Buddhist schools or sects which arose in China, one of the most ancient was the *Lotus*, known as Amidism, founded in China in the fourth century. It was not primitive Buddhism, and possibly received its gods from Persia or Syria; later it was called *Lotus Blanc*, and was a religion of love, pity, and naive devotion, which conquered China and Japan, and is strong to-day.

Later again, under the name "Association of the Lotus Blanc," it ceased to be a religious brotherhood. In the fourteenth century, still Buddhist, the sect burnt perfumes, practised divination, used pentacles, and was, above all, Messianic; they announced the incarnation of Maitreya, the future Buddha, so often looked for at various dates. Here the author notes the probable connection between the name Maitreya, the Persian Mithra, and the Mi che ho, the Manichean Messiah. The *Lotus Blanc* having co-operated in the fall of the Yuan and Ming dynasties, had to assist in the overthrow of the Tsing. The "Nuage Blanc," sometimes confounded with the Lotus Blanc, was, according to Father Wieger, tainted with Manichaeism; its chief affected philanthropy, vegetarianism, invoked spirits, and his adepts, like the Manichaeans, did not marry and refused to procreate. During the nineteenth century the affiliations of the Lotus Blanc exercised considerable influence over historical events in China, and to-day they still exist.

The *Triad* or Hong is an association, known under various names in China, and in the Chinese colonies of Sonde, Straits Settlements, and Indo-China; its origin is unknown, but it first appeared for certain in 1787. It is probable, the author says, that the Hong (Triad) was formed about the beginning of the eighteenth century, as it was spoken of from 1749 to 1832 in several official edicts, in connection with seditious movements in which it participated. The Chinese believe in occultism and magic; it is for them a scientific discipline, a philosophical and practical system which permits them to penetrate beyond the sensible and dominate the forces which surround them; it has its laws and logic. Their chief officer or "Venerable" was known as "Elder Brother." There are also many apparent links between the Triad and Freemasonry: both practise fraternity and aim at the moral perfection of mankind. They have the same conception of the Universe which is shown in the Chinese duality — Yin and Yang, and in Masonry by the Pillars of Jakin and Boaz. Both see the "Light" and a certain number of symbols and rites are common to both; the sign of Fire in Hong is also Masonic. One might ask, are they not both of Sabeist origin? According to Confucius, Chang-ti, the universal principle of existence, is represented under the general emblem of the visible firmament as well as under the particular symbols of Sun, Moon, and Earth.

The political activities of the Triad became intense during the years preceding the revolution of 1911. These secret societies acted for three centuries alternately in the revolutionary domain and in various forms of brigandage. Sun Yat-sen thus explains why the Nationalists from the beginning made use of this collection of men, vagabonds without family; the Nationalists could no longer confide their ideas to the elite, they had to put them into a receptacle of repulsive aspect, the Hong-men, which no one would dream of searching. These ideas were transmitted orally, following the tradition of secret societies, and were kept secret. Sun Yatsen realised that he could no longer utilise them without danger after the overthrow of the Tsing. The survival of the Triad must therefore be looked for among the bands, red or not, who, after the civil wars, swarmed in most provinces devoting themselves to dark exploits.

Concerning these bandits and their societies the author quotes an open letter from a Tientsin journal, *Ta pong pao,* of 4 November, 1930, which was called "Brigands in the region of K'ouang p'ing." It said that after the fall of the Ming dynasty when the revolt aimed at overthrowing the Tsing in order to restore the Ming, secret societies gathered together these vagabonds or bandits into the Society of the Ko-lao houei, the "Old Brothers." Most masters of junks and sampans are affiliated to bandits, and the affiliated members must be closely united, observe justice, be subject to rigorous discipline; those who default must be severely judged; all are equal and must not give themselves up to debauch and robbery. They pay homage to ancestors of dynasties; entering their own houses they must revere the Heaven, the Earth, Sun, Moon and Stars, the saints, the Masters of the three doctrines and the five elements. A secret language is used, and they recognise each other by questions put and answered as required.

Therefore, Colonel Favre adds:

> "These men within these associations have a statute, a ritual; but mystic habits have disappeared; the ritual is democratised, it remains religious and moral. But there is something paradoxical in it since those bands live on cruelty and pillage."

The same apparent paradox is found in modern secret societies in Europe and America; superficially they appear religious and moral bodies, but under all runs the eternal cry of revolt:

"Everything, yes, everything must be destroyed, since everything must be renewed."

CHAPTER XIV

THE SYNARCHY OF AGARTHA

MARCEL LALLEMAND writes in *Notes on Occultism:* "Under the influence of Theosophy, occultism is associated with visions of libraries buried in the caves of the Himalayas." For many years much has been written among certain of these secret societies about the mysterious hierarchy and subterranean libraries of Agartha. Having read *Mission de l'Inde en Europe, Mission de l'Europe en Asie,* written in 1886 by Saint-Yves d'Alveydre, we are led to conclude that it is more or less symbolic, that Agartha is of no one country, of no one nation, but universal; that the hierarchy is, apparently, a group of cabalistic and gnostic magi and initiates, having links with the Jewish School of Alexandria, seeking by means of unification, through many Judaeo-Christian sects, to dominate and secretly rule the Western World and eventually unite the East with the West; that in all probability the mysterious subterranean libraries merely consist of what is known as the "Akashic Records" akasa meaning ether, which according to these initiates has imprinted upon it all past, present, and future world happenings. Therefore they claim to be able to tap the ether and get back the nature and beginnings of prehistoric man and ancient civilisations, as for example their mystical accounts of the Lemurian and Atlantean epochs.

In writing of these ancient epochs of Lemuria and Atlantis Edouard Schure in *From Sphinx to Christ* explains: "Dr. Rudolf Steiner, endowed with esoteric knowledge and highly developed clairvoyance, has furnished us with many novel and striking glimpses of the physical and psychical constitution of the Atlanteans in relation to anterior and posterior human evolution."

There is, however, reason to suspect that Steiner's clairvoyance was more or less the thought-forms of his powerful Masters using him as an instrument to restore the mysteries and illuminise the Western World. Moreover, his teachings on the evolution of the world and man are wholly based on these said visions of the primary, Lemurian, and Atlantean epochs, and the result is like some horrible nightmare, entirely anti-Christian, reeking of ancient Sabeism intermingled with the perverted Christianity of the Hellenised Jews of Alexandria.

Schuré, Max Heindel, and Steiner himself in his *Outline of Occult Science,* all expound this mythological mystery. The early Lemurians are described as eyeless, mindless, vapoury hermaphrodites, ruled by planetary gods, guided by angels, and aided by Luciferian spirits. Later the sexes were separated, bringing terrible sexual disorder, and finally Lemuria was submerged. According to Schure the priests of Ancient Egypt preserved the tradition of a vast Continent which had formerly occupied a great part of the Atlantic Ocean from Africa and Europe to America, and of a powerful civilisation which was engulfed in some prehistoric catastrophe. The priests claimed to have received it from the Atlanteans themselves through some far-back connection; in turn they told Solon of the tradition, and Plato, borrowing from him, wrote of it in his dialogue, the *Timaeus.* The whole tradition is a vast legend, although there are scientific proofs that such a Continent had probably existed. Some of the Lemurians, it is said, survived and settled in Atlantis, which, as Schuré explains, was a tropical Eden with a primitive humanity; then came a long period of wars, followed by a Federation of Initiate Kings, and finally decadence and a reign of black magic, and the Continent was gradually rent and destroyed by subterranean fires.

These primitive people, according to Schuré, were powerful psychics: "His sparkling serpent-like eye seemed to see through the soil and the bark of the trees and to penetrate the souls of animals. His ear could hear the grass growing and the ants walking"; they spent their nights is astral dreams and visions, believing they contacted and conversed with the gods. Again Steiner says that the Atlantean Kings had spirit guides in human form, "Messengers of the Gods" (Elder Brothers), who actually ruled men through the kings. As he explains, these guides were under Luciferian influence, but used it progressively to free themselves from error by becoming initiates of the Solar-Christ Being — they became *Illuminés!* They imparted the mysteries to disciples and in fact became Christ-oracles. Matter in the form of Ahriman came along and intellect was born and the gods receded from among men. In the later Atlantean evolution the mysteries, he said, had to be kept secret so that the knowledge of how to control and direct Nature's forces should not be used for evil and sensual purposes, but in time these powers became known, black magic became rampant, and Atlantis was destroyed.

Then according to Steiner, Europe, Asia, Africa, etc., were colonised by the descendants of Atlantis and with them came the initiates of the oracle-mysteries. Yarker in his *Arcane Schools* states: "When the island of Atlantis sank a pass was reft which drained the Desert of Gobi... Tibet has preserved many details of the wars of this lost Atlantis, charging the cause of its destruction to the cultivation ... of black magic." Further he quotes the *Popul-Vuk,* or *Book of the Azure Veil,* of the Mexicans which tells us that these Atlanteans were a race that "Knew all things by intuition," and repeats the charge of black magic. Yarker adds: "This book allegorises and personifies the forces of nature." Thus we might conclude that much of the legend of Atlantis is also an allegory, personifying Nature's secret and perceptible forces, as found in all mythologies. And upon this web woven out of the astral light Steiner has built up much of his Occult Science and Christian Illuminism.

In support of our opinion of the nature of Agartha we quote from the above book by Saint-Yves d'Alveydre. He explains that "the name Agartha signifies impossible to be taken by violence and inaccessible to anarchy." In itself he says it is a Trinitarian unity and Synarchy of Judaeo-Christians, as opposed to "general government by brute force, that is, military conquest, political tyranny, sectarian intolerance, and colonial rapacity." Everywhere to-day it looks as if an attempt were being made to rule the world by some such Synarchic hierarchy of men, politically, religiously, and economically.

He continues:

> "Suffice it to know that in certain regions of the Himalayas, among twenty-two temples representing the twenty-two Arcana of Hermes (the cabalistic keys of the Tarot Cards) and the twenty-two letters of certain sacred alphabets (among others Greek and Hebrew), Agartha forms the mystic *Zero*, the undiscoverable. The Zero, that is to say, All or Nothing, all by harmonious unity, nothing without it, all by Synarchy, nothing by Anarchy."

The Zero is the *Fool* of these Hermetic Arcana, whose symbol is air, and which is found on one of the paths uniting the Sephiroth of the Supreme Creative Triad at the summit of the Cabalistic Tree of Life. It represents idealism which has lost its foothold on the material world; metaphorically speaking, it is in the air!

"The sacred territory of Agartha is independent, synarchically organised, and composed of a population rising to the figure of nearly 20 million souls." That is, Yogis, adepts, and initiates, who, all over the world, practise Yoga, Eastern or Western, and are united on the astral by the magnetic life-principle which penetrates all peoples and all nature." Agartha is a faithful image of the eternal Word throughout all Creation." Its symbol is the Triangle of Fire, the manifestation of the Creative Principle." The highest circle and the nearest to the mystical Centre is composed of twelve members. These last represent Supreme Initiation, and correspond, among other things, to the Zodiacal Zone. In celebrating their magical Mysteries they wear the symbols of the signs of the Zodiac, as also certain hierarchic letters." They also represent the twelve tribes of Israel.

> "These libraries, which contain the true substance of all ancient arts and sciences going back to 556 centuries, are inaccessible to all profane eyes and to all attacks... Alone in his Supreme Initiation, the Supreme Pontiff, with his principal assessors, holds the complete knowledge of the sacred catalogue of this planetary library."

He alone possesses the key to open it and the knowledge of the contents of this "Cosmic Book." Therefore there is reason to put these libraries down as "Akashic Records," said to be opened and read by means of Hermetic and Cabalistic magical symbols and formulae. Further, he says, the priests and learned men, by entering into this Ancient and Universal Alliance, wherever there was to be found the grave of a vanished civilisation, "not only would the earth deliver up its secrets," but these men would have the golden key of entrance, and would gain complete knowledge of them. "On the spot they would piously rebuild the antiquity of Egypt, Ethiopia, Chaldea, Syria, Armenia, Persia, Thrace, the Caucasus, and even the plateau of High Tartary." By Illuminism all would be known from the highest heaven to the central fire of the earth. There would be no evil, intellectual, moral, or physical, for which union of Man with Divinity could not bring a certain remedy. It is wholly a work of magic, as is Agartha itself.

> "Finally, to pass from the public law of to-day to the Synarchic Alliance of to-morrow, it will be sufficient for us that circumstances should allow a Sovereign Pontiff to rise up at the head of the whole social Judaeo-Christian body, to set up its Authority and synthetic spirit and, supported by the conscience of all peoples who are attentive to the voice of truth, to call Governments to the law of intelligence and love, which should reunite and reorganise them."

Then we appear to come to a League of Nations:

> "For the first time, European States will be able without danger, under guarantee of this great intellectual and arbitral Authority, supported by the public conscience of Europe, to proceed to enthrone a general Government of Justice and not of diplomatic ruse and military antagonism. For the first time under the double guarantee of these two Supreme Councils, the Teaching Authority and this Power of Justice, Emperors, Kings, or Presidents of Republics forming an integral part of the latter, will be able to call Judaeo-Christian nations to form a great economic assembly. Thus the Synarchy can accomplish itself *excathedra* under the banner of the European Sovereign Pontiff, and become accessible to all Judaeo-Christians without exclusion of cults, universities or peoples. This supra-national reorganisation is the possible cornerstone of the whole European social State.

> ... This holy, pacific, synarchic authority, fifty-five thousand years old, uniting Science and religion, blessing all cults, all universities, all nations, embracing entire Humanity and Heaven in one and the same intelligence, in one and the same love... In fact, it is not an ordinary work, nor can any century undertake it without the aid of initiates of the highest grade, this synthetic work which was accomplished at Alexandria under the invisible breath of Christ;

although under the eyes and hand of Caesarism, the Epoptes who, visible or invisible, presided at this synthetic work had to mask esotericism under exotericism, Israelito-Christianity under Helleno-Christianity... It is thus that the Helleno-Christianity included nominally or really all the degrees corresponding to the initiations of the ancient universities, of the Jewish Cabala, of Chaldea, of Egypt, of Thrace, etc.

... In all antiquity the Law signified the Science of things natural, human, and divine."

He further speaks of

"The Cosmic Mysteries such as are revered not only by Judaeo-Christian cabalists. such as are practised in secret, net only by the actual disciples of John the Baptist and certain esoteric schools of Cairo, Sinai, Arabia, but also as are scientifically professed by the Magi of Agartha."

Again he explains: "This spirit is always that of the Universal Alliance of all members of Humanity, that of the indissoluble Union of Science and of Religion in all their universality." Now we know that, according to himself, Steiner's mission was: "To link together Science and Religion. Bring God into Science and nature into religion, and so fecundate anew Art and Life." It was Agartha too "who, at the beginning of modern times, everywhere renewed, through the Judaeo Christians, the thousands of associations developed today under the name of Freemasonry." As Schuré wrote: "The tradition of esoteric Christianity, properly speaking, is directly and uninterruptedly attached to the famous and mysterious Manes, founder of Manichaeism, who lived in Persia in the fourth century." This sect arose out of the influence of the Jewish School of Alexandria.

Like Mazzini who cried: Associate! Associate! Associate! Saint-Yves d'Alveydre's cry was:

"Synarchy! Synarchy! Synarchy! thus save your tiaras, your universities, your crowns, your republics, all that is yours, all, including what was legitimate in the Revolution of 1789 in its social promises, that the Synarchy Judaeo-Christian alone can maintain and accomplish. Unite in that Law, teaching bodies, ecclesiastic or laic; juridical bodies; economic bodies."

Once more Steiner's teaching corresponds, for his "Threefold State" is Economic life; Public Rights; Intellectual and Spiritual life-religion, teaching, art, etc.!

In conclusion:

> "This holy Agartha which I have revealed to you in this present book is anti-sectarian *per excellence,* and far from using its influence over Asia to obstruct a European Synarchy, it only awaits a gesture from you, in this sense, to give you gradually the fraternal communion of all sciences, of all arts which it conceals under the secret of the Mysteries, the nomenclature of which is contained in the texts of our admirable Judaeo-Christian Religion... Thus, finally united anew by the Synarchic Law, the Judaeo-Christians of the Promise and with them the other human communions will see above in the clouds, surrounded by angels, spirits, and souls of saints the glorious body of Christ, and behind the solar aureole of his head, the Triangle of Fire bearing the sacred name of Yod, He, Vau, He [the Tetragrammaton of the Jews and the Gnostic Solar Christ!]."

And to-day are we not fast coming under the three-fold Law of some such secret Synarchy: *Religions* — the cry of unification of sects and cults under the propaganda of the New York Theosophist, Mrs. Alice A. Bailey, under her Tibet Master and Hierarchy of Supermenone family, one humanity, one life? Also in the earlier "Parliament of Religions," in Chicago. *Economic* — the insidious P.E.P. — Political Economic Planning — of Israel Moses Sieff, which has got such a hold upon this country and is in apparent partnership with G. D. H. Cole's Principles of Economic Planning which has appeared under the banner of Zionism and Freemasonry! *International Politics — the* Judaeo-Masonic League of Nations!

In 1869 the Chevalier Gougenot des Mousseaux wrote in his book, *Le Juif, Le Judaïsme et La Judaïsation des Peuples Chrétiens:*

> "The anti-religious but, above all, anti-Christian efforts which distinguish the present epoch have a character of concentration and *universality* which marks the stamp of the Jew, the supreme patron of the unification of peoples, because he is the cosmopolitan people *par excellence;* because the Jew prepares by the licence of *libre-pensée,* the era called by him Messianic — the day of his universal triumph... The character of *universality* will be noted in *L'Alliance-*

israélite-universelle, in the *Universal Association of Freemasonry..."*

Moreover, in support of the above, we quote, in *Jewish World* of 9 and 16 February, 1883:

"The dispersion of the Jews has rendered them a cosmopolitan people. They are the only cosmopolitan people, and in this capacity must act, and are acting, as a solvent of national and racial differences. The great Ideal of Judaism is not that Jews shall be allowed to flock together one day in some hole-and-corner fashion, for, if not tribal, at any rate separatist objects; but that the whole world shall be imbued with Jewish teachings, and that in a Universal Brotherhood of Nations — a greater Judaism, in fact — all the separate races and religions shall disappear.

... The new Constitution of the [Jewish] Board of Deputies marks an epoch in the history of that important institution... The real importance of the new Constitution is ... that it provides a machinery for enabling the Jews of England to work together when the occasion requires — that in short it organises the Jews of the whole Empire, and renders their aggregate force available in cases of emergency."

And of these cabalistic sects, east and west, des Mousseaux, in 1869, raised a voice of warning, all unheeded:

"There will burst forth one fine evening one of these formidable crises which will shake the earth and which occult societies have long prepared for Christian society, and then perhaps will suddenly appear in open day, throughout the entire world, all the militia, all the fraternal and unknown sects of the Cabala. The ignorance, the carelessness in which we live, of their sinister existence, their affinities, and their immense ramifications will in no way prevent them from recognising each other, and under the banner of no matter what universal alliance, giving each other the kiss of Peace, they will hasten to gather together under one Chief..."

The above book of Gougenot des Mousseaux was published in 1869 and was immediately bought up, and save for a few odd copies completely disappeared! It was not until ten years after his mysterious death that a second edition was allowed to be published in 1886, and finally circulated.

In conclusion, these, then, are the results of our further investigations into the many secret and occult societies both of yesterday and to-day, as published in the *Patriot* from 1930 to 1935. Everything seems to point to the cabalistic and revolutionary Jew as the Master-mind working behind them, using them as pawns in his great gamble and world-wide conspiracy, which would disintegrate and destroy, not only the Christian Faith, but the entire traditions of Western civilisation. His weapon of control and attack being the Triangle of Fire, these magnetic-forces of Life which can both slay and make alive, and by which he professes to free and enlighten the peoples, only the more surely to bind, unify, and enslave them under some unknown and alien Ruler. Moreover, to forward this sinister gamble he entraps and blinds them with the ancient catch-words: "Know Thyself" and "Ye shall be as Gods." That is Illuminism or so-called — Liberation of Man — Free not to use his freedom for himself, but to fulfil the Plans of the Great Conspiracy and its Supreme Pontiff!

Other titles

OMNIA VERITAS LTD PRESENTS:

BEYOND the CONSPIRACY
UNMASKING THE INVISIBLE WORLD GOVERNMENT

All great historical events are planned in secret by men who surround themselves with total discretion.

by John Coleman

Highly organized groups always have the advantage over citizens

OMNIA VERITAS LTD PRESENTS:

THE CLUB OF ROME
THE THINK TANK OF THE NEW WORLD ORDER

The many tragic and explosive events of the 20th century didn't happen by themselves, but were planned according to a well-established pattern...

BY JOHN COLEMAN

Who were the planners and creators of these major events?

OMNIA VERITAS LTD PRESENTS:

DIPLOMACY BY DECEPTION
AN ACCOUNT OF THE TREASONOUS CONDUCT BY THE GOVERNMENTS OF BRITAIN AND THE UNITED STATES

BY JOHN COLEMAN

The story of the creation of the United Nations is a classic case of diplomacy by deception

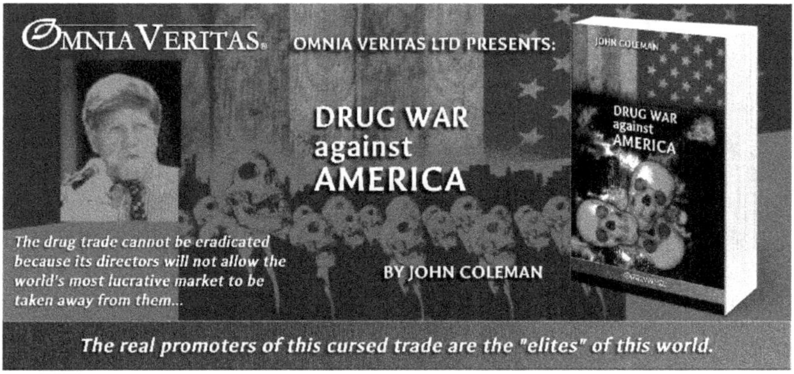
OMNIA VERITAS
OMNIA VERITAS LTD PRESENTS:
DRUG WAR against AMERICA
The drug trade cannot be eradicated because its directors will not allow the world's most lucrative market to be taken away from them...
BY JOHN COLEMAN
The real promoters of this cursed trade are the "elites" of this world.

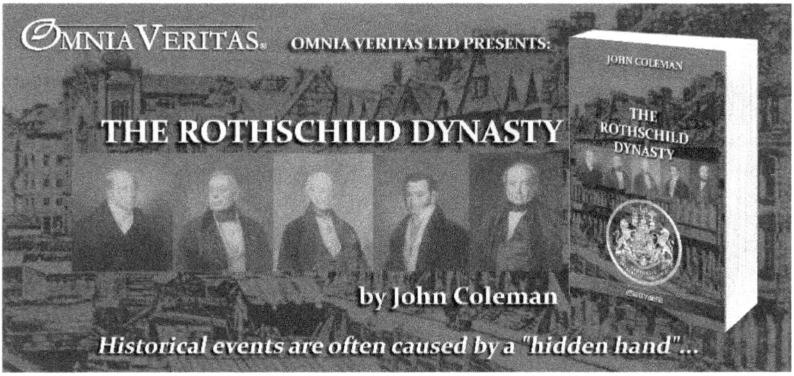
OMNIA VERITAS
OMNIA VERITAS LTD PRESENTS:
THE ROTHSCHILD DYNASTY
by John Coleman
Historical events are often caused by a "hidden hand"...

OMNIA VERITAS
OMNIA VERITAS LTD PRESENTS:
ONE WORLD ORDER SOCIALIST DICTATORSHIP
All these years, while our attention was focused on the evils of communism in Moscow, the socialists in Washington were busy stealing from America!
BY JOHN COLEMAN
"The enemy in Washington is more to be feared than the enemy in Moscow."

ⓞMNIA VERITAS.

MK ULTRA
Ritual Abuse and Mind Control
Tools of domination for the nameless religion

For the first time, a book attempts to explore the complex subjects of traumatic ritual abuse and the mind control that results from it...

How is it possible to mentally program a human being?

ALEXANDRE LEBRETON

MK ULTRA
Ritual Abuse and Mind Control
Tools of domination for the nameless religion

ⓞMNIA VERITAS

OMNIA VERITAS LTD PRESENTS:

English Freemasonry is wealthy and capitalistic, controlling the money and rulers of the world through banking and commerce. French Freemasonry, on the other hand, is poor and communistic, attempting to control state finances through an all-powerful socialistic government.

SCARLET AND THE BEAST
ENGLISH FREEMASONRY, BANKS, AND THE ILLEGAL DRUG TRADE

JOHN DANIEL

SCARLET AND THE BEAST
ENGLISH FREEMASONRY, BANKS, AND THE ILLEGAL DRUG TRADE

The Harlot's abominable cup is in the hands of English Freemasonry

ⓞMNIA VERITAS.

Omnia Veritas Ltd presents:

MYRON FAGAN

The objective is to brainwash the people into accepting the phony peace bait to transform the United States into an enslaved unit of the United Nations' one-world government.

THE ILLUMINATI
AND THE COUNCIL ON FOREIGN RELATIONS

MYRON FAGAN

THE ILLUMINATI AND THE COUNCIL ON FOREIGN RELATIONS

They have seized that power on orders from their masters of the great conspiracy

OMNIA VERITAS

OMNIA VERITAS LTD PRESENTS:

THE HIDDEN AUTHORS
of the
FRENCH REVOLUTION

by HENRI POOGET DE SAINT-ANDRÉ

It seems," Robespierre once said to Amar, "that we are being carried away by an invisible hand beyond our control..."

The more we study the history of the French Revolution, the more we come up against enigmas...

OMNIA VERITAS

Omnia Veritas Ltd presents:

An exclusive and unpublished work of EUSTACE MULLINS

BLOOD AND GOLD
HISTORY OF THE COUNCIL ON FOREIGN RELATIONS

The CFR, founded by internationalists and banking interests, has played a significant role in shaping US foreign policy

Revolutions are not made by the middle class, but by the oligarchy at the top

OMNIA VERITAS

OMNIA VERITAS LTD PRESENTS:

SCARLET AND THE BEAST

My research has revealed that there are two separate and opposing powers in Freemasonry...

One is Scarlet. The other, the Beast.

A HISTORY OF THE WAR BETWEEN ENGLISH AND FRENCH FREEMASONRY

www.ingramcontent.com/pod-product-compliance
Lightning Source LLC
Chambersburg PA
CBHW071640270326
41928CB00010B/1989